Collins
Spanish
Verbs

HarperCollins Publishers
Westerhill Road
Bishopbriggs
Glasgow
G64 2QT
Great Britain

Second Edition 2011

Reprint 10 9 8 7 6 5 4 3 2 1 0

© HarperCollins Publishers 2005, 2007, 2011

ISBN 978-0-00-736975-1

www.collinslanguage.com

A catalogue record for this book is available
from the British Library

Typeset by Davidson Publishing Solutions,
Glasgow

Printed in India by Gopsons Papers Limited

This book is set in Collins Fedra, a typeface
specially created for Collins dictionaries by
Peter Bil'ak

Acknowledgements
We would like to thank those authors and
publishers who kindly gave permission for
copyright material to be used in the Collins
Word Web. We would also like to thank
Times Newspapers Ltd for providing
valuable data.

SERIES EDITOR
Rob Scriven

MANAGING EDITOR
Gaëlle Amiot-Cadey

EDITORIAL COORDINATION
Susanne Reichert
Rachel Smith

CONTRIBUTORS
Cordelia Lilly
Victoria Romero Cerro
José María Ruiz Vaca
Fernando León Solís
Jeremy Butterfield

Contents

Introduction

The *Easy Learning Spanish Verbs* is designed for both young and adult learners. Whether you are starting to learn Spanish for the very first time, brushing up your language skills or revising for exams, the *Easy Learning Spanish Verbs* and its companion volume, the *Easy Learning Spanish Grammar*, are here to help.

Newcomers can sometimes struggle with the technical terms they come across when they start to explore the grammar of a new language. The *Easy Learning Spanish Verbs* contains a glossary which explains verb grammar terms using simple language and cutting out jargon.

The text is divided into sections to help you become confident in using and understanding Spanish verbs. The first section looks at verb formation. Written in clear language, with numerous examples in real Spanish, this section helps you to understand the rules which are used to form verb tenses.

The next section of text looks at certain common prepositions which are used with a number of verbs. Each combination of verb plus preposition is shown with a simple example of real Spanish to show exactly how it is used.

The **Verb Tables** contain 120 important Spanish verbs (both regular and irregular) which are given in full for various tenses. Examples show how to use these verbs in your own work. If you are unsure how a verb goes in Spanish, you can look up the Verb Index at the back of the book to find either the conjugation of the verb itself, or a cross-reference to a model verb, which will show you the patterns that the verb follows.

The *Easy Learning Spanish Grammar* takes you a step further in your language learning. It supplements the information given in the *Easy Learning Spanish Verbs* by offering even more guidance on the usage and meaning of verbs, as well as looking at the most important aspects of Spanish grammar. Together, or individually, the *Easy Learning* titles offer you all the help you need when learning Spanish.

Glossary of Verb Grammar Terms

ACTIVE a form of the verb that is used when the subject of the verb is the person or thing doing the action, for example, *I wrote a letter*. Compare with passive.

AFFIRMATIVE an affirmative sentence or instruction is one that does not contain a negative word such as *not*. Compare with negative.

AGREE (to) in the case of verbs, to have the form which goes with the person or thing carrying out the action.

AUXILIARY VERB a verb such as *be*, *have* or *do* used with a main verb to form tenses.

BASE FORM the form of the verb without any endings added to it, for example, *walk, have, be, go*.

CLAUSE a group of words containing a verb.

CONDITIONAL a verb form used to talk about things that *would* happen or *would* be true under certain conditions, for example, *I would help you if I could*. It is also used to say what you *would* like or need, for example, *Could you give me the bill?*

CONJUGATE (to) to give a verb different endings according to whether you are referring to *I, you, they* and so on, and according to whether you are referring to the present, past or future, for example, *I have, she had, they will have*.

CONJUGATION a group of verbs which have the same endings as each other or change according to the same pattern.

CONTINUOUS TENSE a verb tense formed using *to be* and the *-ing* form of the main verb, for example, *They're swimming* (present continuous); *He was eating* (past continuous).

DIRECT OBJECT a noun or pronoun used with verbs to show who or what is acted on by the verb. For example, in *He wrote a letter* and *He wrote me a letter*, *letter* is the direct object. Compare indirect object.

DIRECT OBJECT PRONOUN a word such as *me, him, us* and *them* which is used instead of a noun to stand in for the person or thing most directly affected by the action expressed by the verb. Compare with indirect object pronoun.

ENDING a form added to something such as a verb, for example, *go > goes*.

FUTURE a verb tense used to talk about something that *will* happen or *will* be true.

GERUND a verb form in English ending in *-ing*, for example, *eating, sleeping*.

IMPERATIVE the form of a verb used when giving orders and instructions, for example, *Shut the door!; Sit down!; Don't go!; Let's eat*.

IMPERFECT one of the verb tenses used to talk about the past in Spanish, especially in descriptions, and to say what *was happening* or *used to happen*, for example, *It was sunny at the weekend; We were living in Spain at the time; I used to walk to school*. Compare with preterite.

IMPERSONAL VERB a verb whose subject is *it*, but where the *it* does not refer to any specific thing, for example, *It's raining; It's 10 o'clock*.

INDICATIVE ordinary verb forms that aren't subjunctive, such as the present, preterite or future. Compare with subjunctive.

INDIRECT OBJECT a noun or pronoun used with verbs to show who benefits or is harmed by an action. For example, in *I gave the carrot to the rabbit*, *the rabbit* is the indirect object and *the carrot* is the direct object. Compare with direct object.

INDIRECT OBJECT PRONOUN a pronoun used with verbs to show who benefits or is harmed by an action. For example, in *I gave him the carrot* and *I gave it to him*, *him* is the indirect object and the *carrot* and *it* are the direct objects. Compare with direct object pronoun.

INDIRECT SPEECH the words you use to report what someone has said when you aren't using their actual words, for example, *He said that he was going out*. Also called reported speech.

INFINITIVE a form of the verb that hasn't any endings added to it and doesn't relate to any particular tense. In English the infinitive is usually shown with *to*, as in *to speak, to eat*.

INTRANSITIVE VERB a type of verb that does not take a direct object, for example, *to sleep, to rise, to laugh*. Compare with transitive verb.

IRREGULAR VERB a verb whose forms do not follow a general pattern. Compare with regular verb.

NEGATIVE a question or statement which contains a word such as *not*, *never* or *nothing*, and is used to say that something is not happening, is not true or is absent, for example,*I never eat meat; Don't you love me?* Compare with positive.

OBJECT a noun or pronoun which refers to a person or thing that is affected by the action described by the verb. Compare with direct object, indirect object and subject.

OBJECT PRONOUN one of the set of pronouns including *me*, *him* and *them*, which are used instead of the noun as the object of a verb or preposition. Compare with subject pronoun.

PASSIVE a form of the verb that is used when the subject of the verb is the person or thing that is affected by the action, for example, *We were told* or *It was sold*.

PAST PARTICIPLE a verb form which is used to form perfect and pluperfect tenses and passives, for example, *watched, swum*. Some past participles are also used as adjectives, for example, *a broken watch*.

PAST PERFECT see pluperfect.

PERFECT a verb form used to talk about what *has* or *hasn't* happened, for example, *I've broken my glasses; We haven't eaten yet*.

PERSON one of three classes: the first person (*I, we*), the second person (*you* singular and *you* plural), and the third person (*he, she, it* and *they*).

PERSONAL PRONOUN one of the group of words including *I, you* and *they* which are used to refer to you, the people you are talking to, or the people or things you are talking about.

PLUPERFECT one of the verb tenses used to describe something that *had* happened or *had* been true at a point in the past, for example, *I'd forgotten to finish my homework*. Also called past perfect.

PLURAL the form of a word which is used to refer to more than one person or thing. Compare with singular.

POSITIVE a positive sentence or instruction is one that does not contain a negative word such as *not*. Compare with negative.

PREPOSITION is a word such as *at, for, with, into* or *from*, which is usually followed by a noun, pronoun or, in English, a word ending in *-ing*. Prepositions show how people and things relate to the rest of the sentence, for example, *She's at home; a tool for cutting grass; It's from David*.

PRESENT a verb form used to talk about what is true at the moment, what happens regularly, and what is happening now, for example, *I'm a student; I travel to college by train; I'm studying languages*.

PRESENT CONTINUOUS see continuous tense.

PRESENT PARTICIPLE a verb form in English ending in *-ing*, for example, *eating, sleeping*.

PRESENT SIMPLE see simple tense.

PRETERITE a verb form used to talk about actions that were completed in the past in Spanish. It often corresponds to the ordinary past tense in English, for example, *I bought a new bike; Mary went to the shops; I typed two reports yesterday*.

PRONOUN a word which you use instead of a noun, when you do not need or want to name someone or something directly, for example, *it, you, none*.

PROPER NOUN the name of a person, place, organization or thing. Proper nouns are always written with a capital letter, for example, *Kevin, Glasgow, Europe*.

RADICAL-CHANGING VERBS in Spanish, verbs which change their stem or root in certain tenses and in certain persons.

REFLEXIVE PRONOUN a word ending in -self or -selves, such as myself or themselves, which refers back to the subject, for example, He hurt himself; Take care of yourself.

REFLEXIVE VERB a verb where the subject and object are the same, and where the action 'reflects back' on the subject. A reflexive verb is used with a reflexive pronoun such as myself, yourself, herself, for example, I washed myself; He shaved himself.

REGULAR VERB a verb whose forms follow a general pattern or the normal rules. Compare with irregular verb.

SIMPLE TENSE a verb tense in which the verb form is made up of one word, rather than being formed from to have and a past participle or to be and an -ing form; for example, She plays tennis; He wrote a book.

SINGULAR the form of a word which is used to refer to one person or thing. Compare with plural.

STEM the main part of a verb to which endings are added.

SUBJECT a noun or pronoun that refers to the person or thing doing the action or being in the state described by the verb, for example, My cat doesn't drink milk. Compare with object.

SUBJECT PRONOUN a word such as I, he, she and they which carries out the action described by the verb. Pronouns stand in for nouns when it is clear who is being talked about, for example, My brother isn't here at the moment. He'll be back in an hour. Compare with object pronoun.

SUBJUNCTIVE a verb form used in certain circumstances to indicate some sort of feeling, or to show doubt about whether something will happen or whether something is true. It is only used occasionally in modern English, for example, If I were you, I wouldn't bother; So be it.

TENSE the form of a verb which shows whether you are referring to the past, present or future.

TRANSITIVE VERB a type of verb that takes a direct object, for example, to spend, to raise, to waste. Compare with intransitive verb.

VERB a 'doing' word which describes what someone or something does, is, or what happens to them, for example, be, sing, live.

Introduction to Verb Formation

Verbs are frequently used with a noun, with somebody's name or, particularly in English, with a pronoun such as *I*, *you* or *she*. They can relate to the present, the past and the future; this is called their <u>tense</u>.

Verbs are either:

> <u>regular</u>; their forms follow the normal rules
> <u>irregular</u>; their forms do not follow the normal rules

Almost all verbs have a form called the <u>infinitive</u>. This is a base form of the verb (for example, *walk*, *see*, *hear*) that hasn't had any endings added to it and doesn't relate to any particular tense.

In English, the infinitive is usually shown with *to*, as in *to speak*, *to eat*, *to live*. In Spanish, the infinitive is always made up of just one word (never two as in *to speak* in English) and ends in -ar, -er or -ir: for example, hab<u>lar</u> (meaning *to speak*), com<u>er</u> (meaning *to eat*) and viv<u>ir</u> (meaning *to live*). All Spanish verbs belong to one of these three types, which are called <u>conjugations</u>. We will look at each of these three conjugations in turn on the next few pages.

Regular English verbs have other forms apart from the infinitive: a form ending in -*s* (*walks*), a form ending in -*ing* (*walking*), and a form ending in -*ed* (*walked*). Spanish verbs have many more forms than this, which are made up of endings added to a <u>stem</u>. The stem of a verb can usually be worked out from the infinitive.

Spanish verb endings change depending on who or what is doing the action and on when the action takes place. In fact, the ending is very often the only thing that shows you <u>who</u> is doing the action, as the Spanish equivalents of *I*, *you*, *he* and so on (yo, tú, él and so on) are not used very much. So, both hablo on its own and yo hablo mean *I speak*. Sometimes there is a name or a noun in the sentence to make it clear who is doing the action.

For further explanation of grammatical terms, please see pages 8-11.

José habla español. José speaks Spanish.

El profesor habla español. The teacher speaks Spanish.

Spanish verb forms also change depending on whether you are talking about the present, past or future, so (yo) hablaré means *I will speak* while (yo) hablé means *I spoke*.

Some verbs in Spanish do not follow the usual patterns. These irregular verbs include some very common and important verbs like ir (meaning *to go*), ser and estar (meaning *to be*) and hacer (meaning *to do* or *to make*). Other verbs are only slightly irregular, changing their stems in certain tenses.

The following sections give you all the help you need on how to form the different verb tenses used in Spanish. If you would like even more information on how Spanish verbs are used, the *Easy Learning Spanish Grammar* shows you when and how numerous different verbs are used when writing and speaking modern Spanish.

The present simple tense

Forming the present simple tense of regular -ar verbs

If the infinitive of the Spanish verb ends in -ar, it means that the verb belongs to the first conjugation, for example, hablar, lavar, llamar.

To know which form of the verb to use in Spanish, you need to work out what the stem of the verb is and then add the correct ending. The stem of regular -ar verbs in the present simple tense is formed by taking the infinitive and chopping off -ar.

Infinitive	Stem (without -ar)
hablar (*to speak*)	habl-
lavar (*to wash*)	lav-

Now you know how to find the stem of a verb you can add the correct ending. The one you choose will depend on who or what is doing the action.

Here are the present simple endings for regular -ar verbs:

Present simple endings	Present simple of hablar	Meaning: *to speak*
-o	(yo) habl<u>o</u>	I speak
-as	(tú) habl<u>as</u>	you speak
-a	(él/ella) habl<u>a</u>	he/she/it speaks
	(usted) habl<u>a</u>	you speak
-amos	(nosotros/nosotras) habl<u>amos</u>	we speak
-áis	(vosotros/vosotras) habl<u>áis</u>	you speak
-an	(ellos/ellas) habl<u>an</u>	they speak
	(ustedes) habl<u>an</u>	you speak

For further explanation of grammatical terms, please see pages 8-11.

Trabajo en un banco. I work in a bank.

No hablo alemán. I don't speak German.

¿Buscas algo? Are you looking for something?

Compra pan cada día. He/She buys bread every day.

Lydia estudia medicina. Lydia studies *or* is studying medicine.

Funciona bien. It works well.

Viajamos mucho. We travel a lot.

¿Recordáis aquella noche? Do you remember that night?

Ustedes fabrican ventanas, ¿no? You make windows, don't you?

Mis profesores me ayudan mucho. My teachers help me a lot.

Forming the present simple tense of regular -er verbs

If the infinitive of the Spanish verb ends in -er, it means that the verb belongs to the second conjugation, for example, comer, depender.

The stem of regular -er verbs in the present simple tense is formed by taking the infinitive and chopping off -er.

Infinitive	Stem (without -er)
comer (*to eat*)	com-
depender (*to depend*)	depend-

Now add the correct ending, depending on who or what is doing the action.

Here are the present simple endings for regular -er verbs:

Present simple endings	Present simple of comer	Meaning: *to eat*
-o	(yo) como	I eat
-es	(tú) comes	you eat
-e	(él/ella) come	he/she/it eats
	(usted) come	you eat
-emos	(nosotros/nosotras) comemos	we eat
-éis	(vosotros/vosotras) coméis	you eat
-en	(ellos/ellas) comen	they eat
	(ustedes) comen	you eat

Juan come demasiado. Juan eats too much.

Mis padres me deben 15 euros. My parents owe me 15 euros.

Depende. It depends.

For further explanation of grammatical terms, please see pages 8-11.

Forming the present simple tense of regular -ir verbs

If the infinitive of the Spanish verb ends in -ir, it means that the verb belongs to the <u>third conjugation</u>, for example, vivir, recibir.

The stem of regular -ir verbs in the present simple tense is formed by taking the <u>infinitive</u> and chopping off -ir.

Infinitive	Stem (without -ir)
vivir (*to live*)	viv-
recibir (*to receive*)	recib-

Now add the correct ending depending on who or what is doing the action.

Here are the present simple endings for regular -ir verbs:

Present simple endings	Present simple of vivir	Meaning: *to live*
-o	(yo) viv<u>o</u>	I live
-es	(tú) viv<u>es</u>	you live
-e	(él/ella) viv<u>e</u>	he/she/it lives
	(usted) viv<u>e</u>	you live
-imos	(nosotros/nosotras) viv<u>imos</u>	we live
-ís	(vosotros/vosotras) viv<u>ís</u>	you live
-en	(ellos/ellas) viv<u>en</u>	they live
	(ustedes) viv<u>en</u>	you live

Mi padre recib<u>e</u> muchas cartas. My father gets a lot of letters.
Javier y Antonia viv<u>en</u> aquí. Javier and Antonia live here.
Ocurr<u>e</u> frecuentemente. It happens frequently.

Forming the present simple tense of less regular verbs

Many Spanish verbs do not follow the regular patterns shown previously. There are lots of verbs that change their <u>stem</u> in the present tense when the stress is on the stem. This means that all forms are affected in the present simple <u>APART FROM</u> the nosotros and vosotros forms. Such verbs are often called <u>radical-changing verbs</u>, meaning root-changing verbs.

For example, some verbs containing an -o in the stem change it to -ue in the present simple for all forms <u>APART FROM</u> the nosotros/nosotras and vosotros/vosotras forms.

	encontrar *to find*	recordar *to remember*	poder *to be able*	dormir *to sleep*
(yo)	encuentro	recuerdo	puedo	duermo
(tú)	encuentras	recuerdas	puedes	duermes
(él/ella/usted)	encuentra	recuerda	puede	duerme
(nosotros/as)	encontramos	recordamos	podemos	dormimos
(vosotros/as)	encontráis	recordáis	podéis	dormís
(ellos/ellas/ustedes)	encuentran	recuerdan	pueden	duermen

Other verbs containing an -e in the stem change it to -ie for all forms <u>APART FROM</u> the nosotros/nosotras and vosotros/vosotras forms.

	cerrar *to close*	pensar *to think*	entender *to understand*	perder *to lose*	preferir *to prefer*
(yo)	cierro	pienso	entiendo	pierdo	prefiero
(tú)	cierras	piensas	entiendes	pierdes	prefieres
(él/ella/usted)	cierra	piensa	entiende	pierde	prefiere
(nosotros/as)	cerramos	pensamos	entendemos	perdemos	preferimos
(vosotros/as)	cerráis	pensáis	entendéis	perdéis	preferís
(ellos/ellas/ustedes)	cierran	piensan	entienden	pierden	prefieren

For further explanation of grammatical terms, please see pages 8-11.

A few -ir verbs containing -e in the stem change this to -i in the present simple for all forms <u>APART FROM</u> the nosotros/nosotras and vosotros/ vosotras forms.

	pedir *to ask (for)*	**servir** *to serve*
(yo)	p<u>i</u>do	s<u>i</u>rvo
(tú)	p<u>i</u>des	s<u>i</u>rves
(él/ella/usted)	p<u>i</u>de	s<u>i</u>rve
(nosotros/as)	p<u>e</u>dimos	s<u>e</u>rvimos
(vosotros/as)	p<u>e</u>dís	s<u>e</u>rvís
(ellos/ellas/ustedes)	p<u>i</u>den	s<u>i</u>rven

The present continuous tense

The Spanish present continuous tense is formed from the <u>present tense</u> of **estar** and the <u>gerund</u> of the verb. The gerund is the form of the verb that ends in **-ando** (for **-ar** verbs) or **-iendo** (for **-er** and **-ir** verbs) and is the same as the *-ing* form of the verb in English (for example, *walking*, *swimming*).

> <u>Estoy</u> traba<u>jando</u>. I'm working.
> No <u>estamos</u> com<u>iendo</u>. We aren't eating.
> ¿<u>Estás</u> escrib<u>iendo</u>? Are you writing?

To form the gerund of an **-ar** verb, take off the **-ar** ending of the infinitive and add **-ando**:

Infinitive	Meaning	Stem (without -ar)	Gerund	Meaning
hablar	to speak	habl-	habl<u>ando</u>	speaking
trabajar	to work	trabaj-	trabaj<u>ando</u>	working

> Coge al niño, que <u>está llorando</u>. Pick the baby up; he's crying.
> <u>Está intentando</u> perder peso. He's trying to lose weight.

To form the gerund of an **-er** or **-ir** verb, take off the **-er** or **-ir** ending of the infinitive and add **-iendo**:

Infinitive	Meaning	Stem (without -er/-ir)	Gerund	Meaning
comer	to eat	com-	com<u>iendo</u>	eating
escribir	to write	escrib-	escrib<u>iendo</u>	writing

> <u>Estoy haciendo</u> los deberes. I'm doing my homework.
> ¿Qué <u>está</u> ocurriendo? What's happening?

For further explanation of grammatical terms, please see pages 8-11.

The imperative

Forming the imperative: instructions not to do something

In orders that tell you <u>NOT</u> to do something and that have no in front of them in Spanish, the imperative forms for tú, usted, nosotros/nosotras, vosotros/vosotras and ustedes are all taken from a verb form called the <u>present subjunctive</u>.
It's easy to remember because the endings for -ar and -er verbs are the opposite of what they are in the ordinary present tense.

In regular -ar verbs, you take off the -as, -a, -amos, -áis and -an endings of the present tense and replace them with: -es, -e, -emos, -éis and -en.

-ar verb	trabajar	*to work*
tú form	¡no trabajes!	Don't work!
usted form	¡no trabaje!	Don't work!
nosotros/as form	¡no trabajemos!	Let's not work!
vosotros/as form	¡no trabajéis!	Don't work!
ustedes form	¡no trabajen!	Don't work!

In regular -er verbs, you take off the -es, -e, -emos, -éis and -en endings of the present tense and replace them with -as, -a, -amos, -áis and -an.

-er verb	comer	*to eat*
tú form	¡no comas!	Don't eat!
usted form	¡no coma!	Don't eat!
nosotros/as form	¡no comamos!	Let's not eat!
vosotros/as form	¡no comáis!	Don't eat!
ustedes form	¡no coman!	Don't eat!

In regular -ir verbs, you take off the -es, -e, -imos, -ís and -en endings of the present tense and replace them with -as, -a, -amos, -áis and -an.

-ir verb	decidir	to decide
tú form	¡no decidas!	Don't decide!
usted form	¡no decida!	Don't decide!
nosotros/as form	¡no decidamos!	Let's not decide!
vosotros/as form	¡no decidáis!	Don't decide!
ustedes form	¡no decidan!	Don't decide!

A number of irregular verbs also have irregular imperative forms. These are shown in the table below.

	dar *to give*	decir *to say*	estar *to be*	hacer *to do/make*	ir *to go*
tú form	¡no des! don't give!	¡no digas! don't say!	¡no estés! don't be!	¡no hagas! don't do/make!	¡no vayas! don't go!
usted form	¡no dé! don't give!	¡no diga! don't say!	¡no esté! don't be!	¡no haga! don't do/make!	¡no vaya! don't go!
nosotros form	¡no demos! let's not give!	¡no digamos! let's not say!	¡no estemos! let's not be!	¡no hagamos! let's not do/make!	¡no vayamos! let's not go!
vosotros form	¡no deis! don't give!	¡no digáis! don't say!	¡no estéis! don't be!	¡no hagáis! don't do/make!	¡no vayáis! don't go!
ustedes form	¡no den! don't give!	¡no digan! don't say!	¡no estén! don't be!	¡no hagan! don't do/make!	¡no vayan! don't go!

	poner *to put*	salir *to leave*	ser *to be*	tener *to have*	venir *to come*
tú form	¡no pongas! don't put!	¡no salgas! don't leave!	¡no seas! don't be!	¡no tengas! don't have!	¡no vengas! don't come!
usted form	¡no ponga! don't put!	¡no salga! don't leave!	¡no sea! don't be!	¡no tenga! don't have!	¡no venga! don't come!
nosotros form	¡no pongamos! let's not put!	¡no salgamos! let's not leave!	¡no seamos! let's not be!	¡no tengamos! let's not have!	¡no vengamos! let's not come!
vosotros form	¡no pongáis! don't put!	¡no salgáis! don't leave!	¡no seáis! don't be!	¡no tengáis! don't have!	¡no vengáis! don't come!
ustedes form	¡no pongan! don't put!	¡no salgan! don't leave!	¡no sean! don't be!	¡no tengan! don't have!	¡no vengan! don't come!

For further explanation of grammatical terms, please see pages 8-11.

Note that if you take the yo form of the present tense, take off the -o and add the endings to this instead for instructions <u>NOT TO DO</u> something, some of these irregular forms will be more predictable.

digo	I say	>	negative imperative stem	>	dig-
hago	I do	>	negative imperative stem	>	hag-
pongo	I put	>	negative imperative stem	>	pong-
salgo	I leave	>	negative imperative stem	>	salg-
tengo	I have	>	negative imperative stem	>	teng-
vengo	I come	>	negative imperative stem	>	veng-

Forming the imperative: instructions to do something

In instructions telling you <u>TO DO</u> something, the forms for usted, nosotros and ustedes are exactly the same as they are in negative instructions (instructions telling you not to do something) except that there isn't a no.

	trabajar to work	comer to eat	decidir to decide
usted form	¡Trabaje!	¡Coma!	¡Decida!
nosotros/as form	¡Trabajemos!	¡Comamos!	¡Decidamos!
ustedes form	¡Trabajen!	¡Coman!	¡Decidan!

There are special forms of the imperative for tú and vosotros/vosotras in positive instructions (instructions telling you to do something). The tú form of the imperative is the same as the tú form of the ordinary present simple tense, but without the final -s.

trabajar	>	¡Trabaja!
to work		Work!
comer	>	¡Come!
to eat		Eat!
decidir	>	¡Decide!
to decide		Decide!

The vosotros/vosotras form of the imperative is the same as the infinitive, except that you take off the final -r and add -d instead.

trabajar	>	Trabajad!
to work		Work!
comer	>	Comed!
to eat		Eat!
decidir	>	Decidid!
to decide		Decide!

There are a number of imperative forms that are irregular in Spanish. The irregular imperative forms for usted, nosotros/nosotras and ustedes are the same as the irregular negative imperative forms without the no. The tú and vosotros/vosotras forms are different again.

	dar *to give*	decir *to say*	estar *to be*	hacer *to do/make*	ir *to go*
tú form	¡da! give!	¡di! say!	¡está! be!	¡haz! do/make!	¡ve! go!
usted form	¡dé! give!	¡diga! say!	¡esté! be!	¡haga! do/make!	¡vaya! go!
nosotros/as form	¡demos! let's give!	¡digamos! let's say!	¡estemos! let's be!	¡hagamos! let's do/make!	¡vamos! let's go!
vosotros/as form	¡dad! give!	¡decid! say!	¡estad! be!	¡haced! do/make!	¡id! go!
ustedes form	¡den! give!	¡digan! say!	¡estén! be!	¡hagan! do/make!	¡vayan! go!

	poner *to put*	salir *to leave*	ser *to be*	tener *to have*	venir *to come*
tú form	¡pon! put!	¡sal! leave!	¡sé! be!	¡ten! have!	¡ven! come!
usted form	¡ponga! put!	¡salga! leave!	¡sea! be!	¡tenga! have!	¡venga! come!
nosotros/as form	¡pongamos! let's put!	¡salgamos! let's leave!	¡seamos! let's be!	¡tengamos! let's have!	¡vengamos! let's come!
vosotros/as form	¡poned! put!	¡salid! leave!	¡sed! be!	¡tened! have!	¡venid! come!
ustedes form	¡pongan! put!	¡salgan! leave!	¡sean! be!	¡tengan! have!	¡vengan! come!

For further explanation of grammatical terms, please see pages 8-11.

Note that the **nosotros/nosotras** form for ir in instructions <u>TO DO</u> something is usually **vamos**; in instructions <u>NOT TO DO</u> something, it is **no vayamos**.

Position of object pronouns

If you are telling someone <u>NOT TO DO</u> something, any object pronouns go <u>BEFORE</u> the verb.

> ¡No <u>me lo</u> mandes! Don't send it to me!
> ¡No <u>me</u> molestes! Don't disturb me!
> ¡No <u>los</u> castigue! Don't punish them!
> ¡No <u>se la</u> devolvamos! Let's not give it back to him/her/them!
> ¡No <u>las</u> contestéis! Don't answer them!

If you are telling someone <u>TO DO</u> something, any object pronouns join on to the <u>END</u> of the verb. An accent is usually added to make sure that the stress in the imperative verb stays the same.

> ¡Explícame<u>lo</u>! Explain it to me!
> ¡Perdóne<u>me</u>! Excuse me!
> ¡Díga<u>me</u>! Tell me!
> ¡Esperémos<u>la</u>! Let's wait for her/it!

Reflexive verbs

Forming the present tense of reflexive verbs

The present tense of a reflexive verb is formed in the same way as that of a non-reflexive verb except that reflexive pronouns are included before the verb.

The following table shows the reflexive verb lavarse in full.

Reflexive forms of lavarse	Meaning
(yo) me lavo	I wash (myself)
(tú) te lavas	you wash (yourself)
(él) se lava	he washes (himself)
(ella) se lava	she washes (herself)
(uno) se lava	one washes (oneself)
se lava	it washes (itself)
(usted) se lava	you wash (yourself)
(nosotros/nosotras) nos lavamos	we wash (ourselves)
(vosotros/vosotras) os laváis	you wash (yourselves)
(ellos) se lavan	they wash (themselves)
(ellas) se lavan	they wash (themselves)
(ustedes) se lavan	you wash (yourselves)

Position of reflexive pronouns

In ordinary tenses such as the present simple, the reflexive pronoun goes <u>BEFORE</u> the verb.

> <u>Me</u> acuesto temprano. I go to bed early.
> ¿Cómo <u>se</u> llama usted? What's your name?

When telling someone <u>NOT TO DO</u> something, you also put the reflexive pronoun <u>BEFORE</u> the verb.

For further explanation of grammatical terms, please see pages 8-11.

No <u>te</u> levantes. Don't get up.
¡No <u>os</u> vayáis! Don't go away!

When telling someone <u>TO DO</u> something, you join the reflexive pronoun onto the end of the verb.

¡Siénten<u>se</u>! Sit down!
¡Cálla<u>te</u>! Be quiet!

When adding reflexive pronouns to the end of the imperative, you drop the final -s of the nosotros form and the final -d of the vosotros form, before the pronoun.

¡Vámo<u>nos</u>! Let's go!
¡Senta<u>os</u>! Sit down!

You always join the reflexive pronoun onto the end of infinitives and gerunds (the -ando or -iendo forms of the verb) unless the infinitive or gerund follows another verb.

Hay que relajar<u>se</u> de vez en cuando. You have to relax from time to time.
Acostándo<u>se</u> temprano, se descansa mejor.
You feel more rested by going to bed early.

Where the infinitive or gerund follows another verb, you can put the reflexive pronoun either at the end of the infinitive or gerund or before the other verb.

Quiero bañar<u>me</u> or <u>Me</u> quiero bañar. I want to have a bath.
Tienes que vestir<u>te</u> or <u>Te</u> tienes que vestir. You must get dressed.
Está vistiéndo<u>se</u> or <u>Se</u> está vistiendo. She's getting dressed.
¿Estás duchándo<u>te</u>? or ¿<u>Te</u> estás duchando? Are you having a shower?

Note that, when adding pronouns to the ends of verb forms, you will often have to add a written accent to preserve the stress.

The future tense

Forming the future tense

To form the future tense of regular **-ar**, **-er** and **-ir** verbs, add the following endings to the <u>infinitive</u> of the verb: **-é, -ás, -á, -emos, -éis, -án**.

The following table shows the future tense of three regular verbs: **hablar** (meaning *to speak*), **comer** (meaning *to eat*) and **vivir** (meaning *to live*).

(yo)	hablaré	comeré	viviré	I'll speak/eat/live
(tú)	hablarás	comerás	vivirás	you'll speak/eat/live
(él, ella) (usted)	hablará	comerá	vivirá	he'll speak/eat/live she'll speak/eat/live it'll speak/eat/live you'll speak/eat/live
(nosotros/nosotras)	hablaremos	comeremos	viviremos	we'll speak/eat/live
(vosotros/vosotras)	hablaréis	comeréis	viviréis	you'll speak/eat/live
(ellos/ellas/ustedes)	hablarán	comerán	vivirán	they'll/you'll speak/eat/live

<u>Hablaré</u> con ella. I'll speak to her.
<u>Comeremos</u> en casa de José. We'll eat at José's.
No <u>volverá</u>. He won't come back.
¿Lo <u>entenderás</u>? Will you understand it?

Note that in the future tense only the **nosotros/nosotras** form doesn't have an accent.

Verbs with irregular stems in the future tense

There are a few verbs that <u>DO NOT</u> use their infinitives as the stem for the future tense. Here are some of the most common.

Verb	Stem	(yo)	(tú)	(él) (ella) (usted)	(nosotros) (nosotras)	(vosotros) (vosotras)	(ellos) (ellas) (ustedes)
decir to say	dir-	diré	dirás	dirá	dir<u>emos</u>	dir<u>éis</u>	dir<u>án</u>
haber to have	habr-	habr<u>é</u>	habrás	habr<u>á</u>	habr<u>emos</u>	habr<u>éis</u>	habr<u>án</u>
hacer to do/make	har-	har<u>é</u>	harás	hará	har<u>emos</u>	har<u>éis</u>	har<u>án</u>
poder to be able	podr-	podr<u>é</u>	podrás	podrá	podr<u>emos</u>	podr<u>éis</u>	podr<u>án</u>
poner to put	pondr-	pondré	pondrás	pondrá	pondr<u>emos</u>	pondr<u>éis</u>	pondrán
querer to want	querr-	querr<u>é</u>	querrás	querrá	querr<u>emos</u>	querr<u>éis</u>	querr<u>án</u>
saber to know	sabr-	sabr<u>é</u>	sabrás	sabrá	sabr<u>emos</u>	sabr<u>éis</u>	sabr<u>án</u>
salir to leave	saldr-	saldré	saldrás	saldrá	saldr<u>emos</u>	saldr<u>éis</u>	saldrán
tener to have	tendr-	tendr<u>é</u>	tendrás	tendrá	tendr<u>emos</u>	tendr<u>éis</u>	tendr<u>án</u>
venir to come	vendr-	vendr<u>é</u>	vendrás	vendrá	vendr<u>emos</u>	vendr<u>éis</u>	vendr<u>án</u>

Lo <u>haré</u> mañana. I'll do it tomorrow.
No <u>podremos</u> hacerlo. We won't be able to do it.
Lo <u>pondré</u> aquí. I'll put it here.
<u>Saldrán</u> por la mañana. They'll leave in the morning.
¿A qué hora <u>vendrás</u>? What time will you come?

Reflexive verbs in the future tense

The future tense of reflexive verbs is formed in just the same way as for ordinary verbs, except that you have to remember to give the reflexive pronoun (me, te, se, nos, os, se).

> <u>Me leventaré</u> temprano. I'll get up early.

The conditional

Forming the conditional

To form the conditional of regular -ar, -er, and -ir verbs, add the following endings to the <u>infinitive</u> of the verb: -ía, -ías, -ía, -íamos, -íais, -ían.

The following table shows the conditional tense of three regular verbs: hablar (meaning to speak), comer (meaning to eat) and vivir (meaning to live).

(yo)	hablaría	comería	viviría	I would speak/eat/live
(tú)	hablarías	comerías	vivirías	you would speak/eat/live
(él, ella) (usted)	hablaría	comería	viviría	he would speak/eat/live she would speak/eat/live it would speak/eat/live you would speak/eat/live
(nosotros/nosotras)	hablaríamos	comeríamos	viviríamos	we would speak/eat/live
(vosotros/vosotras)	hablaríais	comeríais	viviríais	you would speak/eat/live
(ellos/ellas/ustedes)	hablarían	comerían	vivirían	they would/you would speak/eat/live

Me <u>gustaría</u> ir a China. I'd like to go to China.
Dije que <u>hablaría</u> con ella. I said that I would speak to her.
<u>Debería</u> llamar a mis padres. I should ring my parents.

Don't forget to put an accent on the í in the conditional.

Note that the endings in the conditional tense are identical to those of the <u>imperfect tense</u> for -er and -ir verbs. The only difference is that they are added to a different stem.

Verbs with irregular stems in the conditional

To form the conditional of irregular verbs, use the same stem as for the <u>future tense</u>, then add the usual endings for the conditional. The same verbs that are irregular in the future tense are irregular in the conditional.

Verb	Stem	(yo)	(tú)	(él) (ella) (usted)	(nosotros) (nosotras)	(vosotros) (vosotras)	(ellos) (ellas) (ustedes)
decir *to say*	dir-	diría	dirías	diría	diríamos	diríais	dirían
haber *to have*	habr-	habría	habrías	habría	habríamos	habríais	habrían
hacer *to do/make*	har-	haría	harías	haría	haríamos	haríais	harían
poder *to be able*	podr-	podría	podrías	podría	podríamos	podríais	podrían
poner *to put*	pondr-	pondría	pondrías	pondría	pondríamos	pondríais	pondrían
querer *to want*	querr-	querría	querrías	querría	querríamos	querríais	querrían
saber *to know*	sabr-	sabría	sabrías	sabría	sabríamos	sabríais	sabrían
salir *to leave*	saldr-	saldría	saldrías	saldría	saldríamos	saldríais	saldrían
tener *to have*	tendr-	tendría	tendrías	tendría	tendríamos	tendríais	tendrían
venir *to come*	vendr-	vendría	vendrías	vendría	vendríamos	vendríais	vendrían

For further explanation of grammatical terms, please see pages 8-11.

¿Qué harías tú en mi lugar? What would you do if you were me?
¿Podrías ayudarme? Could you help me?
Yo lo pondría aquí. I would put it here.

Reflexive verbs in the conditional

The conditional of reflexive verbs is formed in just the same way as for ordinary verbs, except that you have to remember to give the reflexive pronoun (me, te, se, nos, os, se).

Le dije que me levantaría temprano. I told him I would get up early.

The preterite

Forming the preterite of regular verbs

To form the preterite of any regular -ar verb, you take off the -ar ending to form the stem, and add the endings: -é, -aste, -ó, -amos, -asteis, -aron.

To form the preterite of any regular -er or -ir verb, you also take off the -er or -ir ending to form the stem and add the endings: -í, -iste, -ió, -imos, -isteis, -ieron.

The following table shows the preterite of three regular verbs: hablar (meaning to speak), comer (meaning to eat) and vivir (meaning to live).

(yo)	hablé	comí	viví	I spoke/ate/lived
(tú)	hablaste	comiste	viviste	you spoke/ate/lived
(él, ella) (usted)	habló	comió	vivió	he spoke/ate/lived she spoke/ate/lived it spoke/ate/lived you spoke/ate/lived
(nosotros/nosotras)	hablamos	comimos	vivimos	we spoke/ate/lived
(vosotros/vosotras)	hablasteis	comisteis	vivisteis	you spoke/ate/lived
(ellos/ellas) (ustedes)	hablaron	comieron	vivieron	they spoke/ate/lived you spoke/ate/lived

Bailé con mi hermana. I danced with my sister.
No hablé con ella. I didn't speak to her.
Comimos en un restaurante. We had lunch in a restaurant.
¿Cerraste la ventana? Did you close the window?

Irregular verbs in the preterite

A number of verbs have very irregular forms in the preterite. The table shows some of the most common.

Verb	(yo)	(tú)	(él) (ella) (usted)	(nosotros) (nosotras)	(vosotros) (vosotras)	(ellos) (ellas) (ustedes)
andar *to walk*	anduve	anduviste	anduvo	anduvimos	anduvisteis	anduvieron
conducir *to drive*	conduje	condujiste	condujo	condujimos	condujisteis	condujeron
dar *to give*	di	diste	dio	dimos	disteis	dieron
decir *to say*	dije	dijiste	dijo	dijimos	dijisteis	dijeron
estar *to be*	estuve	estuviste	estuvo	estuvimos	estuvisteis	estuvieron
hacer *to do, to make*	hice	hiciste	hizo	hicimos	hicisteis	hicieron
ir *to go*	fui	fuiste	fue	fuimos	fuisteis	fueron
poder *to be able*	pude	pudiste	pudo	pudimos	pudisteis	pudieron
poner *to put*	puse	pusiste	puso	pusimos	pusisteis	pusieron
querer *to want*	quise	quisiste	quiso	quisimos	quisisteis	quisieron
saber *to know*	supe	supiste	supo	supimos	supisteis	supieron
ser *to be*	fui	fuiste	fue	fuimos	fuisteis	fueron
tener *to have*	tuve	tuviste	tuvo	tuvimos	tuvisteis	tuvieron
traer *to bring*	traje	trajiste	trajo	trajimos	trajisteis	trajeron
venir *to come*	vine	viniste	vino	vinimos	vinisteis	vinieron
ver *to see*	vi	viste	vio	vimos	visteis	vieron

Note that hizo (the él/ella/usted form of hacer) is spelt with a z.

> Fue a Madrid. He went to Madrid.
> Te vi en el parque. I saw you in the park.
> No vinieron. They didn't come.
> ¿Qué hizo? What did she do?
> Se lo di a Teresa. I gave it to Teresa.
> Fue en 1999. It was in 1999.

The preterite forms of ser (meaning *to be*) are the same as the preterite forms of ir (meaning *to go*).

Some other verbs are regular EXCEPT FOR the él/ella/usted and ellos/ellas/ustedes forms (*third persons singular and plural*). In these forms the stem vowel changes.

Verb	(yo)	(tú)	(él) (ella) (usted)	(nosotros) (nosotras)	(vosotros) (vosotras)	(ellos) (ellas) (ustedes)
dormir *to sleep*	dormí	dormiste	durmió	dormimos	dormisteis	durmieron
morir *to die*	morí	moriste	murió	morimos	moristeis	murieron
pedir *to ask for*	pedí	pediste	pidió	pedimos	pedisteis	pidieron
reír *to laugh*	reí	reíste	rió	reímos	reísteis	rieron
seguir *to follow*	seguí	seguiste	siguió	seguimos	seguisteis	siguieron
sentir *to feel*	sentí	sentiste	sintió	sentimos	sentisteis	sintieron

Note that reír also has an accent in all persons apart from the ellos/ellas/ustedes forms.

> Antonio <u>durmió</u> diez horas. Antonio slept for ten hours.
> <u>Murió</u> en 1066. He died in 1066.
> <u>Pidió</u> paella. He asked for paella.
> ¿Los <u>siguió</u>? Did she follow them?
> <u>Sintió</u> un dolor en la pierna. He felt a pain in his leg.
> Nos <u>reímos</u> mucho. We laughed a lot.
> Juan no se <u>rió</u>. Juan didn't laugh.

caer (meaning *to fall*) and leer (meaning *to read*) have an accent in all persons <u>apart from</u> the ellos/ellas/ustedes form (*third person plural*). In addition, the vowel changes to y in the él/ella/usted and ellos/ellas/ustedes forms (*third persons singular and plural*).

Verb	(yo)	(tú)	(él) (ella) (usted)	(nosotros) (nosotras)	(vosotros) (vosotras)	(ellos) (ellas) (ustedes)
caer to fall	caí	caíste	cayó	caímos	caísteis	cayeron
construir to build	construí	construiste	construyó	construimos	construisteis	construyeron
leer to read	leí	leíste	leyó	leímos	leísteis	leyeron

Note that construir also changes to y in the él/ella/usted and ellos/ellas/ustedes forms (*third persons singular and plural*), but only has accents in the yo and él/ella/usted forms.

> Se <u>cayó</u> por la ventana. He fell out of the window.
> Ayer <u>leí</u> un artículo muy interesante.
> I read a very interesting article yesterday.
> <u>Construyeron</u> una nueva autopista. They built a new motorway.

Other spelling changes in the preterite

Spanish verbs that end in -zar, -gar and -car in the infinitive change the z to c, the g to gu and the c to qu in the yo form (*first person singular*).

Verb	(yo)	(tú)	(él) (ella) (usted)	(nosotros) (nosotras)	(vosotros) (vosotras)	(ellos) (ellas) (ustedes)
cruzar *to cross*	crucé	cruzaste	cruzó	cruzamos	cruzasteis	cruzaron
empezar *to begin*	empecé	empezaste	empezó	empezamos	empezasteis	empezaron
pagar *to pay for*	pagué	pagaste	pagó	pagamos	pagasteis	pagaron
sacar *to follow*	saqué	sacaste	sacó	sacamos	sacasteis	sacaron

<u>Crucé</u> el río. I crossed the river.

<u>Empecé</u> a hacer mis deberes. I began doing my homework.

No <u>pagué</u> la cuenta. I didn't pay the bill.

Me <u>saqué</u> las llaves del bolsillo. I took my keys out of my pocket.

Note that the change from g to gu and c to qu before e is to keep the sound hard.

Reflexive verbs in the preterite

The preterite of reflexive verbs is formed in just the same way as for ordinary verbs, except that you have to remember to give the reflexive pronoun (me, te, se, nos, os, se).

<u>Me levanté</u> a las siete. I got up at seven.

For further explanation of grammatical terms, please see pages 8-11.

The imperfect tense

Forming the imperfect tense

To form the imperfect of any regular -ar verb, you take off the -ar ending of the infinitive to form the stem and add the endings: -aba, -abas, -aba, -ábamos, -abais, -aban.

The following table shows the imperfect tense of one regular -ar verb: hablar (meaning *to speak*).

(yo)	hablaba	I spoke
		I was speaking
		I used to speak
(tú)	hablabas	you spoke
		you were speaking
		you used to speak
(él/ella/usted)	hablaba	he/she/it/you spoke
		he/she/it was speaking, you were speaking
		he/she/it/you used to speak
(nosotros/nosotras)	hablábamos	we spoke
		we were speaking
		we used to speak
(vosotros/vosotras)	hablabais	you spoke
		you were speaking
		you used to speak
(ellos/ellas/ustedes)	hablaban	they/you spoke
		they/you were speaking
		they/you used to speak

Note that in the imperfect tense of -ar verbs, the only accent is on the nosotros/nosotras form.

Hablaba francés e italiano. He spoke French and Italian.

Cuando era joven, mi tío trabajaba mucho.

My uncle worked hard when he was young.

Estudiábamos matemáticas e inglés. We were studying maths and English.

To form the imperfect of any regular -er or -ir verb, you take off the -er or -ir ending of the infinitive to form the stem and add the endings: -ía, -ías, -ía, -íamos, -íais, -ían.

The following table shows the imperfect of two regular verbs: comer (meaning *to eat*) and vivir (meaning *to live*).

(yo)	comía	vivía	I ate/lived I was eating/living I used to eat/live
(tú)	comías	vivías	you ate/lived you were eating/living you used to eat/live
(él/ella/usted)	comía	vivía	he/she/it/you ate/lived he/she/it was eating/living, you were eating/living he/she/it was eating/living, you were eating/living
(nosotros/nosotras)	comíamos	vivíamos	we ate/lived we were eating/living we used to eat/live
(vosotros/vosotras)	comíais	vivíais	you ate/lived you were eating/living you used to eat/live
(ellos/ellas/ustedes)	comían	vivían	they/you ate/lived they/you were eating/living they/you used to eat/live

Note that in the imperfect tense of -er and -ir verbs, there's an accent on all the endings.

> A veces, <u>comíamos</u> en casa de Pepe. We sometimes used to eat at Pepe's.
> <u>Vivía</u> en un piso en la Avenida de Barcelona.
> She lived in a flat in Avenida de Barcelona.
> Cuando llegó el médico, ya se <u>sentían</u> mejor.
> They were already feeling better when the doctor arrived.

The imperfect endings for -er and -ir verbs are the same as the endings used to form the conditional for all verbs. The only difference is that, in the conditional, the endings are added to the future stem.

Reflexive verbs in the imperfect tense

The imperfect of reflexive verbs is formed in just the same way as for ordinary verbs, except that you have to remember to give the reflexive pronoun (me, te, se, nos, os, se).

> Antes <u>se levantaba</u> temprano. He used to get up early.

The perfect tense

Forming the perfect tense

As in English, the perfect tense in Spanish has two parts to it. These are:

- the <u>present</u> tense of the verb haber (meaning *to have*)
- a part of the main verb called the <u>past participle</u>.

Forming the past participle

To form the past participle of regular -ar verbs, take off the -ar ending of the infinitive and add -ado.

> hablar (*to speak*) > hablado (*spoken*)

To form the past participle of regular -er or -ir verbs, take off the -er or -ir ending of the infinitive and add -ido.

> comer (*to eat*) > comido (*eaten*)
> vivir (*to live*) > vivido (*lived*)

The perfect tense of some regular verbs

The following table shows how you can combine the present tense of haber with the past participle of any verb to form the perfect tense.

In this case, the past participles are taken from the following regular verbs:

hablar (meaning *to speak*); trabajar (meaning *to work*); comer (meaning *to eat*); vender (meaning *to sell*); vivir (meaning *to live*); decidir (meaning *to decide*).

	Present of haber	**Past participle**	**Meaning**
(yo)	he	hablado	I have spoken
(tú)	has	trabajado	you have worked
(él/ella/usted)	ha	comido	he/she/it has eaten, you have eaten
(nosotros/nosotras)	hemos	vendido	we have sold
(vosotros/vosotras)	habéis	vivido	you have lived
(ellos/ellas/ustedes)	han	decidido	they/you have decided

Has trabajado mucho. You've worked hard.

No he comido nada. I haven't eaten anything.

Verbs with irregular past participles

Some past participles are irregular. There aren't too many, so try to learn them.

abrir (to open)	>	abierto (opened)
cubrir (to cover)	>	cubierto (covered)
decir (to say)	>	dicho (said)
escribir (to write)	>	escrito (written)
freír (to fry)	>	frito (fried)
hacer (to do, to make)	>	hecho (done, made)
morir (to die)	>	muerto (died)
oír (to hear)	>	oído (heard)
poner (to put)	>	puesto (put)
romper (to break)	>	roto (broken)
ver (to see)	>	visto (seen)
volver (to return)	>	vuelto (returned)

No ha dicho nada. He hasn't said anything.

Hoy he hecho muchas cosas. I've done a lot today.

Han muerto tres personas. Three people have died.

Carlos ha roto el espejo. Carlos has broken the mirror.

Jamás he visto una cosa parecida. I've never seen anything like it.

he/has/ha and so on must <u>NEVER</u> be separated from the past participle.
Any object pronouns go before the form of haber being used, and <u>NOT</u> between
the form of haber and the past participle.

> No <u>lo</u> he visto. I haven't seen it.
> ¿<u>Lo</u> has hecho ya? Have you done it yet?

Reflexive verbs in the perfect tense

The perfect tense of reflexive verbs is formed in the same way as for ordinary
verbs. The reflexive pronouns (me, te, se, nos, os, se) come before he, has, ha,
and so on. The table below shows the perfect tense of lavarse in full.

(Subject pronoun)	Reflexive pronoun	Present tense of haber	Past Participle	Meaning
(yo)	me	he	lavado	I have washed
(tú)	te	has	lavado	you have washed
(él, ella, uno) (usted)	se	ha	lavado	he has washed she has washed one has washed it has washed you have washed
(nosotros) (nosotras)	nos	hemos	lavado	we have washed we have washed
(vosotros) (vosotras)	os	habéis	lavado	you have washed you have washed
(ellos) (ellas) (ustedes)	se	han	lavado	they have washed they have washed you have washed

The pluperfect or past perfect tense

Forming the pluperfect tense

Like the perfect tense, the pluperfect tense in Spanish has <u>two</u> parts to it:

- the imperfect tense of the verb haber (meaning *to have*)
- the past participle.

The table below shows how you can combine the imperfect tense of haber with the past participle of any verb to form the pluperfect tense. Here, the past participles are taken from the following regular verbs: hablar (meaning *to speak*); trabajar (meaning *to work*); comer (meaning *to eat*); vender (meaning *to sell*); vivir (meaning *to live*); decidir (meaning *to decide*).

(Subject pronoun)	Imperfect of haber	Past Participle	Meaning
(yo)	había	hablado	I had spoken
(tú)	habías	trabajado	you had worked
(él/ella/usted)	había	comido	he/she/it/you had eaten
(nosotros/nosotras)	habíamos	vendido	we had sold
(vosotros/vosotras)	habíais	vivido	you had lived
(ellos/ellas/ustedes)	habían	decidido	they/you had decided

<u>Había decidido</u> escribirle. I had decided to write to her.
No <u>había trabajado</u> antes. He hadn't worked before.
<u>Había vendido</u> su caballo. She had sold her horse.
Ya <u>habíamos comido</u>. We had already eaten.
<u>Habían hablado</u> con el médico. They had spoken to the doctor.

Remember that some very common verbs have irregular past participles.

abrir (*to open*)	>	abierto (*opened*)
cubrir (*to cover*)	>	cubierto (*covered*)
decir (*to say*)	>	dicho (*said*)
escribir (*to write*)	>	escrito (*written*)
freír (*to fry*)	>	frito (*fried*)
hacer (*to do, to make*)	>	hecho (*done, made*)
morir (*to die*)	>	muerto (*died*)
oír (*to hear*)	>	oído (*heard*)
poner (*to put*)	>	puesto (*put*)
romper (*to break*)	>	roto (*broken*)
ver (*to see*)	>	visto (*seen*)
volver (*to return*)	>	vuelto (*returned*)

No <u>había dicho</u> nada. He hadn't said anything.
Tres personas <u>habían muerto</u>. Three people had died.

había/habías/habían and so on must <u>NEVER</u> be separated from the past participle. Any object pronouns go before the form of haber being used, and <u>NOT</u> between the form of haber and the past participle.

No lo había visto. I hadn't seen it.

Reflexive verbs in the pluperfect tense

The pluperfect tense of reflexive verbs is formed in the same way as for ordinary verbs. The reflexive pronouns (me, te, se, nos, os, se) come before había, habías, había, and so on. The table on the next page shows the pluperfect tense of lavarse in full.

(Subject pronoun)	Reflexive pronoun	Imperfect tense of haber	Past Participle	Meaning
(yo)	me	había	lavado	I had washed
(tú)	te	habías	lavado	you had washed
(él, ella, uno) (usted)	se	había	lavado	he had washed she had washed one had washed it had washed you had washed
(nosotros) (nosotras)	nos	habíamos	lavado	we had washed we had washed
(vosotros) (vosotras)	os	habíais	lavado	you had washed you had washed
(ellos) (ellas) (ustedes)	se	habían	lavado	they had washed they had washed you had washed

The passive

Forming the passive

In English we use the verb *to be* with a <u>past participle</u> (*was painted, were seen, are made*) to form the passive. In Spanish, the passive is formed in exactly the same way, using the verb ser (meaning *to be*) and a <u>past participle</u>. When you say who the action is or was done by, you use the preposition por (meaning *by*).

> <u>Son fabricados</u> en España. They're made in Spain.
> <u>Fue escrito</u> por JK Rowling. It was written by JK Rowling.
> La casa <u>fue construida</u> en 1956. The house was built in 1956.
> El cuadro <u>fue pintado</u> por mi padre. The picture was painted by my father.
> El colegio va a <u>ser modernizado</u>. The school is going to be modernized.

Note that the ending of the past participle agrees with the subject of the verb ser in exactly the same way as an adjective would.

Here is the preterite of the -ar verb enviar (meaning *to send*) in its passive form.

(Subject pronoun)	Preterite of ser	Past Participle	Meaning
(yo)	fui	enviado (masculine) enviada (feminine)	I was sent
(tú)	fuiste	enviado (masculine) enviada (feminine)	you were sent
(él)	fue	enviado	he was sent
(ella)		enviada	she was sent
(usted)		enviado (masculine) enviada (feminine)	you were sent

(Subject pronoun)	Preterite of ser	Past Participle	Meaning
(nosotros)	fuimos	enviados	we were sent
(nosotras)		enviadas	we were sent
(vosotros)	fuisteis	enviados	you were sent
(vosotras)		enviadas	you were sent
(ellos)	fueron	enviados	they were sent
(ellas)		enviadas	they were sent
(ustedes)		enviados (masculine)	you were sent
		enviadas (feminine)	you were sent

You can form other tenses in the passive by changing the tense of the verb ser.

| **Future:** | serán enviados | they will be sent |
| **Perfect:** | han sido enviados | they have been sent |

Irregular past participles are the same as they are in the perfect tense. These are shown for many common verbs in the **Verb Tables** at the back of the book.

The gerund

Forming the gerund of regular verbs

To form the gerund of regular -ar verbs, take off the -ar ending of the infinitive to form the stem, and add -ando.

Infinitive	Stem	Gerund
hablar	habl-	hablando
trabajar	trabaj-	trabajando

To form the gerund of regular -er and -ir verbs, take off the -er and -ir ending of the infinitive to form the stem, and add -iendo.

Infinitive	Stem	Gerund
comer	com-	comiendo
vivir	viv-	viviendo

Position of pronouns with the gerund

Object pronouns and reflexive pronouns are attached to the end of the gerund or alternatively put before estar in continuous tenses.

Estoy hablándote or Te estoy hablando. I'm talking to you.
Está vistiéndose or Se está vistiendo. He's getting dressed.
Estaban mostrándoselo or Se lo estaban mostrando.
They were showing it to him/her/them/you.

Note that you will always have to add an accent to keep the stress in the same place when adding pronouns to the end of a gerund.

For further explanation of grammatical terms, please see pages 8-11.

The subjunctive

Forming the present subjunctive

To form the present subjunctive of most verbs, take off the -o ending of the yo form of the <u>present simple</u>, and add a fixed set of endings.

For -ar verbs, the endings are: -e, -es, -e, -emos, -éis, -en.

For both -er and -ir verbs, the endings are: -a, -as, -a, -amos, -áis, -an.

The following table shows the present subjunctive of three regular verbs: hablar (meaning to speak), comer (meaning to eat) and vivir (meaning to live).

Infinitive	(yo)	(tú)	(él) (ella) (usted)	(nosotros) (nosotras)	(vosotros) (vosotras)	(ellos) (ellas) (ustedes)
hablar to speak	hable	hables	hable	hablemos	habléis	hablen
comer to eat	coma	comas	coma	comamos	comáis	coman
vivir to live	viva	vivas	viva	vivamos	viváis	vivan

Quiero que <u>comas</u> algo. I want you to eat something.

Me sorprende que no <u>hable</u> inglés. I'm surprised he doesn't speak English.

No es verdad que <u>trabajen</u> aquí. It isn't true that they work here.

Some verbs have very irregular yo forms in the ordinary present tense and these irregular forms are reflected in the stem for the present subjunctive.

Infinitive	(yo)	(tú)	(él) (ella) (usted)	(nosotros) (nosotras)	(vosotros) (vosotras)	(ellos) (ellas) (ustedes)
decir to say	diga	digas	diga	digamos	digáis	digan
hacer to do/make	haga	hagas	haga	hagamos	hagáis	hagan
poner to put	ponga	pongas	ponga	pongamos	pongáis	pongan
salir to leave	salga	salgas	salga	salgamos	salgáis	salgan
tener to have	tenga	tengas	tenga	tengamos	tengáis	tengan
venir to come	venga	vengas	venga	vengamos	vengáis	vengan

Voy a limpiar la casa antes de que <u>vengan</u>.
I'm going to clean the house before they come.

Note that only the vosotros form has an accent.

The present subjunctive endings are the opposite of what you'd expect, as -ar verbs have endings starting with -e, and -er and -ir verbs have endings starting with -a.

Forming the present subjunctive of radical changing verbs

Verbs that change their stems (<u>radical-changing verbs</u>) in the ordinary present usually change them in the same way in the present subjunctive.

Infinitive	(yo)	(tú)	(él) (ella) (usted)	(nosotros) (nosotras)	(vosotros) (vosotras)	(ellos) (ellas) (ustedes)
pensar *to think*	piense	pienses	piense	pensemos	penséis	piensen
entender *to understand*	entienda	entiendas	entienda	entendamos	entendáis	entiendan
poder *to be able*	pueda	puedas	pueda	podamos	podáis	puedan
querer *to want*	quiera	quieras	quiera	queramos	queráis	quieran
volver *to return*	vuelva	vuelvas	vuelva	volvamos	volváis	vuelvan

No hace falta que <u>vuelvas</u>. There's no need for you to come back.

Me alegro de que <u>puedas</u> venir. I'm pleased you can come.

Sometimes the stem of the nosotros and vosotros forms isn't the same as it is in the ordinary present tense.

Infinitive	(yo)	(tú)	(él) (ella) (usted)	(nosotros) (nosotras)	(vosotros) (vosotras)	(ellos) (ellas) (ustedes)
dormir *to sleep*	duerma	duermas	duerma	durmamos	durmáis	duerman
morir *to die*	muera	mueras	muera	muramos	muráis	mueran
pedir *to ask for*	pida	pidas	pida	pidamos	pidáis	pidan
seguir *to follow*	siga	sigas	siga	sigamos	sigáis	sigan
sentir *to feel*	sienta	sientas	sienta	sintamos	sintáis	sientan

Queremos hacerlo antes de que nos <u>muramos</u>.
We want to do it before we die.
Vendré a veros cuando os <u>sintáis</u> mejor.
I'll come and see you when you feel better.

Forming the imperfect subjunctive

For all verbs, there are <u>two</u> imperfect subjunctive forms that are exactly the same in meaning.

The stem for both imperfect subjunctive forms is the same: you take off the -aron or -ieron ending of the ellos form of the preterite and add a fixed set of endings to what is left.

For -ar verbs, the endings are: -ara, -aras, -ara, -áramos, -arais, -aran or -ase, -ases, -ase, -ásemos, -aseis, -asen. The first form is more common.

For -er and -ir verbs, the endings are: -iera, -ieras, -iera, -iéramos, -ierais, -ieran or -iese, -ieses, -iese, -iésemos, -ieseis, -iesen. The first form is more common.

The following table shows the subjunctive of three regular verbs: hablar (meaning to speak), comer (meaning to eat) and vivir (meaning to live).

Infinitive	(yo)	(tú)	(él) (ella) (usted)	(nosotros) (nosotras)	(vosotros) (vosotras)	(ellos) (ellas) (ustedes)
hablar	hablara	hablaras	hablara	habláramos	hablarais	hablaran
to speak	hablase	hablases	hablase	hablásemos	hablaseis	hablasen
comer	comiera	comieras	comiera	comiéramos	comierais	comieran
to eat	comiese	comieses	comiese	comiésemos	comieseis	comiesen
vivir	viviera	vivieras	viviera	viviéramos	vivierais	vivieran
to live	viviese	vivieses	viviese	viviésemos	vivieseis	viviesen

Many verbs have irregular preterite forms which are reflected in the stem for the imperfect subjunctive. For example:

Infinitive	(yo)	(tú)	(él) (ella) (usted)	(nosotros) (nosotras)	(vosotros) (vosotras)	(ellos) (ellas) (ustedes)
dar *to give*	diera diese	dieras dieses	diera diese	diéramos diésemos	dierais dieseis	dieran diesen
estar *to be*	estuviera estuviese	estuvieras estuvieses	estuviera estuviese	estuviéramos estuviésemos	estuvierais estuvieseis	estuvieran estuviesen
hacer *to do/make*	hiciera hiciese	hicieras hicieses	hiciera hiciese	hiciéramos hiciésemos	hicierais hicieseis	hicieran hiciesen
poner *to put*	pusiera pusiese	pusieras pusieses	pusiera pusiese	pusiéramos pusiésemos	pusierais pusieseis	pusieran pusiesen
tener *to have*	tuviera tuviese	tuvieras tuvieses	tuviera tuviese	tuviéramos tuviésemos	tuvierais tuvieseis	tuvieran tuviesen
venir *to come*	viniera viniese	vinieras vinieses	viniera viniese	viniéramos viniésemos	vinierais vinieseis	vinieran viniesen

Forming the imperfect subjunctive of some irregular -ir verbs

In some irregular -ir verbs – the ones that don't have an i in the ellos form of the preterite – -era, -eras, -era, -éramos, -erais, -eran or -ese, -eses, -ese, -ésemos, -eseis, -esen are added to the preterite stem instead of -iera and -iese and so on.

Infinitive	(yo)	(tú)	(él) (ella) (usted)	(nosotros) (nosotras)	(vosotros) (vosotras)	(ellos) (ellas) (ustedes)
decir *to say*	dijera dijese	dijeras dijeses	dijera dijese	dijéramos dijésemos	dijerais dijeseis	dijeran dijesen
ir *to go*	fuera fuese	fueras fueses	fuera fuese	fuéramos fuésemos	fuerais fueseis	fueran fuesen
ser *to be*	fuera fuese	fueras fueses	fuera fuese	fuéramos fuésemos	fuerais fueseis	fueran fuesen

Accents

When pronouns are added to the end of gerunds (the -ando/-iendo form of the verb), infinitives (the form of the verb ending in –ar, -er or –ir) or positive imperatives (instructions to do something), you often have to add an accent to show that the stress remains the same.

You should always add an accent to a gerund when attaching one or more pronouns:

> Estoy afeitándome. I'm shaving.
> Está limpiándotelo. He's cleaning it for you.
> Estaba diciéndoselo. I was telling her.

You should only add an accent to an infinitive when adding two pronouns:

> Quiero limpiártelo. I want to clean it for you.
> ¿Podrías hacérmelo? Could you do it for me?
> Habría que decírselo. Somebody should tell her.

Don't add an accent when adding only one pronoun to an infinitive:

> Tengo que bañarme. I must have a bath.
> Debo conseguirlo. I must get it.

In positive imperatives (instructions to do something) an accent is usually required when attaching one or more pronouns:

> Tómalo. Take it.
> Póngame un kilo de azúcar. One kilo of sugar, please.
> Cárguelo a mi cuenta. Put it on my account.
> ¡Levantémonos! Let's get up!
> ¡Digámoselo! Let's tell him!

For further explanation of grammatical terms, please see pages 8-11.

Subídmelo a casa. Bring it up to my house.

Decídmelo claro. Tell me clearly.

Confírmenmelo en cuanto puedan. Confirm it as soon as you can.

¡Arrepentíos! Repent!

However, you wouldn't add an accent when adding just one pronoun to either a vosotros imperative in -ar or -er verbs or to a one-syllable imperative:

Acompañadle. Go with him.

Dadle las gracias. Say thank you to him.

Pensadlo bien. Think it over.

¡Despertaos! Wake up!

Hazlo como te he dicho. Do it the way I told you.

Verb Combinations

Verbs followed by the infinitive with no preposition

Some Spanish verbs and groups of verbs can be followed by an infinitive with no preposition:

- poder (meaning *to be able to, can, may*), saber (meaning *to know how to, can*), querer (meaning *to want*) and deber (meaning *to have to, must*)

     No <u>puede venir</u>. He can't come.
     ¿<u>Sabes esquiar</u>? Can you ski?
     <u>Quiere estudiar</u> medicina. He wants to study medicine.
     <u>Debes hacerlo</u>. You must do it.

- verbs like gustar, encantar and apetecer, where the infinitive is the subject of the verb

     <u>Me gusta estudiar</u>. I like studying.
     <u>Nos encanta bailar</u>. We love dancing.
     ¿<u>Te apetece ir</u> al cine? Do you fancy going to the cinema?

- verbs that relate to seeing or hearing, such as ver (meaning *to see*) and oír (meaning *to hear*)

     Nos <u>ha visto llegar</u>. He saw us arrive.
     Te <u>he oído cantar</u>. I heard you singing.

- the verbs hacer (meaning *to make*) and dejar (meaning *to let*)

     ¡No me <u>hagas reír</u>! Don't make me laugh!
     Mis padres no me <u>dejan salir</u> por la noche.
     My parents don't let me go out at night.

For further explanation of grammatical terms, please see pages 8-11.

- the following common verbs

  decidir to decide
  Han <u>decidido comprarse</u> una casa. They've decided to buy a house.

  desear to wish, want
  No <u>desea tener</u> más hijos. She doesn't want to have any more children.

  esperar to hope
  <u>Espero poder</u> ir. I hope to be able to go.

  evitar to avoid
  <u>Evita gastar</u> demasiado dinero. He avoids spending too much money.

  necesitar to need
  <u>Necesito salir</u> un momento. I need to go out for a moment.

  olvidar to forget
  <u>Olvidó dejar</u> su dirección. She forgot to leave her address.

  pensar to think
  <u>Pienso hacer</u> una paella. I'm thinking of making a paella.

  preferir to prefer
  <u>Prefiero ir</u> mañana. I'd prefer to go tomorrow.

  recordar to remember
  <u>Recuerdo haberlo</u> visto. I remember having seen it.

  sentir to be sorry, to regret
  <u>Siento molestarte</u>. I'm sorry to bother you.

Some of these verbs combine with infinitives to make set phrases with a special meaning:

> querer decir to mean
> ¿Qué <u>quiere decir</u> eso? What does that mean?

> dejar caer to drop
> <u>Dejó caer</u> la bandeja. She dropped the tray.

Verbs followed by the preposition a and the infinitive

The following verbs are the most common ones that can be followed by a and the infinitive:

- verbs relating to movement such as ir (meaning *to go*) and venir (meaning *to come*)

  Se va a comprar un caballo. He's going to buy a horse.
  Viene a vernos. He's coming to see us.

- the following common verbs

  aprender a hacer algo to learn to do something
  Me gustaría aprender a nadar. I'd like to learn to swim.

  comenzar a hacer algo to begin to do something
  Comenzó a llover. It began to rain.

  decidirse a hacer algo to decide to do something
  Ojalá se decida a visitarnos I hope she decides to visit us.

  empezar a hacer algo to begin to do something
  Ha empezado a nevar. It's started snowing.

  llegar a hacer algo to manage to do something
  No llegó a terminarlo. She didn't manage to finish it.

  llegar a ser algo to become something
  Llegó a ser primer ministro. He became prime minister.

  probar a hacer algo to try doing something
  He probado a hacerlo yo sola pero no he podido.
  I tried doing it on my own but I wasn't able to.

volver a hacer algo to do something again
No vuelvas a hacerlo nunca más. Don't ever do it again.

The following verbs can be followed by a and a person's name or else by a and a noun or pronoun referring to a person, and then by another a and an infinitive.

ayudar a alguien a hacer algo to help someone to do something
¿Le podrías ayudar a Antonia a fregar los platos?
Could you help Antonia do the dishes?

enseñar a alguien a hacer algo to teach someone to do something
Le enseñó a su hermano a nadar. He taught his brother to swim.

invitar a alguien a hacer algo to invite someone to do something
Los he invitado a tomar unas copas en casa.
I've invited them over for drinks.

Verbs followed by the preposition de and the infinitive

The following verbs are the most common ones that can be followed by de and the infinitive:

aburrirse de hacer algo to get bored with doing something
Me aburría de no poder salir de casa.
I was getting bored with not being able to leave the house.

acabar de hacer algo to have just done something
Acabo de comprar un móvil. I've just bought a mobile.
Acababan de llegar cuando... They had just arrived when...

acordarse de haber hecho/de hacer algo
to remember having done/to do something
Acuérdate de cerrar la puerta con llave. Remember to lock the door.

alegrarse de hacer algo to be glad to do something
Me alegro de verte. I'm glad to see you.

dejar de hacer algo to stop doing something
¿Quieres dejar de hablar? Will you stop talking?

tener ganas de hacer algo to want to do something
Tengo ganas de volver a España. I want to go back to Spain.

tratar de hacer algo to try to do something
Traté de no pensar en ello. I tried not to think about it.

Verbs followed by the preposition con and the infinitive

The following verbs are the most common ones that can be followed by con and the infinitive:

amenazar <u>con</u> hacer algo to threaten to do someting
Amenazó <u>con</u> denunciarlos. He threatened to report them.

soñar <u>con</u> hacer algo to dream about doing something
Sueño <u>con</u> vivir en España. I dream about living in Spain.

Verbs followed by the preposition en and the infinitive

The verb quedar is the most common one that can be followed by en and the infinitive:

quedar <u>en</u> hacer algo to agree to do something
Habíamos quedado <u>en</u> encontrarnos a las ocho.
We had agreed to meet at eight.

Verbs followed by a and an object

a is often the equivalent of the English word to when it is used with an indirect object after verbs like enviar (meaning to send), dar (meaning to give) and decir (meaning to say).

dar algo a alguien to give something to someone
Se lo di a Teresa. I gave it to Teresa.

decir algo a alguien to say something to someone
¿A quién se lo dijo? Who did she tell?

enviar algo a alguien to send something to someone
Tendrías que enviárselo a mi padre. You should send it to my father.

escribir algo a alguien to write something to someone
¿Le has escrito a tu tía? Have you written to your aunt?

mostrar algo a alguien to show something to someone
Quería mostrárselo al médico. I wanted to show it to the doctor.

Here are some verbs taking a in Spanish that have a different construction in English.

asistir a algo to attend something, to be at something
No asistieron a la ceremonia. They didn't go to the ceremony.

dirigirse a (un lugar) to head for (a place)
Se dirigió a la terminal del aeropuerto. He headed for the airport terminal.

dirigirse a alguien to address somebody
El Rey se dirigió a la nación. The King addressed the nation.

jugar a algo to play something (sports/games)
Están jugando al fútbol. They're playing football.

llegar <u>a</u> (un lugar) to arrive at (a place)
¿A qué hora llegaste <u>a</u> casa? What time did you get home?

oler <u>a</u> algo to smell of something
Este perfume huele <u>a</u> jazmín. This perfume smells of jasmine.

parecerse <u>a</u> alguien/algo to look like somebody/something
Te pareces mucho <u>a</u> tu madre. You look very much like your mother.

subir(se) <u>a</u> un autobús/un coche to get on a bus/into a car
¡De prisa, sube <u>al</u> coche! Get into the car, quick!
No (se) subió <u>al</u> tren. He didn't get on the train.

subir(se) <u>a</u> un árbol to climb a tree
Se cayó al subirse <u>a</u> un árbol. He fell while climbing a tree.

tener miedo <u>a</u> alguien to be afraid of somebody
Nunca tuvieron miedo <u>a</u> su padre. They were never afraid of their father.

Verbs followed by de and an object

Here are some verbs taking de in Spanish that have a different construction in English:

acordarse de algo/alguien to remember something/somebody
¿Te acuerdas de mí? Do you remember me?

alegrarse de algo to be glad about something
Me alegro de tu ascenso. I'm glad about your promotion.

bajarse de un autobús/un coche to get off a bus/out of a car
Se bajó del coche. He got out of the car.

darse cuenta de algo to realize something
Perdona, no me daba cuenta de que eras vegetariano.
Sorry, I didn't realize you were a vegetarian.

depender de algo/alguien to depend on something/somebody
No depende de mí. It doesn't depend on me.

despedirse de alguien to say goodbye to somebody
Se fue sin despedirse de nosotros. He left without saying goodbye to us.

preocuparse de algo/alguien to worry about something/somebody
Se preocupa mucho de su apariencia.
He worries a lot about his appearance.

quejarse de algo to complain about something
Se quejaba de la falta de información.
He was complaining about the lack of information.

reírse de algo/alguien to laugh at something/somebody
¿De qué te ríes? What are you laughing at?

salir de (un cuarto/un edificio) to leave (a room/a building)
¿A qué hora sales de la oficina? What time do you leave the office?

tener miedo de algo to be afraid of something
Tiene miedo de la oscuridad. He's afraid of the dark.

trabajar de (camarero/secretario) to work as (a waiter/secretary)
Trabajo de camarero. I work as a waiter.

tratarse de algo/alguien
to be a question of something/to be about somebody
¿De qué se trata? What's it about?

Verbs followed by **con** and an object

Here are some verbs taking con in Spanish that sometimes have a different construction in English:

comparar algo/a alguien <u>con</u> algo/alguien
to compare something/somebody with something/somebody
Siempre me comparan <u>con</u> mi hermana.
I'm always being compared to my sister.

contar <u>con</u> alguien/algo to rely on somebody/something
Cuento <u>con</u>tigo. I'm relying on you.

encontrarse <u>con</u> alguien to meet somebody (by chance)
Me encontré <u>con</u> ella al entrar en el banco.
I met her as I was going into the bank.

enfadarse <u>con</u> alguien to get annoyed with somebody
No te enfades <u>con</u> él, lo ha hecho sin intención.
Don't be annoyed with him, he didn't mean to do it.

estar de acuerdo <u>con</u> alguien/algo to agree with somebody/something
Estoy totalmente de acuerdo <u>con</u>tigo. I totally agree with you.

hablar <u>con</u> alguien to talk to somebody
¿Puedo hablar <u>con</u> usted un momento? May I talk to you for a moment?

soñar <u>con</u> alguien/algo to dream about somebody/something
Ayer soñé <u>con</u> él. I dreamed about him yesterday.

Verbs followed by en and an object

Here are some verbs taking en in Spanish that sometimes have a different construction in English:

entrar en (un edificio/un cuarto) to enter, go into (a building/a room)
Entré en la casa. I went into the house.

pensar en algo/alguien to think about something/somebody
No quiero pensar en eso. I don't want to think about that.

trabajar en (una oficina/una fábrica) to work in (an office/a factory)
Trabaja en un banco. She works in a bank.

Verbs followed by por and an object

Here are some verbs taking por in Spanish that have a different construction in English:

interesarse <u>por</u> algo/alguien to be interested in something/somebody or to ask about something/somebody
Me interesaba mucho <u>por</u> la arqueología.
I was very interested in archaeology.
Llamó para interesarse por su salud. He called to ask after her health.

preguntar <u>por</u> alguien to ask for/about somebody
Si preguntan <u>por</u> mí, no digas nada.
Don't say anything if they ask about me.

preocuparse <u>por</u> algo/alguien to worry about something/somebody
Se preocupa mucho <u>por</u> su apariencia.
He worries a lot about his appearance.

Verbs taking a direct object in Spanish but not in English

In English there are a few verbs that are followed by *at*, *for* or *to* which, in Spanish, are not followed by any preposition other than the personal *a* where required.

mirar algo/a alguien to look at something/somebody
Mira esta foto. Look at this photo.

escuchar algo/a alguien to listen to something/somebody
Me gusta escuchar música. I like listening to music.

buscar algo/a alguien to look for something/somebody
Estoy buscando las gafas. I'm looking for my glasses.
Estoy buscando a mi hermano. I'm looking for my brother.

pedir algo to ask for something
Pidió una taza de té. He asked for a cup of tea.

esperar algo/a alguien to wait for something/somebody
Estamos esperando el tren. We're waiting for the train.
Estoy esperando a mi hermana. I'm waiting for my sister.

pagar algo to pay for something
Ya he pagado el billete. I've already paid for my ticket.

Verbs followed by personal a

Spanish speakers use a in a way that has no equivalent in English. They use it before nouns referring to specific people and pets when these are the direct object of a verb:

¿Conoces a Maite? Do you know Maite?
Quiere a Pablo. She loves Pablo.
No vi a Juan. I didn't see Juan.
Quiero invitar a Teresa a cenar. I want to invite Teresa to supper.
Llama a un médico. Call a doctor.

Personal a is also used before certain pronouns referring to people (but NOT object pronouns):

No conozco a nadie. I don't know anybody.
¿Viste a alguien? Did you see anyone?
¿A quién llamaste? Who did you call?

Personal a is NOT normally used after tener (meaning *to have*):

Tengo dos hermanas. I've got two sisters.
Tiene un perro. He's got a dog.

VERB TABLES

Introduction

The **Verb Tables** in the following section contain 120 tables of Spanish verbs (some regular and some irregular) in alphabetical order. Each table shows you the following forms: **Present, Present Perfect, Preterite, Imperfect, Future, Conditional, Present Subjunctive, Imperfect Subjunctive, Imperative** and the **Past Participle** and **Gerund**. For more information on these tenses and how they are formed you should look at the section on Verb Formation in the main text on pages 10–55. If you want to find out in more detail how verbs are used in different contexts, the *Easy Learning Spanish Grammar* will give you additional information.

In order to help you use the verbs shown in the **Verb Tables** correctly, there are also a number of example phrases at the bottom of each page to show the verb as it is used in context.

In Spanish there are both **regular** verbs (their forms follow the normal rules) and **irregular** verbs (their forms do not follow the normal rules). The regular verbs in these tables that you can use as models for other regular verbs are:

hablar (regular -**ar** verb, Verb Table 118–119)
comer (regular -**er** verb, Verb Table 52–53)
vivir (regular -**ir** verb, Verb Table 234–235)

The irregular verbs are shown in full.

The **Verb Index** at the end of this section contains over 1200 verbs, each of which is cross-referred to one of the verbs given in the Verb Tables. The table shows the patterns that the verb listed in the index follows.

abolir (to abolish)

	PRESENT	PRESENT PERFECT
(yo)		he abolido
(tú)		has abolido
(él/ella/usted)		ha abolido
(nosotros/as)	abolimos	hemos abolido
(vosotros/as)	abolís	habéis abolido
(ellos/ellas/ ustedes)		han abolido

Present tense only used in persons shown

	PRETERITE	IMPERFECT
(yo)	abolí	abolía
(tú)	aboliste	abolías
(él/ella/usted)	abolió	abolía
(nosotros/as)	abolimos	abolíamos
(vosotros/as)	abolisteis	abolíais
(ellos/ellas/ ustedes)	abolieron	abolían

GERUND
aboliendo

PAST PARTICIPLE
abolido

EXAMPLE PHRASES

Hay que **abolirlo**. It ought to be abolished.

¿Por qué no **abolimos** esta ley? Why don't we abolish this law?

Han abolido la pena de muerte. They have abolished the death penalty.

Abolieron la esclavitud. They abolished slavery.

Remember that subject pronouns are not used very often in Spanish.

abolir

	FUTURE	CONDITIONAL
(yo)	aboliré	aboliría
(tú)	abolirás	abolirías
(él/ella/usted)	abolirá	aboliría
(nosotros/as)	aboliremos	aboliríamos
(vosotros/as)	aboliréis	aboliríais
(ellos/ellas/ ustedes)	abolirán	abolirían

	PRESENT SUBJUNCTIVE	IMPERFECT SUBJUNCTIVE
(yo)	*not used*	aboliera *or* aboliese
(tú)		abolieras *or* abolieses
(él/ella/usted)		aboliera *or* aboliese
(nosotros/as)		aboliéramos *or* aboliésemos
(vosotros/as)		abolierais *or* abolieseis
(ellos/ellas/ ustedes)		abolieran *or* aboliesen

IMPERATIVE
abolid

EXAMPLE PHRASES

Sólo unidos **aboliremos** la injusticia. We will only abolish injustice if we stand together.

Prometieron que **abolirían** la censura. They promised they'd abolish censorship.

Si lo **abolieran**, se producirían disturbios. There would be riots if it were abolished.

Remember that subject pronouns are not used very often in Spanish.

abrir (to open)

	PRESENT	PRESENT PERFECT
(yo)	abro	he abierto
(tú)	abres	has abierto
(él/ella/usted)	abre	ha abierto
(nosotros/as)	abrimos	hemos abierto
(vosotros/as)	abrís	habéis abierto
(ellos/ellas/ ustedes)	abren	han abierto

	PRETERITE	IMPERFECT
(yo)	abrí	abría
(tú)	abriste	abrías
(él/ella/usted)	abrió	abría
(nosotros/as)	abrimos	abríamos
(vosotros/as)	abristeis	abríais
(ellos/ellas/ ustedes)	abrieron	abrían

GERUND

abriendo

PAST PARTICIPLE

abierto

EXAMPLE PHRASES

Hoy **se abre** el plazo de matrícula. Registration begins today.

Han abierto un restaurante cerca de aquí. They've opened a new restaurant near here.

¿Quién **abrió** la ventana? Who opened the window?

La llave **abría** el armario. The key opened the cupboard.

Remember that subject pronouns are not used very often in Spanish.

abrir

	FUTURE	CONDITIONAL
(yo)	abriré	abriría
(tú)	abrirás	abrirías
(él/ella/usted)	abrirá	abriría
(nosotros/as)	abriremos	abriríamos
(vosotros/as)	abriréis	abriríais
(ellos/ellas/ustedes)	abrirán	abrirían

	PRESENT SUBJUNCTIVE	IMPERFECT SUBJUNCTIVE
(yo)	abra	abriera *or* abriese
(tú)	abras	abrieras *or* abrieses
(él/ella/usted)	abra	abriera *or* abriese
(nosotros/as)	abramos	abriéramos *or* abriésemos
(vosotros/as)	abráis	abrierais *or* abrieseis
(ellos/ellas/ustedes)	abran	abrieran *or* abriesen

IMPERATIVE

abre / abrid

Use the present subjunctive in all cases other than these tú and vosotros affirmative forms.

EXAMPLE PHRASES

Abrirán todas las puertas de la catedral. They'll open all the doors of the
cathedral.

Me dijo que hoy **abrirían** sólo por la tarde. He told me that they'd only be
open in the evening.

No creo que **abran** un nuevo supermercado por aquí. I don't think they'll
open a new supermarket here.

No **abras** ese grifo. Don't turn on that tap.

Remember that subject pronouns are not used very often in Spanish.

actuar (to act)

	PRESENT	PRESENT PERFECT
(yo)	actúo	he actuado
(tú)	actúas	has actuado
(él/ella/usted)	actúa	ha actuado
(nosotros/as)	actuamos	hemos actuado
(vosotros/as)	actuáis	habéis actuado
(ellos/ellas/ ustedes)	actúan	han actuado

	PRETERITE	IMPERFECT
(yo)	actué	actuaba
(tú)	actuaste	actuabas
(él/ella/usted)	actuó	actuaba
(nosotros/as)	actuamos	actuábamos
(vosotros/as)	actuasteis	actuabais
(ellos/ellas/ ustedes)	actuaron	actuaban

GERUND

actuando

PAST PARTICIPLE

actuado

EXAMPLE PHRASES

Actúa de una forma muy rara. He's acting very strangely.

Ha actuado siguiendo un impulso. He acted on impulse.

Actuó en varias películas. He was in several films.

Actuaba como si no supiera nada. She was behaving as if she didn't know anything about it.

Remember that subject pronouns are not used very often in Spanish.

actuar

	FUTURE	CONDITIONAL
(yo)	actuaré	actuaría
(tú)	actuarás	actuarías
(él/ella/usted)	actuará	actuaría
(nosotros/as)	actuaremos	actuaríamos
(vosotros/as)	actuaréis	actuaríais
(ellos/ellas/ ustedes)	actuarán	actuarían

	PRESENT SUBJUNCTIVE	IMPERFECT SUBJUNCTIVE
(yo)	actúe	actuara *or* actuase
(tú)	actúes	actuaras *or* actuases
(él/ella/usted)	actúe	actuara *or* actuase
(nosotros/as)	actuemos	actuáramos *or* actuásemos
(vosotros/as)	actuéis	actuarais *or* actuaseis
(ellos/ellas/ ustedes)	actúen	actuaran *or* actuasen

IMPERATIVE

actúa / actuad

*Use the present subjunctive in all cases other than these **tú** and **vosotros** affirmative forms.*

EXAMPLE PHRASES

¿Quién **actuará** en su próxima película? Who will be in his next film?

Yo nunca **actuaría** así. I'd never behave like that.

Si **actuara** de forma más lógica, sería más fácil atraparle. It would be easier to catch him if he behaved in a more logical way.

Actuad como mejor os parezca. Do as you think best.

Remember that subject pronouns are not used very often in Spanish.

adquirir (to acquire)

	PRESENT	PRESENT PERFECT
(yo)	adquiero	he adquirido
(tú)	adquieres	has adquirido
(él/ella/usted)	adquiere	ha adquirido
(nosotros/as)	adquirimos	hemos adquirido
(vosotros/as)	adquirís	habéis adquirido
(ellos/ellas/ ustedes)	adquieren	han adquirido

	PRETERITE	IMPERFECT
(yo)	adquirí	adquiría
(tú)	adquiriste	adquirías
(él/ella/usted)	adquirió	adquiría
(nosotros/as)	adquirimos	adquiríamos
(vosotros/as)	adquiristeis	adquiríais
(ellos/ellas/ ustedes)	adquirieron	adquirían

GERUND
adquiriendo

PAST PARTICIPLE
adquirido

EXAMPLE PHRASES

Adquiere cada vez mayor importancia. It's becoming more and more important.

Está adquiriendo una reputación que no merece. It's getting a reputation it doesn't deserve.

Hemos adquirido una colección de sellos. We've bought a stamp collection.

Con el tiempo **adquirió** cierta madurez. Over the years he gained a certain maturity.

Remember that subject pronouns are not used very often in Spanish.

adquirir

	FUTURE	CONDITIONAL
(yo)	adquiriré	adquiriría
(tú)	adquirirás	adquirirías
(él/ella/usted)	adquirirá	adquiriría
(nosotros/as)	adquiriremos	adquiriríamos
(vosotros/as)	adquiriréis	adquiriríais
(ellos/ellas/ ustedes)	adquirirán	adquirirían

	PRESENT SUBJUNCTIVE	IMPERFECT SUBJUNCTIVE
(yo)	adquiera	adquiriera or adquiriese
(tú)	adquieras	adquirieras or adquirieses
(él/ella/usted)	adquiera	adquiriera or adquiriese
(nosotros/as)	adquiramos	adquiriéramos or adquiriésemos
(vosotros/as)	adquiráis	adquirierais or adquirieseis
(ellos/ellas/ ustedes)	adquieran	adquirieran or adquiriesen

IMPERATIVE
adquiere / adquirid

Use the present subjunctive in all cases other than these tú and vosotros affirmative forms.

EXAMPLE PHRASES
Al final **adquirirán** los derechos de publicación. They will get the publishing rights in the end.

¿Lo **adquirirías** por ese precio? Would you buy it for that price?

Adquiera o no la nacionalidad, podrá permanecer en el país. She'll be able to stay in the country whether she becomes naturalized or not.

Tenía gran interés en que **adquiriera** el cuadro. He was very keen that she should buy the picture.

Remember that subject pronouns are not used very often in Spanish.

advertir (to warn; to notice)

	PRESENT		PRESENT PERFECT
(yo)	advierto		he advertido
(tú)	adviertes		has advertido
(él/ella/usted)	advierte		ha advertido
(nosotros/as)	advertimos		hemos advertido
(vosotros/as)	advertís		habéis advertido
(ellos/ellas/ustedes)	advierten		han advertido

	PRETERITE		IMPERFECT
(yo)	advertí		advertía
(tú)	advertiste		advertías
(él/ella/usted)	advirtió		advertía
(nosotros/as)	advertimos		advertíamos
(vosotros/as)	advertisteis		advertíais
(ellos/ellas/ustedes)	advirtieron		advertían

GERUND

advirtiendo

PAST PARTICIPLE

advertido

EXAMPLE PHRASES

Te **advierto** que no va a ser nada fácil. I must warn you that it won't be at all easy.

No **he advertido** nada extraño en su comportamiento. I haven't noticed anything strange about his behaviour.

Ya te **advertí** que no intervinieras. I warned you not to get involved.

Las señales **advertían** del peligro. The signs warned of danger.

Remember that subject pronouns are not used very often in Spanish.

advertir

	FUTURE	CONDITIONAL
(yo)	advertiré	advertiría
(tú)	advertirás	advertirías
(él/ella/usted)	advertirá	advertiría
(nosotros/as)	advertiremos	advertiríamos
(vosotros/as)	advertiréis	advertiríais
(ellos/ellas/ ustedes)	advertirán	advertirían

	PRESENT SUBJUNCTIVE	IMPERFECT SUBJUNCTIVE
(yo)	advierta	advirtiera or advirtiese
(tú)	adviertas	advirtieras or advirtieses
(él/ella/usted)	advierta	advirtiera or advirtiese
(nosotros/as)	advirtamos	advirtiéramos or advirtiésemos
(vosotros/as)	advirtáis	advirtierais or advirtieseis
(ellos/ellas/ ustedes)	adviertan	advirtieran or advirtiesen

IMPERATIVE
advierte / advertid

Use the present subjunctive in all cases other than these tú and vosotros affirmative forms.

EXAMPLE PHRASES

Si **advirtiera** algún cambio, llámenos. If you should notice any change, give us a call.

Adviértele del riesgo que entraña. Warn him about the risk involved.

Remember that subject pronouns are not used very often in Spanish.

almorzar (to have lunch)

	PRESENT		PRESENT PERFECT
(yo)	almuerzo		he almorzado
(tú)	almuerzas		has almorzado
(él/ella/usted)	almuerza		ha almorzado
(nosotros/as)	almorzamos		hemos almorzado
(vosotros/as)	almorzáis		habéis almorzado
(ellos/ellas/ ustedes)	almuerzan		han almorzado

	PRETERITE		IMPERFECT
(yo)	almorcé		almorzaba
(tú)	almorzaste		almorzabas
(él/ella/usted)	almorzó		almorzaba
(nosotros/as)	almorzamos		almorzábamos
(vosotros/as)	almorzasteis		almorzabais
(ellos/ellas/ ustedes)	almorzaron		almorzaban

GERUND	PAST PARTICIPLE
almorzando	almorzado

EXAMPLE PHRASES

¿Dónde vais a **almorzar**? Where are you going to have lunch?

¿A qué hora **almuerzas**? What time do you have lunch?

Ya **hemos almorzado**. We've already had lunch.

Almorcé en un bar. I had lunch in a bar.

Siempre **almorzaba** un bocadillo. He always had a sandwich for lunch.

Remember that subject pronouns are not used very often in Spanish.

almorzar

	FUTURE	CONDITIONAL
(yo)	almorzaré	almorzaría
(tú)	almorzarás	almorzarías
(él/ella/usted)	almorzará	almorzaría
(nosotros/as)	almorzaremos	almorzaríamos
(vosotros/as)	almorzaréis	almorzaríais
(ellos/ellas/ ustedes)	almorzarán	almorzarían

	PRESENT SUBJUNCTIVE	IMPERFECT SUBJUNCTIVE
(yo)	almuerce	almorzara *or* almorzase
(tú)	almuerces	almorzaras *or* almorzases
(él/ella/usted)	almuerce	almorzara *or* almorzase
(nosotros/as)	almorcemos	almorzáramos *or* almorzásemos
(vosotros/as)	almorcéis	almorzarais *or* almorzaseis
(ellos/ellas/ ustedes)	almuercen	almorzaran *or* almorzasen

IMPERATIVE
almuerza / almorzad

Use the present subjunctive in all cases other than these **tú** *and* **vosotros** *affirmative forms.*

EXAMPLE PHRASES

Mañana **almorzaremos** todos juntos. We'll all have lunch together tomorrow.

Almuerce o no siempre me entra sueño a esta hora. I always feel sleepy at this time of the day, regardless of whether I've had lunch or not.

Si **almorzara** así todos los días, estaría mucho más gordo. I'd be much fatter if I had this sort of lunch every day.

Remember that subject pronouns are not used very often in Spanish.

amanecer (to get light; to wake up)

	PRESENT		PRESENT PERFECT
(yo)	amanezco		he amanecido
(tú)	amaneces		has amanecido
(él/ella/usted)	amanece		ha amanecido
(nosotros/as)	amanecemos		hemos amanecido
(vosotros/as)	amanecéis		habéis amanecido
(ellos/ellas/ ustedes)	amanecen		han amanecido

	PRETERITE		IMPERFECT
(yo)	amanecí		amanecía
(tú)	amaneciste		amanecías
(él/ella/usted)	amaneció		amanecía
(nosotros/as)	amanecimos		amanecíamos
(vosotros/as)	amanecisteis		amanecíais
(ellos/ellas/ ustedes)	amanecieron		amanecían

GERUND
amaneciendo

PAST PARTICIPLE
amanecido

EXAMPLE PHRASES

Siempre **amanece** nublado. The day always starts off cloudy.

Justo en ese momento **estaba amaneciendo**. Just then, dawn was breaking.

Hoy **ha amanecido** a las ocho. Today it got light at eight o'clock.

La ciudad **amaneció** desierta. In the morning, the town was deserted.

Amanecía de un humor de perros. She would wake up in a really bad mood.

Remember that subject pronouns are not used very often in Spanish.

amanecer

	FUTURE	CONDITIONAL
(yo)	amaneceré	amanecería
(tú)	amanecerás	amanecerías
(él/ella/usted)	amanecerá	amanecería
(nosotros/as)	amaneceremos	amaneceríamos
(vosotros/as)	amaneceréis	amaneceríais
(ellos/ellas/ustedes)	amanecerán	amanecerían

	PRESENT SUBJUNCTIVE	IMPERFECT SUBJUNCTIVE
(yo)	amanezca	amaneciera or amaneciese
(tú)	amanezcas	amanecieras or amanecieses
(él/ella/usted)	amanezca	amaneciera or amaneciese
(nosotros/as)	amanezcamos	amaneciéramos or amaneciésemos
(vosotros/as)	amanezcáis	amanecierais or amanecieseis
(ellos/ellas/ustedes)	amanezcan	amanecieran or amaneciesen

IMPERATIVE
amanece / amaneced

*Use the present subjunctive in all cases other than these **tú** and **vosotros** affirmative forms.*

EXAMPLE PHRASES

Pronto **amanecerá**. It will soon be daylight.

Saldremos en cuanto **amanezca**. We'll set off as soon as it gets light.

Si **amanecieras** con fiebre, toma una de estas pastillas. If you should wake up with a temperature, take one of these pills.

Remember that subject pronouns are not used very often in Spanish.

andar (to walk)

	PRESENT		PRESENT PERFECT
(yo)	ando		he andado
(tú)	andas		has andado
(él/ella/usted)	anda		ha andado
(nosotros/as)	andamos		hemos andado
(vosotros/as)	andáis		habéis andado
(ellos/ellas/ ustedes)	andan		han andado

	PRETERITE		IMPERFECT
(yo)	anduve		andaba
(tú)	anduviste		andabas
(él/ella/usted)	anduvo		andaba
(nosotros/as)	anduvimos		andábamos
(vosotros/as)	anduvisteis		andabais
(ellos/ellas/ ustedes)	anduvieron		andaban

GERUND

andando

PAST PARTICIPLE

andado

EXAMPLE PHRASES

Andar es un ejercicio muy sano. Walking is very good exercise.

Hemos andado todo el camino hasta aquí. We walked all the way here.

Anduvimos al menos 10 km. We walked at least 10 km.

Por aquel entonces **andaban** mal de dinero. Back then they were short of money.

Voy **andando** al trabajo todos los días. I walk to work every day.

Remember that subject pronouns are not used very often in Spanish.

andar

	FUTURE	CONDITIONAL
(yo)	andaré	andaría
(tú)	andarás	andarías
(él/ella/usted)	andará	andaría
(nosotros/as)	andaremos	andaríamos
(vosotros/as)	andaréis	andaríais
(ellos/ellas/ustedes)	andarán	andarían

	PRESENT SUBJUNCTIVE	IMPERFECT SUBJUNCTIVE
(yo)	ande	anduviera *or* anduviese
(tú)	andes	anduvieras *or* anduvieses
(él/ella/usted)	ande	anduviera *or* anduviese
(nosotros/as)	andemos	anduviéramos *or* anduviésemos
(vosotros/as)	andéis	anduvierais *or* anduvieseis
(ellos/ellas/ustedes)	anden	anduvieran *or* anduviesen

IMPERATIVE

anda / andad

Use the present subjunctive in all cases other than these tú and vosotros affirmative forms.

EXAMPLE PHRASES

Andará por los cuarenta. He must be about forty.

Yo **me andaría** con pies de plomo. I'd tread very carefully.

El médico le ha aconsejado que **ande** varios kilómetros al día. The doctor has advised him to walk several kilometres a day.

Si **anduvieras** con más cuidado, no te pasarían esas cosas. If you were more careful, this sort of thing wouldn't happen to you.

Remember that subject pronouns are not used very often in Spanish.

apoderarse (to take possession)

	PRESENT	PRESENT PERFECT
(yo)	me apodero	me he apoderado
(tú)	te apoderas	te has apoderado
(él/ella/usted)	se apodera	se ha apoderado
(nosotros/as)	nos apoderamos	nos hemos apoderado
(vosotros/as)	os apoderáis	os habéis apoderado
(ellos/ellas/ ustedes)	se apoderan	se han apoderado

	PRETERITE	IMPERFECT
(yo)	me apoderé	me apoderaba
(tú)	te apoderaste	te apoderabas
(él/ella/usted)	se apoderó	se apoderaba
(nosotros/as)	nos apoderamos	nos apoderábamos
(vosotros/as)	os apoderasteis	os apoderabais
(ellos/ellas/ ustedes)	se apoderaron	se apoderaban

GERUND

apoderando

PAST PARTICIPLE

apoderado

EXAMPLE PHRASES

En esas situaciones, el miedo **se apodera** de mí. In situations like that, I find myself gripped by fear.

Poco a poco **se han ido apoderando** de las riquezas del país. Little by little, they've seized the country's riches.

Se apoderaron de las joyas y huyeron. They ran off with the jewels.

El desánimo **se apoderaba** de nosotros por momentos. We were feeling more and more discouraged by the minute.

Remember that subject pronouns are not used very often in Spanish.

apoderarse

	FUTURE	CONDITIONAL
(yo)	me apoderaré	me apoderaría
(tú)	te apoderarás	te apoderarías
(él/ella/usted)	se apoderará	se apoderaría
(nosotros/as)	nos apoderaremos	nos apoderaríamos
(vosotros/as)	os apoderaréis	os apoderaríais
(ellos/ellas/ustedes)	se apoderarán	se apoderarían

	PRESENT SUBJUNCTIVE	IMPERFECT SUBJUNCTIVE
(yo)	me apodere	me apoderara *or* apoderase
(tú)	te apoderes	te apoderaras *or* apoderases
(él/ella/usted)	se apodere	se apoderara *or* apoderase
(nosotros/as)	nos apoderemos	nos apoderáramos *or* apoderásemos
(vosotros/as)	os apoderéis	os apoderarais *or* apoderaseis
(ellos/ellas/ustedes)	se apoderen	se apoderaran *or* apoderasen

IMPERATIVE

apodérate / apoderaos

Use the present subjunctive in all cases other than these tú and vosotros affirmative forms.

EXAMPLE PHRASES

No dejes que la curiosidad **se apodere** de ti. Don't let curiosity get the better of you.

Remember that subject pronouns are not used very often in Spanish.

aprobar (to pass; to approve of)

	PRESENT		PRESENT PERFECT
(yo)	apruebo		he aprobado
(tú)	apruebas		has aprobado
(él/ella/usted)	aprueba		ha aprobado
(nosotros/as)	aprobamos		hemos aprobado
(vosotros/as)	aprobáis		habéis aprobado
(ellos/ellas/ustedes)	aprueban		han aprobado

	PRETERITE		IMPERFECT
(yo)	aprobé		aprobaba
(tú)	aprobaste		aprobabas
(él/ella/usted)	aprobó		aprobaba
(nosotros/as)	aprobamos		aprobábamos
(vosotros/as)	aprobasteis		aprobabais
(ellos/ellas/ustedes)	aprobaron		aprobaban

GERUND

aprobando

PAST PARTICIPLE

aprobado

EXAMPLE PHRASES

No **apruebo** esa conducta. I don't approve of that sort of behaviour.

Este año lo **estoy aprobando** todo. So far this year I've passed everything.

Han aprobado una ley antitabaco. They've passed an anti-smoking law.

¿**Aprobaste** el examen? Did you pass the exam?

La decisión **fue aprobada** por mayoría. The decision was approved by a majority.

Remember that subject pronouns are not used very often in Spanish.

aprobar

	FUTURE	CONDITIONAL
(yo)	aprobaré	aprobaría
(tú)	aprobarás	aprobarías
(él/ella/usted)	aprobará	aprobaría
(nosotros/as)	aprobaremos	aprobaríamos
(vosotros/as)	aprobaréis	aprobaríais
(ellos/ellas/ ustedes)	aprobarán	aprobarían

	PRESENT SUBJUNCTIVE	IMPERFECT SUBJUNCTIVE
(yo)	apruebe	aprobara or aprobase
(tú)	apruebes	aprobaras or aprobases
(él/ella/usted)	apruebe	aprobara or aprobase
(nosotros/as)	aprobemos	aprobáramos or aprobásemos
(vosotros/as)	aprobéis	aprobarais or aprobaseis
(ellos/ellas/ ustedes)	aprueben	aprobaran or aprobasen

IMPERATIVE
aprueba / aprobad

Use the present subjunctive in all cases other than these tú and vosotros affirmative forms.

arrancar (to pull up)

	PRESENT		PRESENT PERFECT
(yo)	arranco		he arrancado
(tú)	arrancas		has arrancado
(él/ella/usted)	arranca		ha arrancado
(nosotros/as)	arrancamos		hemos arrancado
(vosotros/as)	arrancáis		habéis arrancado
(ellos/ellas/ustedes)	arrancan		han arrancado

	PRETERITE		IMPERFECT
(yo)	arranqué		arrancaba
(tú)	arrancaste		arrancabas
(él/ella/usted)	arrancó		arrancaba
(nosotros/as)	arrancamos		arrancábamos
(vosotros/as)	arrancasteis		arrancabais
(ellos/ellas/ustedes)	arrancaron		arrancaban

GERUND

arrancando

PAST PARTICIPLE

arrancado

EXAMPLE PHRASES

Lo tienes que **arrancar** de raíz. You must pull it up by its roots.

Estaba arrancando malas hierbas. I was pulling up weeds.

Me **has arrancado** un botón. You've pulled off one of my buttons.

El viento **arrancó** varios árboles. Several trees were uprooted in the wind.

arrancar

	FUTURE	CONDITIONAL
(yo)	arrancaré	arrancaría
(tú)	arrancarás	arrancarías
(él/ella/usted)	arrancará	arrancaría
(nosotros/as)	arrancaremos	arrancaríamos
(vosotros/as)	arrancaréis	arrancaríais
(ellos/ellas/ ustedes)	arrancarán	arrancarían

	PRESENT SUBJUNCTIVE	IMPERFECT SUBJUNCTIVE
(yo)	arranque	arrancara *or* arrancase
(tú)	arranques	arrancaras *or* arrancases
(él/ella/usted)	arranque	arrancara *or* arrancase
(nosotros/as)	arranquemos	arrancáramos *or* arrancásemos
(vosotros/as)	arranquéis	arrancarais *or* arrancaseis
(ellos/ellas/ ustedes)	arranquen	arrancaran *or* arrancasen

IMPERATIVE

arranca / arrancad

*Use the present subjunctive in all cases other than these **tú** and **vosotros** affirmative forms.*

EXAMPLE PHRASES

No **arranques** hojas del cuaderno. Don't go tearing pages out of the exercise book.

Arranca y vámonos. Start the engine and let's get going.

arrepentirse (to be sorry)

	PRESENT	PRESENT PERFECT
(yo)	me arrepiento	me he arrepentido
(tú)	te arrepientes	te has arrepentido
(él/ella/usted)	se arrepiente	se ha arrepentido
(nosotros/as)	nos arrepentimos	nos hemos arrepentido
(vosotros/as)	os arrepentís	os habéis arrepentido
(ellos/ellas/ustedes)	se arrepienten	se han arrepentido

	PRETERITE	IMPERFECT
(yo)	me arrepentí	me arrepentía
(tú)	te arrepentiste	te arrepentías
(él/ella/usted)	se arrepintió	se arrepentía
(nosotros/as)	nos arrepentimos	nos arrepentíamos
(vosotros/as)	os arrepentisteis	os arrepentíais
(ellos/ellas/ustedes)	se arrepintieron	se arrepentían

GERUND
arrepintiéndose, etc

PAST PARTICIPLE
arrepentido

EXAMPLE PHRASES

¡**Te** vas a **arrepentir** de esto! You'll be sorry you did that!

No **me arrepiento** de nada. I don't regret anything.

Arrepintiéndote en serio, seguro que te perdonarán. If you're truly sorry,
I'm sure they'll forgive you.

Se arrepintieron y decidieron no vender la casa. They changed their minds
and decided not to sell the house.

Remember that subject pronouns are not used very often in Spanish.

arrepentirse

	FUTURE	CONDITIONAL
(yo)	me arrepentiré	me arrepentiría
(tú)	te arrepentirás	te arrepentirías
(él/ella/usted)	se arrepentirá	se arrepentiría
(nosotros/as)	nos arrepentiremos	nos arrepentiríamos
(vosotros/as)	os arrepentiréis	os arrepentiríais
(ellos/ellas/ ustedes)	se arrepentirán	se arrepentirían

	PRESENT SUBJUNCTIVE	IMPERFECT SUBJUNCTIVE
(yo)	me arrepienta	me arrepintiera or arrepintiese
(tú)	te arrepientas	te arrepintieras or arrepintieses
(él/ella/usted)	se arrepienta	se arrepintiera or arrepintiese
(nosotros/as)	nos arrepintamos	nos arrepintiéramos or arrepintiésemos
(vosotros/as)	os arrepintáis	os arrepintierais or arrepintieseis
(ellos/ellas/ ustedes)	se arrepientan	se arrepintieran or arrepintiesen

IMPERATIVE

arrepiéntete / arrepentíos

Use the present subjunctive in all cases other than these tú and vosotros affirmative forms.

EXAMPLE PHRASES

Algún día **se arrepentirá** de no haber estudiado una carrera. One day he'll be sorry he didn't go to university.

No **te arrepientas** nunca de haber dicho la verdad. Don't ever regret having told the truth.

atravesar (to cross; to go through)

	PRESENT		PRESENT PERFECT
(yo)	atravieso		he atravesado
(tú)	atraviesas		has atravesado
(él/ella/usted)	atraviesa		ha atravesado
(nosotros/as)	atravesamos		hemos atravesado
(vosotros/as)	atravesáis		habéis atravesado
(ellos/ellas/ ustedes)	atraviesan		han atravesado

	PRETERITE		IMPERFECT
(yo)	atravesé		atravesaba
(tú)	atravesaste		atravesabas
(él/ella/usted)	atravesó		atravesaba
(nosotros/as)	atravesamos		atravesábamos
(vosotros/as)	atravesasteis		atravesabais
(ellos/ellas/ ustedes)	atravesaron		atravesaban

GERUND

atravesando

PAST PARTICIPLE

atravesado

EXAMPLE PHRASES

Atravesamos un mal momento. We're going through a bad patch.

En este momento **está atravesando** la ciudad en un coche descubierto.
 Right now he's driving through the city in an open-topped vehicle.

Hemos atravesado el río a nado. We swam across the river.

La bala le **atravesó** el cráneo. The bullet went through his skull.

Un camión **se** nos **atravesó** en la carretera. A lorry pulled out in front of us
 on the road.

Remember that subject pronouns are not used very often in Spanish.

atravesar

	FUTURE	CONDITIONAL
(yo)	atravesaré	atravesaría
(tú)	atravesarás	atravesarías
(él/ella/usted)	atravesará	atravesaría
(nosotros/as)	atravesaremos	atravesaríamos
(vosotros/as)	atravesaréis	atravesaríais
(ellos/ellas/ ustedes)	atravesarán	atravesarían

	PRESENT SUBJUNCTIVE	IMPERFECT SUBJUNCTIVE
(yo)	atraviese	atravesara *or* atravesase
(tú)	atravieses	atravesaras *or* atravesases
(él/ella/usted)	atraviese	atravesara *or* atravesase
(nosotros/as)	atravesemos	atravesáramos *or* atravesásemos
(vosotros/as)	atraveséis	atravesarais *or* atravesaseis
(ellos/ellas/ ustedes)	atraviesen	atravesaran *or* atravesasen

IMPERATIVE
atraviesa / atravesad

Use the present subjunctive in all cases other than these tú and vosotros affirmative forms.

EXAMPLE PHRASES
El túnel **atravesará** la montaña. The tunnel will go through the mountain.

Remember that subject pronouns are not used very often in Spanish.

aunar (to join together)

	PRESENT	PRESENT PERFECT
(yo)	aúno	he aunado
(tú)	aúnas	has aunado
(él/ella/usted)	aúna	ha aunado
(nosotros/as)	aunamos	hemos aunado
(vosotros/as)	aunáis	habéis aunado
(ellos/ellas/ustedes)	aúnan	han aunado

	PRETERITE	IMPERFECT
(yo)	auné	aunaba
(tú)	aunaste	aunabas
(él/ella/usted)	aunó	aunaba
(nosotros/as)	aunamos	aunábamos
(vosotros/as)	aunasteis	aunabais
(ellos/ellas/ustedes)	aunaron	aunaban

GERUND
aunando

PAST PARTICIPLE
aunado

EXAMPLE PHRASES

En esta obra **se han aunado** imaginación y técnica. This play combines imagination and technique.

Aunaron esfuerzos. They joined forces.

La pintura barroca **aunaba** conocimientos de geometría y anatomía. Baroque painting brought knowledge of geometry and anatomy together.

Remember that subject pronouns are not used very often in Spanish.

aunar

	FUTURE	CONDITIONAL
(yo)	aunaré	aunaría
(tú)	aunarás	aunarías
(él/ella/usted)	aunará	aunaría
(nosotros/as)	aunaremos	aunaríamos
(vosotros/as)	aunaréis	aunaríais
(ellos/ellas/ ustedes)	aunarán	aunarían

	PRESENT SUBJUNCTIVE	IMPERFECT SUBJUNCTIVE
(yo)	aúne	aunara or aunase
(tú)	aúnes	aunaras or aunases
(él/ella/usted)	aúne	aunara or aunase
(nosotros/as)	aunemos	aunáramos or aunásemos
(vosotros/as)	aunéis	aunarais or aunaseis
(ellos/ellas/ ustedes)	aúnen	aunaran or aunasen

IMPERATIVE
aúna / aunad

Use the present subjunctive in all cases other than these **tú** and **vosotros** affirmative forms.

Remember that subject pronouns are not used very often in Spanish.

avergonzar (to shame)

	PRESENT	PRESENT PERFECT
(yo)	avergüenzo	he avergonzado
(tú)	avergüenzas	has avergonzado
(él/ella/usted)	avergüenza	ha avergonzado
(nosotros/as)	avergonzamos	hemos avergonzado
(vosotros/as)	avergonzáis	habéis avergonzado
(ellos/ellas/ustedes)	avergüenzan	han avergonzado

	PRETERITE	IMPERFECT
(yo)	avergoncé	avergonzaba
(tú)	avergonzaste	avergonzabas
(él/ella/usted)	avergonzó	avergonzaba
(nosotros/as)	avergonzamos	avergonzábamos
(vosotros/as)	avergonzasteis	avergonzabais
(ellos/ellas/ustedes)	avergonzaron	avergonzaban

GERUND

avergonzando

PAST PARTICIPLE

avergonzado

EXAMPLE PHRASES

Tendrías que **avergonzarte**. You should be ashamed of yourself.

Le **avergüenza** no tener dinero. He's ashamed of having no money.

Cuando me lo dijo **me avergoncé**. I was embarrassed when he told me.

Se avergonzaba de su familia. He was ashamed of his family.

Avergonzándote no arreglas nada. Being ashamed doesn't solve anything.

Remember that subject pronouns are not used very often in Spanish.

avergonzar

	FUTURE	CONDITIONAL
(yo)	avergonzaré	avergonzaría
(tú)	avergonzarás	avergonzarías
(él/ella/usted)	avergonzará	avergonzaría
(nosotros/as)	avergonzaremos	avergonzaríamos
(vosotros/as)	avegonzaréis	avergonzaríais
(ellos/ellas/ ustedes)	avergonzarán	avergonzarían

	PRESENT SUBJUNCTIVE	IMPERFECT SUBJUNCTIVE
(yo)	avergüence	avergonzara or avergonzase
(tú)	avergüences	avergonzaras or avergonzases
(él/ella/usted)	avergüence	avergonzara or avergonzase
(nosotros/as)	avergoncemos	avergonzáramos or avergonzásemos
(vosotros/as)	avergoncéis	avergonzarais or avergonzaseis
(ellos/ellas/ ustedes)	avergüencen	avergonzaran or avergonzasen

IMPERATIVE
avergüenza / avergonzad

Use the present subjunctive in all cases other than these tú and vosotros affirmative forms.

EXAMPLE PHRASES
Si hubiera sabido que **te avergonzarías** tanto, no te lo habría dicho.
  I wouldn't have told you if I'd known you'd be so embarrassed.
Si de verdad **se avergonzaran**, no se comportarían así. They wouldn't behave
  like that if they were really ashamed.

Remember that subject pronouns are not used very often in Spanish.

averiguar (to find out)

	PRESENT		PRESENT PERFECT
(yo)	averiguo		he averiguado
(tú)	averiguas		has averiguado
(él/ella/usted)	averigua		ha averiguado
(nosotros/as)	averiguamos		hemos averiguado
(vosotros/as)	averiguáis		habéis averiguado
(ellos/ellas/ ustedes)	averiguan		han averiguado

	PRETERITE		IMPERFECT
(yo)	averigüé		averiguaba
(tú)	averiguaste		averiguabas
(él/ella/usted)	averiguó		averiguaba
(nosotros/as)	averiguamos		averiguábamos
(vosotros/as)	averiguasteis		averiguabais
(ellos/ellas/ ustedes)	averiguaron		averiguaban

GERUND

averiguando

PAST PARTICIPLE

averiguado

EXAMPLE PHRASES

Trataron de **averiguar** su paradero. They tried to find out his whereabouts.

Poco a poco van **averiguando** más cosas sobre su vida. They're gradually finding out more about his life.

¿Cómo **has averiguado** dónde vivo? How did you find out where I lived?

¿Cuándo lo **averiguaron**? When did they find out?

Remember that subject pronouns are not used very often in Spanish.

averiguar

	FUTURE	CONDITIONAL
(yo)	averiguaré	averiguaría
(tú)	averiguarás	averiguarías
(él/ella/usted)	averiguará	averiguaría
(nosotros/as)	averiguaremos	averiguaríamos
(vosotros/as)	averiguaréis	averiguaríais
(ellos/ellas/ ustedes)	averiguarán	averiguarían

	PRESENT SUBJUNCTIVE	IMPERFECT SUBJUNCTIVE
(yo)	averigüe	averiguara or averiguase
(tú)	averigües	averiguaras or averiguases
(él/ella/usted)	averigüe	averiguara or averiguase
(nosotros/as)	averigüemos	averiguáramos or averiguásemos
(vosotros/as)	averigüéis	averiguarais or averiguaseis
(ellos/ellas/ ustedes)	averigüen	averiguaran or averiguasen

IMPERATIVE
averigua / averiguad

Use the present subjunctive in all cases other than these tú and vosotros affirmative forms.

EXAMPLE PHRASES

Lo **averiguaré** pronto. I'll find out soon.

Dijo que si le dábamos tiempo lo **averiguaría**. She said that she'd find out if we gave her time.

En cuanto lo **averigüe** te lo digo. I'll tell you as soon as I find out.

¡**Averígualo** inmediatamente! Check it out immediately!

Remember that subject pronouns are not used very often in Spanish.

bendecir (to bless)

	PRESENT	PRESENT PERFECT
(yo)	bendigo	he bendecido
(tú)	bendices	has bendecido
(él/ella/usted)	bendice	ha bendecido
(nosotros/as)	bendecimos	hemos bendecido
(vosotros/as)	bendecís	habéis bendecido
(ellos/ellas/ustedes)	bendicen	han bendecido

	PRETERITE	IMPERFECT
(yo)	bendije	bendecía
(tú)	bendijiste	bendecías
(él/ella/usted)	bendijo	bendecía
(nosotros/as)	bendijimos	bendecíamos
(vosotros/as)	bendijisteis	bendecíais
(ellos/ellas/ustedes)	bendijeron	bendecían

GERUND
bendiciendo

PAST PARTICIPLE
bendecido

EXAMPLE PHRASES

Su padre **bendice** siempre la mesa. His father always says grace.

La vida me **ha bendecido** con unos hijos maravillosos. I've been blessed with wonderful children.

Jesús **bendijo** los panes y los peces. Jesus blessed the fish and the bread.

Bendecía el día en que lo conoció. She blessed the day she met him.

Remember that subject pronouns are not used very often in Spanish.

bendecir

	FUTURE	CONDITIONAL
(yo)	bendeciré	bendeciría
(tú)	bendecirás	bendecirías
(él/ella/usted)	bendecirá	bendeciría
(nosotros/as)	bendeciremos	bendeciríamos
(vosotros/as)	bendeciréis	bendeciríais
(ellos/ellas/ ustedes)	bendecirán	bendecirían

	PRESENT SUBJUNCTIVE	IMPERFECT SUBJUNCTIVE
(yo)	bendiga	bendijera or bendijese
(tú)	bendigas	bendijeras or bendijeses
(él/ella/usted)	bendiga	bendijera or bendijese
(nosotros/as)	bendigamos	bendijéramos or bendijésemos
(vosotros/as)	bendigáis	bendijerais or bendijeseis
(ellos/ellas/ ustedes)	bendigan	bendijeran or bendijesen

IMPERATIVE
bendice / bendecid

Use the present subjunctive in all cases other than these tú and vosotros affirmative forms.

EXAMPLE PHRASES

El Papa **bendecirá** a los fieles desde el balcón. The Pope will bless the faithful from the balcony.

Quieren que sea él quien **bendiga** su unión. They want him to marry them.

Pidieron a un sacerdote que **bendijera** su nueva casa. They asked a priest to bless their new house.

Remember that subject pronouns are not used very often in Spanish.

caber (to fit)

	PRESENT	PRESENT PERFECT
(yo)	quepo	he cabido
(tú)	cabes	has cabido
(él/ella/usted)	cabe	ha cabido
(nosotros/as)	cabemos	hemos cabido
(vosotros/as)	cabéis	habéis cabido
(ellos/ellas/ustedes)	caben	han cabido

	PRETERITE	IMPERFECT
(yo)	cupe	cabía
(tú)	cupiste	cabías
(él/ella/usted)	cupo	cabía
(nosotros/as)	cupimos	cabíamos
(vosotros/as)	cupisteis	cabíais
(ellos/ellas/ustedes)	cupieron	cabían

GERUND

cabiendo

PAST PARTICIPLE

cabido

EXAMPLE PHRASES

No te preocupes, que va a **caber**. Don't worry, it will fit.

Aquí no **cabe**. There isn't enough room for it here.

Al final **ha cabido** todo. In the end everything went in.

No le **cupo** la menor duda. She wasn't in any doubt.

No **cabía** en sí de gozo. She was beside herself with joy.

Remember that subject pronouns are not used very often in Spanish.

caber

	FUTURE	CONDITIONAL
(yo)	cabré	cabría
(tú)	cabrás	cabrías
(él/ella/usted)	cabrá	cabría
(nosotros/as)	cabremos	cabríamos
(vosotros/as)	cabréis	cabríais
(ellos/ellas/ustedes)	cabrán	cabrían

	PRESENT SUBJUNCTIVE	IMPERFECT SUBJUNCTIVE
(yo)	quepa	cupiera or cupiese
(tú)	quepas	cupieras or cupieses
(él/ella/usted)	quepa	cupiera or cupiese
(nosotros/as)	quepamos	cupiéramos or cupiésemos
(vosotros/as)	quepáis	cupierais or cupieseis
(ellos/ellas/ustedes)	quepan	cupieran or cupiesen

IMPERATIVE

cabe / cabed

Use the present subjunctive in all cases other than these tú and vosotros affirmative forms.

EXAMPLE PHRASES

¿Crees que **cabrá**? Do you think there will be enough room for it?

Cabría cuestionarse si es la mejor solución. We should ask ourselves whether it's the best solution.

Hizo lo imposible para que le **cupiera** la redacción en una página.
He did everything he could to fit the composition onto one page.

Remember that subject pronouns are not used very often in Spanish.

caer (to fall)

	PRESENT	PRESENT PERFECT
(yo)	caigo	he caído
(tú)	caes	has caído
(él/ella/usted)	cae	ha caído
(nosotros/as)	caemos	hemos caído
(vosotros/as)	caéis	habéis caído
(ellos/ellas/ustedes)	caen	han caído

	PRETERITE	IMPERFECT
(yo)	caí	caía
(tú)	caíste	caías
(él/ella/usted)	cayó	caía
(nosotros/as)	caímos	caíamos
(vosotros/as)	caísteis	caíais
(ellos/ellas/ustedes)	cayeron	caían

GERUND
cayendo

PAST PARTICIPLE
caído

EXAMPLE PHRASES

Su cumpleaños **cae** en viernes. Her birthday falls on a Friday.

Ese edificio se **está cayendo**. That building's falling down.

Se me **ha caído** un guante. I've dropped one of my gloves.

Me **caí** por las escaleras. I fell down the stairs.

Me **caía** muy bien. I really liked him.

Remember that subject pronouns are not used very often in Spanish.

caer

	FUTURE	CONDITIONAL
(yo)	caeré	caería
(tú)	caerás	caerías
(él/ella/usted)	caerá	caería
(nosotros/as)	caeremos	caeríamos
(vosotros/as)	caeréis	caeríais
(ellos/ellas/ustedes)	caerán	caerían

	PRESENT SUBJUNCTIVE	IMPERFECT SUBJUNCTIVE
(yo)	caiga	cayera or cayese
(tú)	caigas	cayeras or cayeses
(él/ella/usted)	caiga	cayera or cayese
(nosotros/as)	caigamos	cayéramos or cayésemos
(vosotros/as)	caigáis	cayerais or cayeseis
(ellos/ellas/ustedes)	caigan	cayeran or cayesen

IMPERATIVE

cae / caed

Use the present subjunctive in all cases other than these tú and vosotros affirmative forms.

EXAMPLE PHRASES

Tarde o temprano, **caerá** en manos del enemigo. Sooner or later, it will fall into enemy hands.

Yo me **caería** con esos tacones. I'd fall over if I wore heels like those.

Seguirá adelante **caiga** quien **caiga**. She'll go ahead no matter how many heads have to roll.

No **caigas** tan bajo. Don't stoop so low.

Remember that subject pronouns are not used very often in Spanish.

cambiar (to change)

	PRESENT		PRESENT PERFECT
(yo)	cambio		he cambiado
(tú)	cambias		has cambiado
(él/ella/usted)	cambia		ha cambiado
(nosotros/as)	cambiamos		hemos cambiado
(vosotros/as)	cambiáis		habéis cambiado
(ellos/ellas/ ustedes)	cambian		han cambiado

	PRETERITE		IMPERFECT
(yo)	cambié		cambiaba
(tú)	cambiaste		cambiabas
(él/ella/usted)	cambió		cambiaba
(nosotros/as)	cambiamos		cambiábamos
(vosotros/as)	cambiasteis		cambiabais
(ellos/ellas/ ustedes)	cambiaron		cambiaban

GERUND
cambiando

PAST PARTICIPLE
cambiado

EXAMPLE PHRASES

Necesito **cambiar** de ambiente. I need a change of scene.

Te **cambio** mi bolígrafo por tu goma. I'll swap my pen for your rubber.

He cambiado de idea. I've changed my mind.

Cambié varias veces de trabajo. I changed jobs several times.

Cambiaban de coche cada año. They changed their car every year.

Remember that subject pronouns are not used very often in Spanish.

cambiar

	FUTURE	CONDITIONAL
(yo)	cambiaré	cambiaría
(tú)	cambiarás	cambiarías
(él/ella/usted)	cambiará	cambiaría
(nosotros/as)	cambiaremos	cambiaríamos
(vosotros/as)	cambiaréis	cambiaríais
(ellos/ellas/ustedes)	cambiarán	cambiarían

	PRESENT SUBJUNCTIVE	IMPERFECT SUBJUNCTIVE
(yo)	cambie	cambiara or cambiase
(tú)	cambies	cambiaras or cambiases
(él/ella/usted)	cambie	cambiara or cambiase
(nosotros/as)	cambiemos	cambiáramos or cambiásemos
(vosotros/as)	cambiéis	cambiarais or cambiaseis
(ellos/ellas/ustedes)	cambien	cambiaran or cambiasen

IMPERATIVE

cambia / cambiad

Use the present subjunctive in all cases other than these tú and vosotros affirmative forms.

EXAMPLE PHRASES

Cuando la conozcas, **cambiarás** de idea. You'll change your mind when you meet her.

Si pudiéramos, **nos cambiaríamos** de casa. If we could, we'd move house.

No quiero que **cambies**. I don't want you to change.

Cámbiate, que se nos hace tarde. Get changed, it's getting late.

Remember that subject pronouns are not used very often in Spanish.

cazar (to hunt; to shoot)

	PRESENT		PRESENT PERFECT
(yo)	cazo		he cazado
(tú)	cazas		has cazado
(él/ella/usted)	caza		ha cazado
(nosotros/as)	cazamos		hemos cazado
(vosotros/as)	cazáis		habéis cazado
(ellos/ellas/ustedes)	cazan		han cazado

	PRETERITE		IMPERFECT
(yo)	cacé		cazaba
(tú)	cazaste		cazabas
(él/ella/usted)	cazó		cazaba
(nosotros/as)	cazamos		cazábamos
(vosotros/as)	cazasteis		cazabais
(ellos/ellas/ustedes)	cazaron		cazaban

GERUND

cazando

PAST PARTICIPLE

cazado

EXAMPLE PHRASES

Salieron a **cazar** ciervos. They went deer-hunting.

Caza las cosas al vuelo. She's very quick on the uptake.

No **he cazado** nada de lo que ha dicho. I didn't understand a word he said.

Los **cacé** robando. I caught them stealing.

Cazaban con lanza. They hunted with spears.

Remember that subject pronouns are not used very often in Spanish.

cazar

	FUTURE	**CONDITIONAL**
(yo)	cazaré	cazaría
(tú)	cazarás	cazarías
(él/ella/usted)	cazará	cazaría
(nosotros/as)	cazaremos	cazaríamos
(vosotros/as)	cazaréis	cazaríais
(ellos/ellas/ustedes)	cazarán	cazarían

	PRESENT SUBJUNCTIVE	**IMPERFECT SUBJUNCTIVE**
(yo)	cace	cazara or cazase
(tú)	caces	cazaras or cazases
(él/ella/usted)	cace	cazara or cazase
(nosotros/as)	cacemos	cazáramos or cazásemos
(vosotros/as)	cacéis	cazarais or cazaseis
(ellos/ellas/ustedes)	cacen	cazaran or cazasen

IMPERATIVE

caza / cazad

Use the present subjunctive in all cases other than these tú and vosotros affirmative forms.

EXAMPLE PHRASES

¡Quién **cazara** a un millonario! I wish I could land myself a millionaire!

Remember that subject pronouns are not used very often in Spanish.

cerrar (to close)

	PRESENT		PRESENT PERFECT
(yo)	cierro		he cerrado
(tú)	cierras		has cerrado
(él/ella/usted)	cierra		ha cerrado
(nosotros/as)	cerramos		hemos cerrado
(vosotros/as)	cerráis		habéis cerrado
(ellos/ellas/ ustedes)	cierran		han cerrado

	PRETERITE		IMPERFECT
(yo)	cerré		cerraba
(tú)	cerraste		cerrabas
(él/ella/usted)	cerró		cerraba
(nosotros/as)	cerramos		cerrábamos
(vosotros/as)	cerrasteis		cerrabais
(ellos/ellas/ ustedes)	cerraron		cerraban

GERUND
cerrando

PAST PARTICIPLE
cerrado

EXAMPLE PHRASES

No puedo **cerrar** la maleta. I can't shut my suitcase.

No **cierran** al mediodía. They don't close at lunchtime.

Ha cerrado la puerta con llave. She's locked the door.

Cerró el libro. He closed the book.

Se le **cerraban** los ojos. She couldn't keep her eyes open.

Remember that subject pronouns are not used very often in Spanish.

cerrar

	FUTURE	CONDITIONAL
(yo)	cerraré	cerraría
(tú)	cerrarás	cerrarías
(él/ella/usted)	cerrará	cerraría
(nosotros/as)	cerraremos	cerraríamos
(vosotros/as)	cerraréis	cerraríais
(ellos/ellas/ustedes)	cerrrarán	cerrarían

	PRESENT SUBJUNCTIVE	IMPERFECT SUBJUNCTIVE
(yo)	cierre	cerrara or cerrase
(tú)	cierres	cerraras or cerrases
(él/ella/usted)	cierre	cerrara or cerrase
(nosotros/as)	cerremos	cerráramos or cerrásemos
(vosotros/as)	cerréis	cerrarais or cerraseis
(ellos/ellas/ustedes)	cierren	cerraran or cerrasen

IMPERATIVE

cierra / cerrad

*Use the present subjunctive in all cases other than these **tú** and **vosotros** affirmative forms.*

EXAMPLE PHRASES

No dejes que **se cierre** la puerta de golpe. Don't let the door slam shut.

No **cierres** la ventana. Don't close the window.

Cierra el grifo. Turn off the tap.

Remember that subject pronouns are not used very often in Spanish.

cocer (to boil; to cook)

	PRESENT		PRESENT PERFECT
(yo)	cuezo		he cocido
(tú)	cueces		has cocido
(él/ella/usted)	cuece		ha cocido
(nosotros/as)	cocemos		hemos cocido
(vosotros/as)	cocéis		habéis cocido
(ellos/ellas/ ustedes)	cuecen		han cocido

	PRETERITE		IMPERFECT
(yo)	cocí		cocía
(tú)	cociste		cocías
(él/ella/usted)	coció		cocía
(nosotros/as)	cocimos		cocíamos
(vosotros/as)	cocisteis		cocíais
(ellos/ellas/ ustedes)	cocieron		cocían

GERUND

cociendo

PAST PARTICIPLE

cocido

EXAMPLE PHRASES

Las gambas **se cuecen** en un momento. Prawns take no time to cook.

Aquí nos **estamos cociendo**. It's boiling in here.

He cocido todo junto. I've cooked everything together.

Coció el pan en el horno. He baked the bread in the oven.

Remember that subject pronouns are not used very often in Spanish.

cocer

	FUTURE	CONDITIONAL
(yo)	coceré	cocería
(tú)	cocerás	cocerías
(él/ella/usted)	cocerá	cocería
(nosotros/as)	coceremos	coceríamos
(vosotros/as)	coceréis	coceríais
(ellos/ellas/ ustedes)	cocerán	cocerían

	PRESENT SUBJUNCTIVE	IMPERFECT SUBJUNCTIVE
(yo)	cueza	cociera or cociese
(tú)	cuezas	cocieras or cocieses
(él/ella/usted)	cueza	cociera or cociese
(nosotros/as)	cozamos	cociéramos or cociésemos
(vosotros/as)	cozáis	cocierais or cocieseis
(ellos/ellas/ ustedes)	cuezan	cocieran or cociesen

IMPERATIVE

cuece / coced

*Use the present subjunctive in all cases other than these **tú** and **vosotros** affirmative forms.*

EXAMPLE PHRASES

Así se **cocerá** antes. This way it will be ready sooner.

Te dije que lo **cocieras** tapado. I told you to cook it with the lid on.

No lo **cuezas** demasiado. Don't overcook it.

Cuécelo a fuego lento. Cook it over a gentle heat.

Remember that subject pronouns are not used very often in Spanish.

coger (to catch; to take)

	PRESENT		PRESENT PERFECT
(yo)	cojo		he cogido
(tú)	coges		has cogido
(él/ella/usted)	coge		ha cogido
(nosotros/as)	cogemos		hemos cogido
(vosotros/as)	cogéis		habéis cogido
(ellos/ellas/ ustedes)	cogen		han cogido

	PRETERITE		IMPERFECT
(yo)	cogí		cogía
(tú)	cogiste		cogías
(él/ella/usted)	cogió		cogía
(nosotros/as)	cogimos		cogíamos
(vosotros/as)	cogisteis		cogíais
(ellos/ellas/ ustedes)	cogieron		cogían

GERUND
cogiendo

PAST PARTICIPLE
cogido

EXAMPLE PHRASES

¿Por qué no **coges** el tren de las seis? Why don't you get the six o'clock train?
Estuvimos cogiendo setas. We were picking mushrooms.
Le **he cogido** cariño al gato. I've grown fond of the cat.
La **cogí** entre mis brazos. I took her in my arms.
Cogía el metro todos los días. I used to take the tube every day.

Remember that subject pronouns are not used very often in Spanish.

coger

	FUTURE	CONDITIONAL
(yo)	cogeré	cogería
(tú)	cogerás	cogerías
(él/ella/usted)	cogerá	cogería
(nosotros/as)	cogeremos	cogeríamos
(vosotros/as)	cogeréis	cogeríais
(ellos/ellas/ ustedes)	cogerán	cogerían

	PRESENT SUBJUNCTIVE	IMPERFECT SUBJUNCTIVE
(yo)	coja	cogiera or cogiese
(tú)	cojas	cogieras or cogieses
(él/ella/usted)	coja	cogiera or cogiese
(nosotros/as)	cojamos	cogiéramos or cogiésemos
(vosotros/as)	cojáis	cogierais or cogieseis
(ellos/ellas/ ustedes)	cojan	cogieran or cogiesen

IMPERATIVE

coge / coged

Use the present subjunctive in all cases other than these tú and vosotros affirmative forms.

EXAMPLE PHRASES

Se cogerá un resfriado. He'll catch a cold.

Yo **cogería** el azul. I'd take the blue one.

No le **cojas** los juguetes a tu hermana. Don't take your sister's toys.

Coja la primera calle a la derecha. Take the first street on the right.

Remember that subject pronouns are not used very often in Spanish.

colgar (to hang)

	PRESENT	PRESENT PERFECT
(yo)	cuelgo	he colgado
(tú)	cuelgas	has colgado
(él/ella/usted)	cuelga	ha colgado
(nosotros/as)	colgamos	hemos colgado
(vosotros/as)	colgáis	habéis colgado
(ellos/ellas/ ustedes)	cuelgan	han colgado

	PRETERITE	IMPERFECT
(yo)	colgué	colgaba
(tú)	colgaste	colgabas
(él/ella/usted)	colgó	colgaba
(nosotros/as)	colgamos	colgábamos
(vosotros/as)	colgasteis	colgabais
(ellos/ellas/ ustedes)	colgaron	colgaban

GERUND
colgando

PAST PARTICIPLE
colgado

EXAMPLE PHRASES

Cada día **cuelgan** el cartel de "no hay billetes". Every day the "sold out" sign goes up.

Hay telarañas **colgando** del techo. There are cobwebs hanging from the ceiling.

Te **he colgado** la chaqueta en la percha. I've hung your jacket on the hanger.

Me **colgó** el teléfono. He hung up on me.

De la pared **colgaba** un espejo. There was a mirror hanging on the wall.

Remember that subject pronouns are not used very often in Spanish.

colgar

	FUTURE	**CONDITIONAL**
(yo)	colgaré	colgaría
(tú)	colgarás	colgarías
(él/ella/usted)	colgará	colgaría
(nosotros/as)	colgaremos	colgaríamos
(vosotros/as)	colgaréis	colgaríais
(ellos/ellas/ustedes)	colgarán	colgarían

	PRESENT SUBJUNCTIVE	**IMPERFECT SUBJUNCTIVE**
(yo)	cuelgue	colgara or colgase
(tú)	cuelgues	colgaras or colgases
(él/ella/usted)	cuelgue	colgara or colgase
(nosotros/as)	colguemos	colgáramos or colgásemos
(vosotros/as)	colguéis	colgarais or colgaseis
(ellos/ellas/ustedes)	cuelguen	colgaran or colgasen

IMPERATIVE

cuelga / colgad

Use the present subjunctive in all cases other than these tú and vosotros affirmative forms.

EXAMPLE PHRASES

Colgaremos el cuadro en esa pared. We'll hang the picture on that wall.

¡Que lo **cuelguen**! Hang him!

No **cuelgue**, por favor. Please don't hang up.

¡**Cuelga**, por favor, que quiero hacer una llamada! Please hang up. I want to use the phone!

Remember that subject pronouns are not used very often in Spanish.

comer (to eat)

	PRESENT		PRESENT PERFECT
(yo)	como		he comido
(tú)	comes		has comido
(él/ella/usted)	come		ha comido
(nosotros/as)	comemos		hemos comido
(vosotros/as)	coméis		habéis comido
(ellos/ellas/ ustedes)	comen		han comido

	PRETERITE		IMPERFECT
(yo)	comí		comía
(tú)	comiste		comías
(él/ella/usted)	comió		comía
(nosotros/as)	comimos		comíamos
(vosotros/as)	comisteis		comíais
(ellos/ellas/ ustedes)	comieron		comían

GERUND
comiendo

PAST PARTICIPLE
comido

EXAMPLE PHRASES

No **come** carne. He doesn't eat meat.

Se lo **ha comido** todo. He's eaten it all.

Comimos en un restaurante. We had lunch in a restaurant.

Siempre **comían** demasiado. They always ate too much.

Remember that subject pronouns are not used very often in Spanish.

comer

	FUTURE	CONDITIONAL
(yo)	comeré	comería
(tú)	comerás	comerías
(él/ella/usted)	comerá	comería
(nosotros/as)	comeremos	comeríamos
(vosotros/as)	comeréis	comeríais
(ellos/ellas/ ustedes)	comerán	comerían

	PRESENT SUBJUNCTIVE	IMPERFECT SUBJUNCTIVE
(yo)	coma	comiera or comiese
(tú)	comas	comieras or comieses
(él/ella/usted)	coma	comiera or comiese
(nosotros/as)	comamos	comiéramos or comiésemos
(vosotros/as)	comáis	comierais or comieseis
(ellos/ellas/ ustedes)	coman	comieran or comiesen

IMPERATIVE
come / comed

*Use the present subjunctive in all cases other than these **tú** and **vosotros** affirmative forms.*

EXAMPLE PHRASES

Me lo **comeré** yo. I'll eat it.

Si no fuera por mí, no **comeríamos**. We wouldn't eat if it weren't for me.

Si **comieras** más, no estarías tan delgado. You wouldn't be so thin if you ate more.

No **comas** tan deprisa. Don't eat so fast.

Remember that subject pronouns are not used very often in Spanish.

conducir (to drive; to lead)

	PRESENT		PRESENT PERFECT
(yo)	conduzco		he conducido
(tú)	conduces		has conducido
(él/ella/usted)	conduce		ha conducido
(nosotros/as)	conducimos		hemos conducido
(vosotros/as)	conducís		habéis conducido
(ellos/ellas/ ustedes)	conducen		han conducido

	PRETERITE		IMPERFECT
(yo)	conduje		conducía
(tú)	condujiste		conducías
(él/ella/usted)	condujo		conducía
(nosotros/as)	condujimos		conducíamos
(vosotros/as)	condujisteis		conducíais
(ellos/ellas/ ustedes)	condujeron		conducían

GERUND
conduciendo

PAST PARTICIPLE
conducido

EXAMPLE PHRASES

No sé **conducir**. I can't drive.

Conduces muy bien. You're a very good driver.

Enfadarte no te **ha conducido** a nada. Getting angry hasn't got you anywhere.

La pista nos **condujo** hasta él. The clue led us to him.

¿**Conducías** tú? Was it you driving?

Remember that subject pronouns are not used very often in Spanish.

conducir

	FUTURE	**CONDITIONAL**
(yo)	conduciré	conduciría
(tú)	conducirás	conducirías
(él/ella/usted)	conducirá	conduciría
(nosotros/as)	conduciremos	conduciríamos
(vosotros/as)	conduciréis	conduciríais
(ellos/ellas/ ustedes)	conducirán	conducirían

	PRESENT SUBJUNCTIVE	**IMPERFECT SUBJUNCTIVE**
(yo)	conduzca	condujera or condujese
(tú)	conduzcas	condujeras or condujeses
(él/ella/usted)	conduzca	condujera or condujese
(nosotros/as)	conduzcamos	condujéramos or condujésemos
(vosotros/as)	conduzcáis	condujerais or condujeseis
(ellos/ellas/ ustedes)	conduzcan	condujeran or condujesen

IMPERATIVE
conduce / conducid

Use the present subjunctive in all cases other than these tú and vosotros affirmative forms.

EXAMPLE PHRASES
El camarero les **conducirá** a su mesa. The waiter will show you to your table.

Si bebes, no **conduzcas**. Don't drink and drive.

Le pedí que **condujera** más despacio. I asked him to drive more slowly.

Conduzca con cuidado. Drive carefully.

Remember that subject pronouns are not used very often in Spanish.

conocer (to know)

	PRESENT		PRESENT PERFECT
(yo)	conozco		he conocido
(tú)	conoces		has conocido
(él/ella/usted)	conoce		ha conocido
(nosotros/as)	conocemos		hemos conocido
(vosotros/as)	conocéis		habéis conocido
(ellos/ellas/ ustedes)	conocen		han conocido

	PRETERITE		IMPERFECT
(yo)	conocí		conocía
(tú)	conociste		conocías
(él/ella/usted)	conoció		conocía
(nosotros/as)	conocimos		conocíamos
(vosotros/as)	conocisteis		conocíais
(ellos/ellas/ ustedes)	conocieron		conocían

GERUND

conociendo

PAST PARTICIPLE

conocido

EXAMPLE PHRASES

Conozco un restaurante donde se come bien. I know a restaurant where the food is very good.

Nunca **he conocido** a nadie así. I've never met anybody like that.

La **conocí** en una fiesta. I met her at a party.

Nos conocíamos desde hacía años. We'd known each other for years.

Remember that subject pronouns are not used very often in Spanish.

conocer

	FUTURE	CONDITIONAL
(yo)	conoceré	conocería
(tú)	conocerás	conocerías
(él/ella/usted)	conocerá	conocería
(nosotros/as)	conoceremos	conoceríamos
(vosotros/as)	conoceréis	conoceríais
(ellos/ellas/ustedes)	conocerán	conocerían

	PRESENT SUBJUNCTIVE	IMPERFECT SUBJUNCTIVE
(yo)	conozca	conociera or conociese
(tú)	conozcas	conocieras or conocieses
(él/ella/usted)	conozca	conociera or conociese
(nosotros/as)	conozcamos	conociéramos or conociésemos
(vosotros/as)	conozcáis	conocierais or conocieseis
(ellos/ellas/ustedes)	conozcan	conocieran or conociesen

IMPERATIVE
conoce / conoced

Use the present subjunctive in all cases other than these tú and vosotros affirmative forms.

EXAMPLE PHRASES

No sé si la **conocerás** cuando la veas. I don't know if you'll recognize her when you see her.

No quiero que mis padres le **conozcan**. I don't want my parents to meet him.

Si no la **conociera**, pensaría que lo hizo queriendo. If I didn't know her better, I'd think she had done it on purpose.

Remember that subject pronouns are not used very often in Spanish.

construir (to build)

	PRESENT	PRESENT PERFECT
(yo)	construyo	he construido
(tú)	construyes	has construido
(él/ella/usted)	construye	ha construido
(nosotros/as)	construimos	hemos construido
(vosotros/as)	construís	habéis construido
(ellos/ellas/ ustedes)	construyen	han construido

	PRETERITE	IMPERFECT
(yo)	construí	construía
(tú)	construiste	construías
(él/ella/usted)	construyó	construía
(nosotros/as)	construimos	construíamos
(vosotros/as)	construisteis	construíais
(ellos/ellas/ ustedes)	construyeron	construían

GERUND	PAST PARTICIPLE
construyendo	construido

EXAMPLE PHRASES

Construyen casas de madera. They build wooden houses.

Están construyendo una escuela. They're building a new school.

Ha construido la casa él solo. He built the house on his own.

Lo **construyó** sin planos. He built it without any plans.

Su empresa **construía** puentes. His company built bridges.

Remember that subject pronouns are not used very often in Spanish.

construir

	FUTURE	**CONDITIONAL**
(yo)	construiré	construiría
(tú)	construirás	construirías
(él/ella/usted)	construirá	construiría
(nosotros/as)	construiremos	construiríamos
(vosotros/as)	construiréis	construiríais
(ellos/ellas/ustedes)	construirán	construirían

	PRESENT SUBJUNCTIVE	**IMPERFECT SUBJUNCTIVE**
(yo)	construya	construyera or construyese
(tú)	construyas	construyeras or construyeses
(él/ella/usted)	construya	construyera or construyese
(nosotros/as)	construyamos	construyéramos or construyésemos
(vosotros/as)	construyáis	construyerais or construyeseis
(ellos/ellas/ustedes)	construyan	construyeran or construyesen

IMPERATIVE

construye / construid

Use the present subjunctive in all cases other than these tú and vosotros affirmative forms.

EXAMPLE PHRASES

Aquí **construirán** una autopista. They're going to build a new motorway here.

Yo **construiría** la oración de otra forma. I'd construct the sentence differently.

Le pedí que lo **construyera** así. I asked him to build it like this.

Remember that subject pronouns are not used very often in Spanish.

contar (to tell; to count)

	PRESENT		PRESENT PERFECT
(yo)	cuento		he contado
(tú)	cuentas		has contado
(él/ella/usted)	cuenta		ha contado
(nosotros/as)	contamos		hemos contado
(vosotros/as)	contáis		habéis contado
(ellos/ellas/ ustedes)	cuentan		han contado

	PRETERITE		IMPERFECT
(yo)	conté		contaba
(tú)	contaste		contabas
(él/ella/usted)	contó		contaba
(nosotros/as)	contamos		contábamos
(vosotros/as)	contasteis		contabais
(ellos/ellas/ ustedes)	contaron		contaban

GERUND

contando

PAST PARTICIPLE

contado

EXAMPLE PHRASES

Sabe **contar** hasta diez. She can count up to ten.

Estoy contando los días. I'm counting the days.

¿**Has contado** el dinero? Have you counted the money?

Nos **contó** un secreto. He told us a secret.

Para él sólo **contaba** su carrera. The only thing that mattered to him was his career.

Remember that subject pronouns are not used very often in Spanish.

contar

	FUTURE	CONDITIONAL
(yo)	contaré	contaría
(tú)	contarás	contarías
(él/ella/usted)	contará	contaría
(nosotros/as)	contaremos	contaríamos
(vosotros/as)	contaréis	contaríais
(ellos/ellas/ ustedes)	contarán	contarían

	PRESENT SUBJUNCTIVE	IMPERFECT SUBJUNCTIVE
(yo)	cuente	contara or contase
(tú)	cuentes	contaras or contases
(él/ella/usted)	cuente	contara or contase
(nosotros/as)	contemos	contáramos or contásemos
(vosotros/as)	contéis	contarais or contaseis
(ellos/ellas/ ustedes)	cuenten	contaran or contasen

IMPERATIVE

cuenta / contad

*Use the present subjunctive in all cases other than these **tú** and **vosotros** affirmative forms.*

EXAMPLE PHRASES

Prométeme que no se lo **contarás** a nadie. Promise you won't tell anyone.

Quiero que me **cuente** exactamente qué pasó. I want you to tell me exactly what happened.

Quería que le **contara** un cuento. She wanted me to tell her a story.

No **cuentes** conmigo. Don't count on me.

Venga, **cuéntamelo**. Come on, tell me.

Remember that subject pronouns are not used very often in Spanish.

crecer (to grow)

	PRESENT	PRESENT PERFECT
(yo)	crezco	he crecido
(tú)	creces	has crecido
(él/ella/usted)	crece	ha crecido
(nosotros/as)	crecemos	hemos crecido
(vosotros/as)	crecéis	habéis crecido
(ellos/ellas/ustedes)	crecen	han crecido

	PRETERITE	IMPERFECT
(yo)	crecí	crecía
(tú)	creciste	crecías
(él/ella/usted)	creció	crecía
(nosotros/as)	crecimos	crecíamos
(vosotros/as)	crecisteis	crecíais
(ellos/ellas/ustedes)	crecieron	crecían

GERUND
creciendo

PAST PARTICIPLE
crecido

EXAMPLE PHRASES

Esas plantas **crecen** en Chile. Those plants grow in Chile.

¡Cómo **has crecido**! Haven't you grown!

Crecimos juntos. We grew up together.

La ciudad **crecía** a pasos agigantados. The city was growing by leaps and bounds.

Sigue **creciendo** la inflación. Inflation is still going up.

Remember that subject pronouns are not used very often in Spanish.

crecer

	FUTURE	CONDITIONAL
(yo)	creceré	crecería
(tú)	crecerás	crecerías
(él/ella/usted)	crecerá	crecería
(nosotros/as)	creceremos	creceríamos
(vosotros/as)	creceréis	creceríais
(ellos/ellas/ustedes)	crecerán	crecerían

	PRESENT SUBJUNCTIVE	IMPERFECT SUBJUNCTIVE
(yo)	crezca	creciera or creciese
(tú)	crezcas	crecieras or crecieses
(él/ella/usted)	crezca	creciera or creciese
(nosotros/as)	crezcamos	creciéramos or creciésemos
(vosotros/as)	crezcáis	crecierais or crecieseis
(ellos/ellas/ustedes)	crezcan	crecieran or creciesen

IMPERATIVE
crece / creced

*Use the present subjunctive in all cases other than these **tú** and **vosotros** affirmative forms.*

EXAMPLE PHRASES
Este año la economía **crecerá** un 2%. The economy will grow by 2% this year.

Crecería mejor en un ambiente húmedo. It would grow better in a humid environment.

Cuando **crezca**, ya verás. When he grows up, you'll see.

Quería que sus hijos **crecieran** en otro ambiente. She wanted her children to grow up in a different environment.

Remember that subject pronouns are not used very often in Spanish.

cruzar (to cross)

	PRESENT		PRESENT PERFECT
(yo)	cruzo		he cruzado
(tú)	cruzas		has cruzado
(él/ella/usted)	cruza		ha cruzado
(nosotros/as)	cruzamos		hemos cruzado
(vosotros/as)	cruzáis		habéis cruzado
(ellos/ellas/ustedes)	cruzan		han cruzado

	PRETERITE		IMPERFECT
(yo)	crucé		cruzaba
(tú)	cruzaste		cruzabas
(él/ella/usted)	cruzó		cruzaba
(nosotros/as)	cruzamos		cruzábamos
(vosotros/as)	cruzasteis		cruzabais
(ellos/ellas/ustedes)	cruzaron		cruzaban

GERUND
cruzando

PAST PARTICIPLE
cruzado

EXAMPLE PHRASES

Hace tiempo que no **me cruzo** con él. I haven't seen him for a long time.

La caravana **está cruzando** el desierto. The caravan is crossing the dessert.

Se me **han cruzado** los cables. I got mixed up.

Cruzaron el puente. They crossed the bridge.

La carretera **cruzaba** la urbanización. The road went through the housing estate.

Remember that subject pronouns are not used very often in Spanish.

cruzar

	FUTURE	CONDITIONAL
(yo)	cruzaré	cruzaría
(tú)	cruzarás	cruzarías
(él/ella/usted)	cruzará	cruzaría
(nosotros/as)	cruzaremos	cruzaríamos
(vosotros/as)	cruzaréis	cruzaríais
(ellos/ellas/ ustedes)	cruzarán	cruzarían

	PRESENT SUBJUNCTIVE	IMPERFECT SUBJUNCTIVE
(yo)	cruce	cruzara or cruzase
(tú)	cruces	cruzaras or cruzases
(él/ella/usted)	cruce	cruzara or cruzase
(nosotros/as)	crucemos	cruzáramos or cruzásemos
(vosotros/as)	crucéis	cruzarais or cruzaseis
(ellos/ellas/ ustedes)	crucen	cruzaran or cruzasen

IMPERATIVE

cruza / cruzad

Use the present subjunctive in all cases other than these tú and vosotros affirmative forms.

EXAMPLE PHRASES

Cruzarán varias especies distintas. They'll cross several different species.

Crucemos los dedos. Let's keep our fingers crossed.

Le dije que **cruzara** por el paso de cebra. I told her to cross at the pedestrian crossing.

No **cruces** la calle con el semáforo en rojo. Don't cross the road when the lights are red.

Remember that subject pronouns are not used very often in Spanish.

cubrir (to cover)

	PRESENT		PRESENT PERFECT
(yo)	cubro		he cubierto
(tú)	cubres		has cubierto
(él/ella/usted)	cubre		ha cubierto
(nosotros/as)	cubrimos		hemos cubierto
(vosotros/as)	cubrís		habéis cubierto
(ellos/ellas/ustedes)	cubren		han cubierto

	PRETERITE		IMPERFECT
(yo)	cubrí		cubría
(tú)	cubriste		cubrías
(él/ella/usted)	cubrió		cubría
(nosotros/as)	cubrimos		cubríamos
(vosotros/as)	cubristeis		cubríais
(ellos/ellas/ustedes)	cubrieron		cubrían

GERUND
cubriendo

PAST PARTICIPLE
cubierto

EXAMPLE PHRASES

Esto no **cubre** los gastos. This isn't enough to cover expenses.

Le **han cubierto** con una manta. They've covered him with a blanket.

Se cubrió la cara con las manos. She covered her face with her hands.

La nieve **cubría** la montaña. The mountain was covered in snow.

Remember that subject pronouns are not used very often in Spanish.

cubrir

	FUTURE	CONDITIONAL
(yo)	cubriré	cubriría
(tú)	cubrirás	cubrirías
(él/ella/usted)	cubrirá	cubriría
(nosotros/as)	cubriremos	cubriríamos
(vosotros/as)	cubriréis	cubriríais
(ellos/ellas/ustedes)	cubrirán	cubrirían

	PRESENT SUBJUNCTIVE	IMPERFECT SUBJUNCTIVE
(yo)	cubra	cubriera or cubriese
(tú)	cubras	cubrieras or cubrieses
(él/ella/usted)	cubra	cubriera or cubriese
(nosotros/as)	cubramos	cubriéramos or cubriésemos
(vosotros/as)	cubráis	cubrierais or cubrieseis
(ellos/ellas/ustedes)	cubran	cubrieran or cubriesen

IMPERATIVE

cubre / cubrid

Use the present subjunctive in all cases other than these tú and vosotros affirmative forms.

EXAMPLE PHRASES

Los corredores **cubrirán** una distancia de 2 km. The runners will cover a distance of 2 km.

¿Quién **cubriría** la vacante? Who'd fill the vacancy?

Quiero que **cubras** la noticia. I want you to cover the story.

dar (to give)

	PRESENT		PRESENT PERFECT
(yo)	doy		he dado
(tú)	das		has dado
(él/ella/usted)	da		ha dado
(nosotros/as)	damos		hemos dado
(vosotros/as)	dais		habéis dado
(ellos/ellas/ ustedes)	dan		han dado

	PRETERITE		IMPERFECT
(yo)	di		daba
(tú)	diste		dabas
(él/ella/usted)	dio		daba
(nosotros/as)	dimos		dábamos
(vosotros/as)	disteis		dabais
(ellos/ellas/ ustedes)	dieron		daban

GERUND
dando

PAST PARTICIPLE
dado

EXAMPLE PHRASES

Me **da** miedo la oscuridad. I'm afraid of the dark.

Le **han dado** varios premios a su película. His film has been awarded several prizes.

Nos **dieron** un par de entradas gratis. They gave us a couple of free tickets.

Mi ventana **daba** al jardín. My window looked out on the garden.

Remember that subject pronouns are not used very often in Spanish.

dar

	FUTURE	CONDITIONAL
(yo)	**daré**	**daría**
(tú)	**darás**	**darías**
(él/ella/usted)	**dará**	**daría**
(nosotros/as)	**daremos**	**daríamos**
(vosotros/as)	**daréis**	**daríais**
(ellos/ellas/ustedes)	**darán**	**darían**

	PRESENT SUBJUNCTIVE	IMPERFECT SUBJUNCTIVE
(yo)	**dé**	**diera** or **diese**
(tú)	**des**	**dieras** or **dieses**
(él/ella/usted)	**dé**	**diera** or **diese**
(nosotros/as)	**demos**	**diéramos** or **diésemos**
(vosotros/as)	**deis**	**dierais** or **dieseis**
(ellos/ellas/ustedes)	**den**	**dieran** or **diesen**

IMPERATIVE

da / dad

*Use the present subjunctive in all cases other than these **tú** and **vosotros** affirmative forms.*

EXAMPLE PHRASES

Te **daré** el número de mi móvil. I'll give you my mobile phone number.

Me **daría** mucha alegría volver a verla. It would be really good to see her again.

Quiero que me lo **des** ahora mismo. I want you to give it to me right now.

Déme 2 kilos. 2 kilos please.

Remember that subject pronouns are not used very often in Spanish.

decir (to say; to tell)

	PRESENT		PRESENT PERFECT
(yo)	digo		he dicho
(tú)	dices		has dicho
(él/ella/usted)	dice		ha dicho
(nosotros/as)	decimos		hemos dicho
(vosotros/as)	decís		habéis dicho
(ellos/ellas/ ustedes)	dicen		han dicho

	PRETERITE		IMPERFECT
(yo)	dije		decía
(tú)	dijiste		decías
(él/ella/usted)	dijo		decía
(nosotros/as)	dijimos		decíamos
(vosotros/as)	dijisteis		decíais
(ellos/ellas/ ustedes)	dijeron		decían

GERUND

diciendo

PAST PARTICIPLE

dicho

EXAMPLE PHRASES

Pero ¿qué **dices**? What are you saying?

¿Te **ha dicho** lo de la boda? Has he told you about the wedding?

Me lo **dijo** ayer. He told me yesterday.

Siempre nos **decía** que tuviéramos cuidado. She always used to tell us to be careful.

Remember that subject pronouns are not used very often in Spanish.

decir

	FUTURE	CONDITIONAL
(yo)	diré	diría
(tú)	dirás	dirías
(él/ella/usted)	dirá	diría
(nosotros/as)	diremos	diríamos
(vosotros/as)	diréis	diríais
(ellos/ellas/ ustedes)	dirán	dirían

	PRESENT SUBJUNCTIVE	IMPERFECT SUBJUNCTIVE
(yo)	diga	dijera or dijese
(tú)	digas	dijeras or dijeses
(él/ella/usted)	diga	dijera or dijese
(nosotros/as)	digamos	dijéramos or dijésemos
(vosotros/as)	digáis	dijerais or dijeseis
(ellos/ellas/ ustedes)	digan	dijeran or dijesen

IMPERATIVE
di / decid

*Use the present subjunctive in all cases other than these **tú** and **vosotros** affirmative forms.*

EXAMPLE PHRASES
Yo **diría** que miente. I'd say he's lying.

Diga lo que **diga**, no le voy a creer. Whatever he says, I won't believe him.

Si me **dijeras** lo que pasa, a lo mejor podría ayudar. If you told me what was going on, I could maybe help.

No le **digas** que me has visto. Don't tell him you've seen me.

Remember that subject pronouns are not used very often in Spanish.

despreocuparse (to stop worrying)

	PRESENT	PRESENT PERFECT
(yo)	me despreocupo	me he despreocupado
(tú)	te despreocupas	te has despreocupado
(él/ella/usted)	se despreocupa	se ha despreocupado
(nosotros/as)	nos despreocupamos	nos hemos despreocupado
(vosotros/as)	os despreocupáis	os habéis despreocupado
(ellos/ellas/ ustedes)	se despreocupan	se han despreocupado

	PRETERITE	IMPERFECT
(yo)	me despreocupé	me despreocupaba
(tú)	te despreocupaste	te despreocupabas
(él/ella/usted)	se despreocupó	se despreocupaba
(nosotros/as)	nos despreocupamos	nos despreocupábamos
(vosotros/as)	os despreocupasteis	os despreocupabais
(ellos/ellas/ ustedes)	se despreocuparon	se despreocupaban

GERUND

despreocupándose, etc

PAST PARTICIPLE

despreocupado

EXAMPLE PHRASES

Deberías **despreocuparte** un poco más de las cosas. You shouldn't worry so much about things.

Se **despreocupa** de todo. He shows no concern for anything.

Se **despreocupó** del asunto. He forgot about the matter.

Remember that subject pronouns are not used very often in Spanish.

despreocuparse

	FUTURE	CONDITIONAL
(yo)	me despreocuparé	me despreocuparía
(tú)	te despreocuparás	te despreocuparías
(él/ella/usted)	se despreocupará	se despreocuparía
(nosotros/as)	nos despreocuparemos	nos despreocuparíamos
(vosotros/as)	os despreocuparéis	os despreocuparíais
(ellos/ellas/ustedes)	se despreocuparán	se despreocuparían

	PRESENT SUBJUNCTIVE	IMPERFECT SUBJUNCTIVE
(yo)	me despreocupe	me despreocupara or despreocupase
(tú)	te despreocupes	te despreocuparas or despreocupases
(él/ella/usted)	se despreocupe	se despreocupara or despreocupase
(nosotros/as)	nos despreocupemos	nos despreocupáramos or despreocupásemos
(vosotros/as)	os despreocupéis	os despreocuparais or despreocupaseis
(ellos/ellas/ustedes)	se despreocupen	se despreocuparan or despreocupasen

IMPERATIVE

despreocúpate / despreocupaos

Use the present subjunctive in all cases other than these tú and vosotros affirmative forms.

EXAMPLE PHRASES

Yo **me despreocuparía** de él. I wouldn't worry about him.

Despreocúpate porque ya no tiene remedio. Stop worrying because there's nothing we can do about it now.

detener (to stop; to arrest)

	PRESENT	PRESENT PERFECT
(yo)	detengo	he detenido
(tú)	detienes	has detenido
(él/ella/usted)	detiene	ha detenido
(nosotros/as)	detenemos	hemos detenido
(vosotros/as)	detenéis	habéis detenido
(ellos/ellas/ustedes)	detienen	han detenido

	PRETERITE	IMPERFECT
(yo)	detuve	detenía
(tú)	detuviste	detenías
(él/ella/usted)	detuvo	detenía
(nosotros/as)	detuvimos	deteníamos
(vosotros/as)	detuvisteis	deteníais
(ellos/ellas/ustedes)	detuvieron	detenían

GERUND

deteniendo

PAST PARTICIPLE

detenido

EXAMPLE PHRASES

Han detenido a los ladrones. They've arrested the thieves.

Nos detuvimos en el semáforo. We stopped at the lights.

¡Queda **detenido**! You are under arrest!

Remember that subject pronouns are not used very often in Spanish.

detener

	FUTURE	CONDITIONAL
(yo)	detendré	detendría
(tú)	detendrás	detendrías
(él/ella/usted)	detendrá	detendría
(nosotros/as)	detendremos	detendríamos
(vosotros/as)	detendréis	detendríais
(ellos/ellas/ustedes)	detendrán	detendrían

	PRESENT SUBJUNCTIVE	IMPERFECT SUBJUNCTIVE
(yo)	detenga	detuviera or detuviese
(tú)	detengas	detuvieras or detuvieses
(él/ella/usted)	detenga	detuviera or detuviese
(nosotros/as)	detengamos	detuviéramos or detuviésemos
(vosotros/as)	detengáis	detuvierais or detuvieseis
(ellos/ellas/ustedes)	detengan	detuvieran or detuviesen

IMPERATIVE

detén / detened

Use the present subjunctive in all cases other than these tú and vosotros affirmative forms.

EXAMPLE PHRASES

Nada la **detendrá**. Nothing will stop her.

Si **te detuvieras** a pensar, nunca harías nada. If you stopped to think, you'd never do anything.

¡**Deténgase**! Stop!

¡No **te detengas**! Don't stop!

Remember that subject pronouns are not used very often in Spanish.

dirigir (to direct; to run)

	PRESENT		PRESENT PERFECT
(yo)	dirijo		he dirigido
(tú)	diriges		has dirigido
(él/ella/usted)	dirige		ha dirigido
(nosotros/as)	dirigimos		hemos dirigido
(vosotros/as)	dirigís		habéis dirigido
(ellos/ellas/ustedes)	dirigen		han dirigido

	PRETERITE		IMPERFECT
(yo)	dirigí		dirigía
(tú)	dirigiste		dirigías
(él/ella/usted)	dirigió		dirigía
(nosotros/as)	dirigimos		dirigíamos
(vosotros/as)	dirigisteis		dirigíais
(ellos/ellas/ustedes)	dirigieron		dirigían

GERUND
dirigiendo

PAST PARTICIPLE
dirigido

EXAMPLE PHRASES

Dirijo esta empresa desde hace dos años. I've been running this company for two years.

Ha dirigido varias películas. She has directed several films.

No le **dirigió** la palabra. She didn't say a word to him.

Se dirigía a la parada de autobús. He was making his way to the bus stop.

Remember that subject pronouns are not used very often in Spanish.

dirigir

	FUTURE	CONDITIONAL
(yo)	dirigiré	dirigiría
(tú)	dirigirás	dirigirías
(él/ella/usted)	dirigirá	dirigiría
(nosotros/as)	dirigiremos	dirigiríamos
(vosotros/as)	dirigiréis	dirigiríais
(ellos/ellas/ ustedes)	dirigirán	dirigirían

	PRESENT SUBJUNCTIVE	IMPERFECT SUBJUNCTIVE
(yo)	dirija	dirigiera *or* dirigiese
(tú)	dirijas	dirigieras *or* dirigieses
(él/ella/usted)	dirija	dirigiera *or* dirigiese
(nosotros/as)	dirijamos	dirigiéramos *or* dirigiésemos
(vosotros/as)	dirijáis	dirigierais *or* dirigieseis
(ellos/ellas/ ustedes)	dirijan	dirigieran *or* dirigiesen

IMPERATIVE

dirige / dirigid

Use the present subjunctive in all cases other than these **tú** *and* **vosotros** *affirmative forms.*

EXAMPLE PHRASES

Dirigirá la expedición. He'll be leading the expedition.

Para más información **diríjase** al apartado de correos número 1002.

    For further information write to PO Box 1002.

distinguir (to distinguish)

	PRESENT		PRESENT PERFECT
(yo)	distingo		he distinguido
(tú)	distingues		has distinguido
(él/ella/usted)	distingue		ha distinguido
(nosotros/as)	distinguimos		hemos distinguido
(vosotros/as)	distinguís		habéis distinguido
(ellos/ellas/ustedes)	distinguen		han distinguido

	PRETERITE		IMPERFECT
(yo)	distinguí		distinguía
(tú)	distinguiste		distinguías
(él/ella/usted)	distinguió		distinguía
(nosotros/as)	distinguimos		distinguíamos
(vosotros/as)	distinguisteis		distinguíais
(ellos/ellas/ustedes)	distinguieron		distinguían

GERUND

distinguiendo

PAST PARTICIPLE

distinguido

EXAMPLE PHRASES

No lo **distingo** del azul. I can't tell the difference between it and the blue one.

Nos **ha distinguido** con su presencia. He has honoured us with his presence.

Se **distinguió** por su gran valentía. He distinguished himself by his bravery.

Se **distinguía** desde lejos. You could see it from the distance.

Remember that subject pronouns are not used very often in Spanish.

distinguir

	FUTURE	CONDITIONAL
(yo)	distinguiré	distinguiría
(tú)	distinguirás	distinguirías
(él/ella/usted)	distinguirá	distinguiría
(nosotros/as)	distinguiremos	distinguiríamos
(vosotros/as)	distinguiréis	distinguiríais
(ellos/ellas/ ustedes)	distinguirán	distinguirían

	PRESENT SUBJUNCTIVE	IMPERFECT SUBJUNCTIVE
(yo)	distinga	distinguiera or distinguiese
(tú)	distingas	distinguieras or distinguieses
(él/ella/usted)	distinga	distinguiera or distinguiese
(nosotros/as)	distingamos	distinguiéramos or distinguiésemos
(vosotros/as)	distingáis	distinguierais or distinguieseis
(ellos/ellas/ ustedes)	distingan	distinguieran or distinguiesen

IMPERATIVE
distingue / distinguid

*Use the present subjunctive in all cases other than these **tú** and **vosotros** affirmative forms.*

EXAMPLE PHRASES
Al final **distinguirás** unas notas de otras. Eventually you'll be able to tell one note from another.

No los **distinguiría**. I wouldn't be able to tell them apart.

Remember that subject pronouns are not used very often in Spanish.

divertir (to entertain)

	PRESENT		PRESENT PERFECT
(yo)	divierto		he divertido
(tú)	diviertes		has divertido
(él/ella/usted)	divierte		ha divertido
(nosotros/as)	divertimos		hemos divertido
(vosotros/as)	divertís		habéis divertido
(ellos/ellas/ustedes)	divierten		han divertido

	PRETERITE		IMPERFECT
(yo)	divertí		divertía
(tú)	divertiste		divertías
(él/ella/usted)	divirtió		divertía
(nosotros/as)	divertimos		divertíamos
(vosotros/as)	divertisteis		divertíais
(ellos/ellas/ustedes)	divirtieron		divertían

GERUND

divirtiendo

PAST PARTICIPLE

divertido

EXAMPLE PHRASES

Cantamos sólo para **divertirnos**. We sing just for fun.

Me **divierte** verlos tan serios. It's amusing to see them looking so serious.

¿**Os habéis divertido** en la fiesta? Did you enjoy the party?

Nos **divirtió** con sus anécdotas. He entertained us with his stories.

Nos divertíamos mucho jugando en la playa. We were having a great time playing on the beach.

Remember that subject pronouns are not used very often in Spanish.

divertir

	FUTURE	CONDITIONAL
(yo)	divertiré	divertiría
(tú)	divertirás	divertirías
(él/ella/usted)	divertirá	divertiría
(nosotros/as)	divertiremos	divertiríamos
(vosotros/as)	divertiréis	divertiríais
(ellos/ellas/ ustedes)	divertirán	divertirían

	PRESENT SUBJUNCTIVE	IMPERFECT SUBJUNCTIVE
(yo)	divierta	divirtiera or divirtiese
(tú)	diviertas	divirtieras or divirtieses
(él/ella/usted)	divierta	divirtiera or divirtiese
(nosotros/as)	divirtamos	divirtiéramos or divirtiésemos
(vosotros/as)	divirtáis	divirtierais or divirtieseis
(ellos/ellas/ ustedes)	diviertan	divirtieran or divirtiesen

IMPERATIVE
divierte / divertid

*Use the present subjunctive in all cases other than these **tú** and **vosotros** affirmative forms.*

EXAMPLE PHRASES
Si fueras, **te divertirías** mucho. If you went you'd have a great time.

Hizo lo posible por que **se divirtieran**. He did everything he could to make it fun for them.

¡Que **te diviertas**! Have a good time!

dormir (to sleep)

	PRESENT		PRESENT PERFECT
(yo)	duermo		he dormido
(tú)	duermes		has dormido
(él/ella/usted)	duerme		ha dormido
(nosotros/as)	dormimos		hemos dormido
(vosotros/as)	dormís		habéis dormido
(ellos/ellas/ ustedes)	duermen		han dormido

	PRETERITE		IMPERFECT
(yo)	dormí		dormía
(tú)	dormiste		dormías
(él/ella/usted)	durmió		dormía
(nosotros/as)	dormimos		dormíamos
(vosotros/as)	dormisteis		dormíais
(ellos/ellas/ ustedes)	durmieron		dormían

GERUND
durmiendo

PAST PARTICIPLE
dormido

EXAMPLE PHRASES

No **duermo** muy bien. I don't sleep very well.
Está durmiendo. She's asleep.
He dormido de un tirón. I slept like a log.
Se me **durmió** la pierna. My leg went to sleep.
Se dormía en clase. She would fall asleep in class.

Remember that subject pronouns are not used very often in Spanish.

dormir

	FUTURE	CONDITIONAL
(yo)	dormiré	dormiría
(tú)	dormirás	dormirías
(él/ella/usted)	dormirá	dormiría
(nosotros/as)	dormiremos	dormiríamos
(vosotros/as)	dormiréis	dormiríais
(ellos/ellas/ustedes)	dormirán	dormirían

	PRESENT SUBJUNCTIVE	IMPERFECT SUBJUNCTIVE
(yo)	duerma	durmiera or durmiese
(tú)	duermas	durmieras or durmieses
(él/ella/usted)	duerma	durmiera or durmiese
(nosotros/as)	durmamos	durmiéramos or durmiésemos
(vosotros/as)	durmáis	durmierais or durmieseis
(ellos/ellas/ustedes)	duerman	durmieran or durmiesen

IMPERATIVE
duerme / dormid

Use the present subjunctive in all cases other than these **tú** *and* **vosotros** *affirmative forms.*

EXAMPLE PHRASES

Si no tomo café, **me dormiré**. I'll fall asleep if I don't have some coffee.

Yo no **dormiría** en esa casa. I wouldn't sleep in that house.

Quiero que **duermas** la siesta. I want you to have a nap.

Si **durmieras** más horas, no estarías tan cansada. You wouldn't be so tired if you slept for longer.

Remember that subject pronouns are not used very often in Spanish.

elegir (to choose)

	PRESENT		PRESENT PERFECT
(yo)	elijo		he elegido
(tú)	eliges		has elegido
(él/ella/usted)	elige		ha elegido
(nosotros/as)	elegimos		hemos elegido
(vosotros/as)	elegís		habéis elegido
(ellos/ellas/ustedes)	eligen		han elegido

	PRETERITE		IMPERFECT
(yo)	elegí		elegía
(tú)	elegiste		elegías
(él/ella/usted)	eligió		elegía
(nosotros/as)	elegimos		elegíamos
(vosotros/as)	elegisteis		elegíais
(ellos/ellas/ustedes)	eligieron		elegían

GERUND
eligiendo

PAST PARTICIPLE
elegido

EXAMPLE PHRASES

Te dan a **elegir** entre dos modelos. You get a choice of two models.

Nosotros no **elegimos** a nuestros padres, ni ellos nos **eligen** a nosotros.
  We don't choose our parents and they don't choose us either.

Creo que **ha elegido** bien. I think he's made a good choice.

No lo **eligieron** ellos. It wasn't them who chose it.

Remember that subject pronouns are not used very often in Spanish.

elegir

	FUTURE	CONDITIONAL
(yo)	**elegiré**	**elegiría**
(tú)	**elegirás**	**elegirías**
(él/ella/usted)	**elegirá**	**elegiría**
(nosotros/as)	**elegiremos**	**elegiríamos**
(vosotros/as)	**elegiréis**	**elegiríais**
(ellos/ellas/ustedes)	**elegirán**	**elegirían**

	PRESENT SUBJUNCTIVE	IMPERFECT SUBJUNCTIVE
(yo)	**elija**	**eligiera** or **eligiese**
(tú)	**elijas**	**eligieras** or **eligieses**
(él/ella/usted)	**elija**	**eligiera** or **eligiese**
(nosotros/as)	**elijamos**	**eligiéramos** or **eligiésemos**
(vosotros/as)	**elijáis**	**eligierais** or **eligieseis**
(ellos/ellas/ustedes)	**elijan**	**eligieran** or **eligiesen**

IMPERATIVE
elige / elegid

*Use the present subjunctive in all cases other than these **tú** and **vosotros** affirmative forms.*

EXAMPLE PHRASES

Yo **elegiría** el más caro. I'd choose the most expensive one.

Elija una carta. Choose a card.

Remember that subject pronouns are not used very often in Spanish.

empezar (to begin)

	PRESENT		PRESENT PERFECT
(yo)	empiezo		he empezado
(tú)	empiezas		has empezado
(él/ella/usted)	empieza		ha empezado
(nosotros/as)	empezamos		hemos empezado
(vosotros/as)	empezáis		habéis empezado
(ellos/ellas/ ustedes)	empiezan		han empezado

	PRETERITE		IMPERFECT
(yo)	empecé		empezaba
(tú)	empezaste		empezabas
(él/ella/usted)	empezó		empezaba
(nosotros/as)	empezamos		empezábamos
(vosotros/as)	empezasteis		empezabais
(ellos/ellas/ ustedes)	empezaron		empezaban

GERUND

empezando

PAST PARTICIPLE

empezado

EXAMPLE PHRASES

Está a punto de **empezar**. It's about to start.

¿Cuándo **empiezas** a trabajar en el sitio nuevo? When do you start work at the new place?

Ha empezado a nevar. It's started snowing.

Las vacaciones **empezaron** el quince. The holidays started on the fifteenth.

Empezaba por *p*. It began with *p*.

Remember that subject pronouns are not used very often in Spanish.

empezar

	FUTURE	CONDITIONAL
(yo)	empezaré	empezaría
(tú)	empezarás	empezarías
(él/ella/usted)	empezará	empezaría
(nosotros/as)	empezaremos	empezaríamos
(vosotros/as)	empezaréis	empezaríais
(ellos/ellas/ ustedes)	empezarán	empezarían

	PRESENT SUBJUNCTIVE	IMPERFECT SUBJUNCTIVE
(yo)	empiece	empezara or empezase
(tú)	empieces	empezaras or empezases
(él/ella/usted)	empiece	empezara or empezase
(nosotros/as)	empecemos	empezáramos or empezásemos
(vosotros/as)	empecéis	empezarais or empezaseis
(ellos/ellas/ ustedes)	empiecen	empezaran or empezasen

IMPERATIVE
empieza / empezad

*Use the present subjunctive in all cases other than these **tú** and **vosotros** affirmative forms.*

EXAMPLE PHRASES
La semana que viene **empezaremos** un curso nuevo. We'll start a new course next week.

Yo **empezaría** desde cero. I'd start from scratch.

Quiero que **empieces** ya. I want you to start now.

Si **empezáramos** ahora, acabaríamos a las diez. If we started now, we'd be finished by ten.

Empieza por aquí. Start here.

Remember that subject pronouns are not used very often in Spanish.

enfrentarse (a) (to face)

	PRESENT	PRESENT PERFECT
(yo)	me enfrento	me he enfrentado
(tú)	te enfrentas	te has enfrentado
(él/ella/usted)	se enfrenta	se ha enfrentado
(nosotros/as)	nos enfrentamos	nos hemos enfrentado
(vosotros/as)	os enfrentáis	os habéis enfrentado
(ellos/ellas/ ustedes)	se enfrentan	se han enfrentado

	PRETERITE	IMPERFECT
(yo)	me enfrenté	me enfrentaba
(tú)	te enfrentaste	te enfrentabas
(él/ella/usted)	se enfrentó	se enfrentaba
(nosotros/as)	nos enfrentamos	nos enfrentábamos
(vosotros/as)	os enfrentasteis	os enfrentabais
(ellos/ellas/ ustedes)	se enfrentaron	se enfrentaban

GERUND
enfrentándose, etc

PAST PARTICIPLE
enfrentado

EXAMPLE PHRASES

Tienes que **enfrentarte al** problema. You have to face up to the problem.

Hoy **se enfrentan** los dos semifinalistas. The two semifinalists meet today.

Padre e hijo **se han enfrentado** varias veces. Father and son have had several confrontations.

Se enfrentaban a un futuro incierto. They faced an uncertain future.

Remember that subject pronouns are not used very often in Spanish.

enfrentarse

	FUTURE	CONDITIONAL
(yo)	me enfrentaré	me enfrentaría
(tú)	te enfrentarás	te enfrentarías
(él/ella/usted)	se enfrentará	se enfrentaría
(nosotros/as)	nos enfrentaremos	nos enfrentaríamos
(vosotros/as)	os enfrentaréis	os enfrentaríais
(ellos/ellas/ ustedes)	se enfrentarán	se enfrentarían

	PRESENT SUBJUNCTIVE	IMPERFECT SUBJUNCTIVE
(yo)	me enfrente	me enfrentara or enfrentase
(tú)	te enfrentes	te enfrentaras or enfrentases
(él/ella/usted)	se enfrente	se enfrentara or enfrentase
(nosotros/as)	nos enfrentemos	nos enfrentáramos or enfrentásemos
(vosotros/as)	os enfrentéis	os enfrentarais or enfrentaseis
(ellos/ellas/ ustedes)	se enfrenten	se enfrentaran or enfrentasen

IMPERATIVE

enfréntate / enfrentaos

Use the present subjunctive in all cases other than these tú and vosotros affirmative forms.

EXAMPLE PHRASES

El héroe **se enfrentará** a todo tipo de peligros. The hero will have to face all kinds of dangers.

No **te enfrentes** con él. Don't confront him.

entender (to understand)

	PRESENT	PRESENT PERFECT
(yo)	entiendo	he entendido
(tú)	entiendes	has entendido
(él/ella/usted)	entiende	ha entendido
(nosotros/as)	entendemos	hemos entendido
(vosotros/as)	entendéis	habéis entendido
(ellos/ellas/ ustedes)	entienden	han entendido

	PRETERITE	IMPERFECT
(yo)	entendí	entendía
(tú)	entendiste	entendías
(él/ella/usted)	entendió	entendía
(nosotros/as)	entendimos	entendíamos
(vosotros/as)	entendisteis	entendíais
(ellos/ellas/ ustedes)	entendieron	entendían

GERUND

entendiendo

PAST PARTICIPLE

entendido

EXAMPLE PHRASES

No lo vas a **entender**. You won't understand.

No lo **entiendo**. I don't understand.

Estás entendiéndolo todo al revés. You're getting the wrong end of the stick.

Creo que lo **he entendido** mal. I think I've misunderstood.

¿**Entendiste** lo que dijo? Did you understand what she said?

Mi padre **entendía** mucho de caballos. My father knew a lot about horses.

Remember that subject pronouns are not used very often in Spanish.

entender

	FUTURE	CONDITIONAL
(yo)	entenderé	entendería
(tú)	entenderás	entenderías
(él/ella/usted)	entenderá	entendería
(nosotros/as)	entenderemos	entenderíamos
(vosotros/as)	entenderéis	entenderíais
(ellos/ellas/ ustedes)	entenderán	entenderían

	PRESENT SUBJUNCTIVE	IMPERFECT SUBJUNCTIVE
(yo)	entienda	entendiera or entendiese
(tú)	entiendas	entendieras or entendieses
(él/ella/usted)	entienda	entendiera or entendiese
(nosotros/as)	entendamos	entendiéramos or entendiésemos
(vosotros/as)	entendáis	entendierais or entendieseis
(ellos/ellas/ ustedes)	entiendan	entendieran or entendiesen

IMPERATIVE

entiende / entended

Use the present subjunctive in all cases other than these tú and vosotros affirmative forms.

EXAMPLE PHRASES

Con el tiempo lo **entenderás**. You'll understand one day.

Yo no lo **entendería** así. I wouldn't interpret it like that.

Si de verdad me **entendieras**, no habrías dicho eso. If you really understood me, you would never have said that.

No me **entiendas** mal. Don't misunderstand me.

Remember that subject pronouns are not used very often in Spanish.

enviar (to send)

	PRESENT	PRESENT PERFECT
(yo)	envío	he enviado
(tú)	envías	has enviado
(él/ella/usted)	envía	ha enviado
(nosotros/as)	enviamos	hemos enviado
(vosotros/as)	enviáis	habéis enviado
(ellos/ellas/ ustedes)	envían	han enviado

	PRETERITE	IMPERFECT
(yo)	envié	enviaba
(tú)	enviaste	enviabas
(él/ella/usted)	envió	enviaba
(nosotros/as)	enviamos	enviábamos
(vosotros/as)	enviasteis	enviabais
(ellos/ellas/ ustedes)	enviaron	enviaban

GERUND

enviando

PAST PARTICIPLE

enviado

EXAMPLE PHRASES

¿Cómo lo vas a **enviar**? How are you going to send it?

Les **envío** el trabajo por correo electrónico. I send them my work by email.

Ya **está enviando** las invitaciones. She has already started sending out the invitations.

La **han enviado** a Guatemala. They've sent her to Guatemala.

Le **envió** el regalo por correo. He posted her the present.

Me **enviaba** siempre a mí a hacer los recados. She always sent me to do the errands.

Remember that subject pronouns are not used very often in Spanish.

enviar

	FUTURE	CONDITIONAL
(yo)	enviaré	enviaría
(tú)	enviarás	enviarías
(él/ella/usted)	enviará	enviaría
(nosotros/as)	enviaremos	enviaríamos
(vosotros/as)	enviaréis	enviaríais
(ellos/ellas/ustedes)	enviarán	enviarían

	PRESENT SUBJUNCTIVE	IMPERFECT SUBJUNCTIVE
(yo)	envíe	enviara or enviase
(tú)	envíes	enviaras or enviases
(él/ella/usted)	envíe	enviara or enviase
(nosotros/as)	enviemos	enviáramos or enviásemos
(vosotros/as)	enviéis	enviarais or enviaseis
(ellos/ellas/ustedes)	envíen	enviaran or enviasen

IMPERATIVE

envía / enviad

Use the present subjunctive in all cases other than these tú and vosotros affirmative forms.

EXAMPLE PHRASES

Nos **enviarán** más información. They'll send us further information.

Yo lo **enviaría** por mensajero. I'd send it by courier.

Necesitamos que lo **envíes** inmediatamente. We need you to send it immediately.

Si lo **enviaras** ahora, llegaría el lunes. If you sent it now it would get there on Monday.

No lo **envíes** sin repasarlo antes. Don't send it in without checking it first.

Envíe sus datos personales. Send in your details.

Remember that subject pronouns are not used very often in Spanish.

equivocarse (to make a mistake; to be wrong)

	PRESENT		PRESENT PERFECT
(yo)	me equivoco		me he equivocado
(tú)	te equivocas		te has equivocado
(él/ella/usted)	se equivoca		se ha equivocado
(nosotros/as)	nos equivocamos		nos hemos equivocado
(vosotros/as)	os equivocáis		os habéis equivocado
(ellos/ellas/ ustedes)	se equivocan		se han equivocado

	PRETERITE		IMPERFECT
(yo)	me equivoqué		me equivocaba
(tú)	te equivocaste		te equivocabas
(él/ella/usted)	se equivocó		se equivocaba
(nosotros/as)	nos equivocamos		nos equivocábamos
(vosotros/as)	os equivocasteis		os equivocabais
(ellos/ellas/ ustedes)	se equivocaron		se equivocaban

GERUND
equivocándose, etc

PAST PARTICIPLE
equivocado

EXAMPLE PHRASES

Si crees que voy a dejarte ir, **te equivocas**. If you think I'm going to let you go, you're mistaken.

Perdone, **me he equivocado** de número. Sorry, I've got the wrong number.

Se equivocaron de tren. They got the wrong train.

Siempre **se equivocaba** de calle. He always went down the wrong street.

Remember that subject pronouns are not used very often in Spanish.

equivocarse

	FUTURE	CONDITIONAL
(yo)	me equivocaré	me equivocaría
(tú)	te equivocarás	te equivocarías
(él/ella/usted)	se equivocará	se equivocaría
(nosotros/as)	nos equivocaremos	nos equivocaríamos
(vosotros/as)	os equivocaréis	os equivocaríais
(ellos/ellas/ ustedes)	se equivocarán	se equivocarían

	PRESENT SUBJUNCTIVE	IMPERFECT SUBJUNCTIVE
(yo)	me equivoque	me equivocara or equivocase
(tú)	te equivoques	te equivocaras or equivocases
(él/ella/usted)	se equivoque	se equivocara or equivocase
(nosotros/as)	nos equivoquemos	nos equivocáramos or equivocásemos
(vosotros/as)	os equivoquéis	os equivocarais or equivocaseis
(ellos/ellas/ ustedes)	se equivoquen	se equivocaran or equivocasen

IMPERATIVE

equivócate / equivocaos

*Use the present subjunctive in all cases other than these **tú** and **vosotros** affirmative forms.*

EXAMPLE PHRASES

Sobre todo, no **te equivoques** de hora. Above all, don't get the time wrong.

Si **te equivocaras**, quedarías eliminado del juego. If you made a mistake, you'd be out of the game.

erguir (to erect)

	PRESENT	PRESENT PERFECT
(yo)	yergo	he erguido
(tú)	yergues	has erguido
(él/ella/usted)	yergue	ha erguido
(nosotros/as)	erguimos	hemos erguido
(vosotros/as)	erguís	habéis erguido
(ellos/ellas/ ustedes)	yerguen	han erguido

	PRETERITE	IMPERFECT
(yo)	erguí	erguía
(tú)	erguiste	erguías
(él/ella/usted)	irguió	erguía
(nosotros/as)	erguimos	erguíamos
(vosotros/as)	erguisteis	erguías
(ellos/ellas/ ustedes)	irguieron	erguían

GERUND	PAST PARTICIPLE
irguiendo	erguido

EXAMPLE PHRASES

El perro **irguió** las orejas. The dog pricked up its ears.

La montaña **se erguía** majestuosa sobre el valle. The mountain rose majestically above the valley.

Tú mantén siempre la cabeza bien **erguida**. You must always hold your head high.

Remember that subject pronouns are not used very often in Spanish.

erguir

	FUTURE	**CONDITIONAL**
(yo)	erguiré	erguiría
(tú)	erguirás	erguirías
(él/ella/usted)	erguirá	erguiría
(nosotros/as)	erguiremos	erguiríamos
(vosotros/as)	erguiréis	erguiríais
(ellos/ellas/ ustedes)	erguirán	erguirían

	PRESENT SUBJUNCTIVE	**IMPERFECT SUBJUNCTIVE**
(yo)	yerga	irguiera or irguiese
(tú)	yergas	irguieras or irguieses
(él/ella/usted)	yerga	irguiera or irguiese
(nosotros/as)	irgamos	irguiéramos or irguiésemos
(vosotros/as)	irgáis	irguierais or irguieseis
(ellos/ellas/ ustedes)	yergan	irguieran or irguiesen

IMPERATIVE

yergue / erguid

Use the present subjunctive in all cases other than these tú and vosotros affirmative forms.

Remember that subject pronouns are not used very often in Spanish.

errar (to err)

	PRESENT	PRESENT PERFECT
(yo)	yerro	he errado
(tú)	yerras	has errado
(él/ella/usted)	yerra	ha errado
(nosotros/as)	erramos	hemos errado
(vosotros/as)	erráis	habéis errado
(ellos/ellas/ustedes)	yerran	han errado

	PRETERITE	IMPERFECT
(yo)	erré	erraba
(tú)	erraste	errabas
(él/ella/usted)	erró	erraba
(nosotros/as)	erramos	errábamos
(vosotros/as)	errasteis	errabais
(ellos/ellas/ustedes)	erraron	erraban

GERUND
errando

PAST PARTICIPLE
errado

EXAMPLE PHRASES

Errar es humano. To err is human.

Ha errado en su decisión. She has made the wrong decision.

Erró el tiro. He missed.

errar

	FUTURE	CONDITIONAL
(yo)	erraré	erraría
(tú)	errarás	errarías
(él/ella/usted)	errará	erraría
(nosotros/as)	erraremos	erraríamos
(vosotros/as)	erraréis	erraríais
(ellos/ellas/ ustedes)	errarán	errarían

	PRESENT SUBJUNCTIVE	IMPERFECT SUBJUNCTIVE
(yo)	yerre	errara or errase
(tú)	yerres	erraras or errases
(él/ella/usted)	yerre	errara or errase
(nosotros/as)	erremos	erráramos or errásemos
(vosotros/as)	erréis	errarais or erraseis
(ellos/ellas/ ustedes)	yerren	erraran or errasen

IMPERATIVE

yerra / errad

Use the present subjunctive in all cases other than these tú and vosotros affirmative forms.

escribir (to write)

	PRESENT	PRESENT PERFECT
(yo)	escribo	he escrito
(tú)	escribes	has escrito
(él/ella/usted)	escribe	ha escrito
(nosotros/as)	escribimos	hemos escrito
(vosotros/as)	escribís	habéis escrito
(ellos/ellas/ustedes)	escriben	han escrito

	PRETERITE	IMPERFECT
(yo)	escribí	escribía
(tú)	escribiste	escribías
(él/ella/usted)	escribió	escribía
(nosotros/as)	escribimos	escribíamos
(vosotros/as)	escribisteis	escribíais
(ellos/ellas/ustedes)	escribieron	escribían

GERUND
escribiendo

PAST PARTICIPLE
escrito

EXAMPLE PHRASES

¿Cómo **se escribe** su nombre? How do you spell your name?

¿**Estás escribiendo** la carta? Are you writing the letter?

Eso lo **he escrito** yo. I wrote that.

Nos escribimos durante un tiempo. We wrote to each other for a while.

Escribía canciones. She wrote songs.

Remember that subject pronouns are not used very often in Spanish.

escribir

	FUTURE	CONDITIONAL
(yo)	escribiré	escribiría
(tú)	escribirás	escribirías
(él/ella/usted)	escribirá	escribiría
(nosotros/as)	escribiremos	escribiríamos
(vosotros/as)	escribiréis	escribiríais
(ellos/ellas/ustedes)	escribirán	escribirían

	PRESENT SUBJUNCTIVE	IMPERFECT SUBJUNCTIVE
(yo)	escriba	escribiera *or* escribiese
(tú)	escribas	escribieras *or* escribieses
(él/ella/usted)	escriba	escribiera *or* escribiese
(nosotros/as)	escribamos	escribiéramos *or* escribiésemos
(vosotros/as)	escribáis	escribierais *or* escribieseis
(ellos/ellas/ustedes)	escriban	escribieran *or* escribiesen

IMPERATIVE

escribe / escribid

*Use the present subjunctive in all cases other than these tú and **vosotros** affirmative forms.*

EXAMPLE PHRASES

¿Me **escribirás**? Will you write to me?

Yo lo **escribiría** con mayúscula. I'd write it with a capital letter.

Te he dicho que no **escribas** en la mesa. I've told you not to write on the table.

Si de verdad **escribiera** bien, ya le habrían publicado algún libro. If he really was a good writer, he'd have had a book published by now.

Escríbelo en la pizarra. Write it on the blackboard.

Remember that subject pronouns are not used very often in Spanish.

esforzarse (to make an effort)

	PRESENT	PRESENT PERFECT
(yo)	me esfuerzo	me he esforzado
(tú)	te esfuerzas	te has esforzado
(él/ella/usted)	se esfuerza	se ha esforzado
(nosotros/as)	nos esforzamos	nos hemos esforzado
(vosotros/as)	os esforzáis	os habéis esforzado
(ellos/ellas/ustedes)	se esfuerzan	se han esforzado

	PRETERITE	IMPERFECT
(yo)	me esforcé	me esforzaba
(tú)	te esforzaste	te esforzabas
(él/ella/usted)	se esforzó	se esforzaba
(nosotros/as)	nos esforzamos	nos esforzábamos
(vosotros/as)	os esforzasteis	os esforzabais
(ellos/ellas/ustedes)	se esforzaron	se esforzaban

GERUND
esforzándose, etc

PAST PARTICIPLE
esforzado

EXAMPLE PHRASES

Tienes que **esforzarte** si quieres ganar. You have to make an effort if you want to win.

No **te esfuerzas** lo suficiente. You don't make enough effort.

Me he esforzado, pero nada. I've tried my best but haven't got anywhere.

Se esforzó todo lo que pudo por aprobar el examen. He did his best to pass the exam.

Me esforzaba por entenderla. I tried hard to understand her.

Remember that subject pronouns are not used very often in Spanish.

esforzarse

	FUTURE	CONDITIONAL
(yo)	me esforzaré	me esforzaría
(tú)	te esforzarás	te esforzarías
(él/ella/usted)	se esforzará	se esforzaría
(nosotros/as)	nos esforzaremos	nos esforzaríamos
(vosotros/as)	os esforzaréis	os esforzaríais
(ellos/ellas/ustedes)	se esforzarán	se esforzarían

	PRESENT SUBJUNCTIVE	IMPERFECT SUBJUNCTIVE
(yo)	me esfuerce	me esforzara or esforzase
(tú)	te esfuerces	te esforzaras or esforzases
(él/ella/usted)	se esfuerce	se esforzara or esforzase
(nosotros/as)	nos esforcemos	nos esforzáramos or esforzásemos
(vosotros/as)	os esforcéis	os esforzarais or esforzaseis
(ellos/ellas/ustedes)	se esfuercen	se esforzaran or esforzasen

IMPERATIVE
esfuérzate / esforzaos

*Use the present subjunctive in all cases other than these **tú** and **vosotros** affirmative forms.*

EXAMPLE PHRASES
No **te esfuerces**, no me vas a convencer. Stop struggling, you're not going to convince me.

Si **te esforzaras** un poco más, lo conseguirías. You'd manage it if you made a bit more of an effort.

Remember that subject pronouns are not used very often in Spanish.

establecer (to establish)

	PRESENT		PRESENT PERFECT
(yo)	establezco		he establecido
(tú)	estableces		has establecido
(él/ella/usted)	establece		ha establecido
(nosotros/as)	establecemos		hemos establecido
(vosotros/as)	establecéis		habéis establecido
(ellos/ellas/ ustedes)	establecen		han establecido

	PRETERITE		IMPERFECT
(yo)	establecí		establecía
(tú)	estableciste		establecías
(él/ella/usted)	estableció		establecía
(nosotros/as)	establecimos		establecíamos
(vosotros/as)	establecisteis		establecíais
(ellos/ellas/ ustedes)	establecieron		establecían

GERUND

estableciendo

PAST PARTICIPLE

establecido

EXAMPLE PHRASES

Han logrado **establecer** contacto con el barco. They've managed to make contact with the boat.

La ley **establece** que... The law states that...

Se ha establecido una buena relación entre los dos países. A good relationship has been established between the two countries.

En 1945, la familia **se estableció** en Madrid. In 1945, the family settled in Madrid.

Remember that subject pronouns are not used very often in Spanish.

establecer

	FUTURE	CONDITIONAL
(yo)	estableceré	establecería
(tú)	establecerás	establecerías
(él/ella/usted)	establecerá	establecería
(nosotros/as)	estableceremos	estableceríamos
(vosotros/as)	estableceréis	estableceríais
(ellos/ellas/ustedes)	establecerán	establecerían

	PRESENT SUBJUNCTIVE	IMPERFECT SUBJUNCTIVE
(yo)	establezca	estableciera or estableciese
(tú)	establezcas	establecieras or establecieses
(él/ella/usted)	establezca	estableciera or estableciese
(nosotros/as)	establezcamos	estableciéramos or estableciésemos
(vosotros/as)	establezcáis	establecierais or establecieseis
(ellos/ellas/ustedes)	establezcan	establecieran or estableciesen

IMPERATIVE

establece / estableced

Use the present subjunctive in all cases other than these tú and vosotros affirmative forms.

EXAMPLE PHRASES

El año que viene **se establecerá** por su cuenta. Next year she'll set up on her own.

estar (to be)

	PRESENT	PRESENT PERFECT
(yo)	estoy	he estado
(tú)	estás	has estado
(él/ella/usted)	está	ha estado
(nosotros/as)	estamos	hemos estado
(vosotros/as)	estáis	habéis estado
(ellos/ellas/ustedes)	están	han estado

	PRETERITE	IMPERFECT
(yo)	estuve	estaba
(tú)	estuviste	estabas
(él/ella/usted)	estuvo	estaba
(nosotros/as)	estuvimos	estábamos
(vosotros/as)	estuvisteis	estabais
(ellos/ellas/ustedes)	estuvieron	estaban

GERUND
estando

PAST PARTICIPLE
estado

EXAMPLE PHRASES

Estoy cansado. I'm tired.

¿Cómo **estás**? How are you?

¿**Has estado** alguna vez en París? Have you ever been to Paris?

Estuvimos en casa de mis padres. We were at my parents'.

¿Dónde **estabas**? Where were you?

Remember that subject pronouns are not used very often in Spanish.

estar

	FUTURE	CONDITIONAL
(yo)	estaré	estaría
(tú)	estarás	estarías
(él/ella/usted)	estará	estaría
(nosotros/as)	estaremos	estaríamos
(vosotros/as)	estaréis	estaríais
(ellos/ellas/ustedes)	estarán	estarían

	PRESENT SUBJUNCTIVE	IMPERFECT SUBJUNCTIVE
(yo)	esté	estuviera or estuviese
(tú)	estés	estuvieras or estuvieses
(él/ella/usted)	esté	estuviera or estuviese
(nosotros/as)	estemos	estuviéramos or estuviésemos
(vosotros/as)	estéis	estuvierais or estuvieseis
(ellos/ellas/ustedes)	estén	estuvieran or estuviesen

IMPERATIVE

está / estad

Use the present subjunctive in all cases other than these tú and vosotros affirmative forms.

EXAMPLE PHRASES

¿A qué hora **estarás** en casa? What time will you be home?

Dijo que **estaría** aquí a las ocho. She said she'd be here at eight o'clock.

Avísame cuando **estés** lista. Let me know when you're ready.

No sabía que **estuviera** tan lejos. I didn't know it was so far.

¡**Estáte** quieto! Stay still!

Remember that subject pronouns are not used very often in Spanish.

evacuar (to evacuate)

	PRESENT		PRESENT PERFECT
(yo)	evacuo		he evacuado
(tú)	evacuas		has evacuado
(él/ella/usted)	evacua		ha evacuado
(nosotros/as)	evacuamos		hemos evacuado
(vosotros/as)	evacuáis		habéis evacuado
(ellos/ellas/ustedes)	evacuan		han evacuado

	PRETERITE		IMPERFECT
(yo)	evacué		evacuaba
(tú)	evacuaste		evacuabas
(él/ella/usted)	evacuó		evacuaba
(nosotros/as)	evacuamos		evacuábamos
(vosotros/as)	evacuasteis		evacuabais
(ellos/ellas/ustedes)	evacuaron		evacuaban

GERUND
evacuando

PAST PARTICIPLE
evacuado

EXAMPLE PHRASES

Van a **evacuar** a los heridos. They're going to evacuate the injured.

Han evacuado la zona. The area has been evacuated.

evacuar

	FUTURE	**CONDITIONAL**
(yo)	evacuaré	evacuaría
(tú)	evacuarás	evacuarías
(él/ella/usted)	evacuará	evacuaría
(nosotros/as)	evacuaremos	evacuaríamos
(vosotros/as)	evacuaréis	evacuaríais
(ellos/ellas/ustedes)	evacuarán	evacuarían

	PRESENT SUBJUNCTIVE	**IMPERFECT SUBJUNCTIVE**
(yo)	evacue	evacuara or evacuase
(tú)	evacues	evacuaras or evacuases
(él/ella/usted)	evacue	evacuara or evacuase
(nosotros/as)	evacuemos	evacuáramos or evacuásemos
(vosotros/as)	evacuéis	evacuarais or evacuaseis
(ellos/ellas/ustedes)	evacuen	evacuaran or evacuasen

IMPERATIVE

evacua / evacuad

Use the present subjunctive in all cases other than these **tú** *and* **vosotros** *affirmative forms.*

EXAMPLE PHRASES

Seguirá existiendo peligro mientras no **evacuen** el edificio. The danger won't be over until the building has been evacuated.

Remember that subject pronouns are not used very often in Spanish.

freír (to fry)

	PRESENT		PRESENT PERFECT
(yo)	frío		he frito
(tú)	fríes		has frito
(él/ella/usted)	fríe		ha frito
(nosotros/as)	freímos		hemos frito
(vosotros/as)	freís		habéis frito
(ellos/ellas/ustedes)	fríen		han frito

	PRETERITE		IMPERFECT
(yo)	freí		freía
(tú)	freíste		freías
(él/ella/usted)	frio		freía
(nosotros/as)	freímos		freíamos
(vosotros/as)	freísteis		freíais
(ellos/ellas/ustedes)	frieron		freían

GERUND
friendo

PAST PARTICIPLE
frito

EXAMPLE PHRASES

No sabe ni **freír** un huevo. He can't even fry an egg.

He frito el pescado. I've fried the fish.

Se está friendo demasiado por ese lado. It's getting overdone on that side.

Lo **frio** en manteca. She fried it in lard.

Nos **freíamos** de calor. We were roasting in the heat.

Remember that subject pronouns are not used very often in Spanish.

freír

	FUTURE	CONDITIONAL
(yo)	freiré	freiría
(tú)	freirás	freirías
(él/ella/usted)	freirá	freiría
(nosotros/as)	freiremos	freiríamos
(vosotros/as)	freiréis	freiríais
(ellos/ellas/ ustedes)	freirán	freirían

	PRESENT SUBJUNCTIVE	IMPERFECT SUBJUNCTIVE
(yo)	fría	friera *or* friese
(tú)	frías	frieras *or* frieses
(él/ella/usted)	fría	friera *or* friese
(nosotros/as)	friamos	friéramos *or* friésemos
(vosotros/as)	friais	frierais *or* frieseis
(ellos/ellas/ ustedes)	frían	frieran *or* friesen

IMPERATIVE
fríe / freíd

Use the present subjunctive in all cases other than these **tú** *and* **vosotros** *affirmative forms.*

EXAMPLE PHRASES

Yo lo **freiría** con menos aceite. I'd fry it using less oil.

Fríelo en esa sartén. Fry it in that pan.

gruñir (to grumble; to growl)

	PRESENT	PRESENT PERFECT
(yo)	gruño	he gruñido
(tú)	gruñes	has gruñido
(él/ella/usted)	gruñe	ha gruñido
(nosotros/as)	gruñimos	hemos gruñido
(vosotros/as)	gruñís	habéis gruñido
(ellos/ellas/ustedes)	gruñen	han gruñido

	PRETERITE	IMPERFECT
(yo)	gruñí	gruñía
(tú)	gruñiste	gruñías
(él/ella/usted)	gruñó	gruñía
(nosotros/as)	gruñimos	gruñíamos
(vosotros/as)	gruñisteis	gruñíais
(ellos/ellas/ustedes)	gruñeron	gruñían

GERUND
gruñendo

PAST PARTICIPLE
gruñido

EXAMPLE PHRASES

¿A quién **gruñe** el perro? Who's the dog growling at?

Siempre **está gruñendo**. He's always grumbling.

El oso nos **gruñía** sin parar. The bear kept growling at us.

Remember that subject pronouns are not used very often in Spanish.

gruñir

	FUTURE	CONDITIONAL
(yo)	gruñiré	gruñiría
(tú)	gruñirás	gruñirías
(él/ella/usted)	gruñirá	gruñiría
(nosotros/as)	gruñiremos	gruñiríamos
(vosotros/as)	gruñiréis	gruñiríais
(ellos/ellas/ ustedes)	gruñirán	gruñirían

	PRESENT SUBJUNCTIVE	IMPERFECT SUBJUNCTIVE
(yo)	gruña	gruñera or gruñese
(tú)	gruñas	gruñeras or gruñeses
(él/ella/usted)	gruña	gruñera or gruñese
(nosotros/as)	gruñamos	gruñéramos or gruñésemos
(vosotros/as)	gruñáis	gruñerais or gruñeseis
(ellos/ellas/ ustedes)	gruñan	gruñeran or gruñesen

IMPERATIVE
gruñe / gruñid

Use the present subjunctive in all cases other than these tú and vosotros affirmative forms.

EXAMPLE PHRASES
¡No **gruñas** tanto! Don't grumble so much.

guiar (to guide)

	PRESENT		PRESENT PERFECT
(yo)	guío		he guiado
(tú)	guías		has guiado
(él/ella/usted)	guía		ha guiado
(nosotros/as)	guiamos		hemos guiado
(vosotros/as)	guiais		habéis guiado
(ellos/ellas/ ustedes)	guían		han guiado

	PRETERITE		IMPERFECT
(yo)	guie		guiaba
(tú)	guiaste		guiabas
(él/ella/usted)	guio		guiaba
(nosotros/as)	guiamos		guiábamos
(vosotros/as)	guiasteis		guiabais
(ellos/ellas/ ustedes)	guiaron		guiaban

GERUND
guiando

PAST PARTICIPLE
guiado

EXAMPLE PHRASES

Los perros **se guían** por su olfato. Dogs follow their sense of smell.

Me he guiado por el instinto. I followed my instinct.

Nos guiamos por un mapa que teníamos. We found our way using a map we had.

Siempre me protegía y me **guiaba**. He always protected me and guided me.

guiar

	FUTURE	CONDITIONAL
(yo)	guiaré	guiaría
(tú)	guiarás	guiarías
(él/ella/usted)	guiará	guiaría
(nosotros/as)	guiaremos	guiaríamos
(vosotros/as)	guiaréis	guiaríais
(ellos/ellas/ustedes)	guiarán	guiarían

	PRESENT SUBJUNCTIVE	IMPERFECT SUBJUNCTIVE
(yo)	guíe	guiara or guiase
(tú)	guíes	guiaras or guiases
(él/ella/usted)	guíe	guiara or guiase
(nosotros/as)	guiemos	guiáramos or guiásemos
(vosotros/as)	guieis	guiarais or guiaseis
(ellos/ellas/ustedes)	guíen	guiaran or guiasen

IMPERATIVE

guía / guiad

Use the present subjunctive in all cases other than these tú and vosotros affirmative forms.

EXAMPLE PHRASES

Les **guiaré** hasta allí. I'll take you there.

Guíate por la razón. Use reason as your guide.

haber (to have – *auxiliary*)

	PRESENT	PRESENT PERFECT
(yo)	he	*not used except impersonally*
(tú)	has	*See* hay
(él/ella/usted)	ha	
(nosotros/as)	hemos	
(vosotros/as)	habéis	
(ellos/ellas/ustedes)	han	

	PRETERITE	IMPERFECT
(yo)	hube	había
(tú)	hubiste	habías
(él/ella/usted)	hubo	había
(nosotros/as)	hubimos	habíamos
(vosotros/as)	hubisteis	habíais
(ellos/ellas/ustedes)	hubieron	habían

GERUND

habiendo

PAST PARTICIPLE

habido

EXAMPLE PHRASES

De **haberlo** sabido, **habría** ido. If I'd known, I would have gone.

¿**Has** visto eso? Did you see that?

Eso nunca **había** pasado antes. That had never happened before.

haber

	FUTURE	CONDITIONAL
(yo)	habré	habría
(tú)	habrás	habrías
(él/ella/usted)	habrá	habría
(nosotros/as)	habremos	habríamos
(vosotros/as)	habréis	habríais
(ellos/ellas/ ustedes)	habrán	habrían

	PRESENT SUBJUNCTIVE	IMPERFECT SUBJUNCTIVE
(yo)	haya	hubiera or hubiese
(tú)	hayas	hubieras or hubieses
(él/ella/usted)	haya	hubiera or hubiese
(nosotros/as)	hayamos	hubiéramos or hubiésemos
(vosotros/as)	hayáis	hubierais or hubieseis
(ellos/ellas/ ustedes)	hayan	hubieran or hubiesen

IMPERATIVE

not used

EXAMPLE PHRASES

Habrá que repasarlo. We'll have to check it.

Habría que limpiarlo. We should clean it.

Como se **hayan** olvidado los mato. I'll kill them if they've forgotten.

Si me lo **hubieras** dicho, te lo **habría** traído. I'd have brought it, if you'd said.

Remember that subject pronouns are not used very often in Spanish.

hablar (to speak; to talk)

	PRESENT	PRESENT PERFECT
(yo)	hablo	he hablado
(tú)	hablas	has hablado
(él/ella/usted)	habla	ha hablado
(nosotros/as)	hablamos	hemos hablado
(vosotros/as)	habláis	habéis hablado
(ellos/ellas/ ustedes)	hablan	han hablado

	PRETERITE	IMPERFECT
(yo)	hablé	hablaba
(tú)	hablaste	hablabas
(él/ella/usted)	habló	hablaba
(nosotros/as)	hablamos	hablábamos
(vosotros/as)	hablasteis	hablabais
(ellos/ellas/ ustedes)	hablaron	hablaban

GERUND

hablando

PAST PARTICIPLE

hablado

EXAMPLE PHRASES

María no **habla** inglés. María doesn't speak English.

No **nos hablamos** desde hace tiempo. We haven't spoken to each other for a long time.

Está **hablando** por teléfono. He's on the phone.

Hoy **he hablado** con mi hermana. I've spoken to my sister today.

¿**Has hablado** ya con el profesor? Have you spoken to the teacher yet?

Remember that subject pronouns are not used very often in Spanish.

hablar

	FUTURE	CONDITIONAL
(yo)	hablaré	hablaría
(tú)	hablarás	hablarías
(él/ella/usted)	hablará	hablaría
(nosotros/as)	hablaremos	hablaríamos
(vosotros/as)	hablaréis	hablaríais
(ellos/ellas/ ustedes)	hablarán	hablarían

	PRESENT SUBJUNCTIVE	IMPERFECT SUBJUNCTIVE
(yo)	hable	hablara or hablase
(tú)	hables	hablaras or hablases
(él/ella/usted)	hable	hablara or hablase
(nosotros/as)	hablemos	habláramos or hablásemos
(vosotros/as)	habléis	hablarais or hablaseis
(ellos/ellas/ ustedes)	hablen	hablaran or hablasen

IMPERATIVE

habla / hablad

*Use the present subjunctive in all cases other than these tú and **vosotros** affirmative forms.*

EXAMPLE PHRASES

Luego **hablaremos** de ese tema. We'll talk about that later.

Recuérdame que **hable** con Daniel. Remind me to speak to Daniel.

¿Quieres que **hablemos**? Shall we talk?

Hay que darles una oportunidad para que **hablen**. We need to give them an opportunity to speak.

Remember that subject pronouns are not used very often in Spanish.

hacer (to do; to make)

	PRESENT		PRESENT PERFECT
(yo)	hago		he hecho
(tú)	haces		has hecho
(él/ella/usted)	hace		ha hecho
(nosotros/as)	hacemos		hemos hecho
(vosotros/as)	hacéis		habéis hecho
(ellos/ellas/ ustedes)	hacen		han hecho

	PRETERITE		IMPERFECT
(yo)	hice		hacía
(tú)	hiciste		hacías
(él/ella/usted)	hizo		hacía
(nosotros/as)	hicimos		hacíamos
(vosotros/as)	hicisteis		hacíais
(ellos/ellas/ ustedes)	hicieron		hacían

GERUND
haciendo

PAST PARTICIPLE
hecho

EXAMPLE PHRASES

¿Qué **hace** tu padre? What does your father do?

Están haciendo mucho ruido. They're making a lot of noise.

¿Quién **hizo** eso? Who did that?

Hicieron pintar la fachada del colegio. They had the front of the school painted.

Lo **hacía** para fastidiarme. He did it to annoy me.

Remember that subject pronouns are not used very often in Spanish.

hacer

	FUTURE	**CONDITIONAL**
(yo)	haré	haría
(tú)	harás	harías
(él/ella/usted)	hará	haría
(nosotros/as)	haremos	haríamos
(vosotros/as)	haréis	haríais
(ellos/ellas/ ustedes)	harán	harían

	PRESENT SUBJUNCTIVE	**IMPERFECT SUBJUNCTIVE**
(yo)	haga	hiciera or hiciese
(tú)	hagas	hicieras or hicieses
(él/ella/usted)	haga	hiciera or hiciese
(nosotros/as)	hagamos	hiciéramos or hiciésemos
(vosotros/as)	hagáis	hicierais or hicieseis
(ellos/ellas/ ustedes)	hagan	hicieran or hiciesen

IMPERATIVE

haz / haced

Use the present subjunctive in all cases other than these tú and vosotros affirmative forms.

EXAMPLE PHRASES

Lo **haré** yo mismo. I'll do it myself.

Dijiste que lo **harías.** You said you'd do it.

¿Quieres que **haga** las camas? Do you want me to make the beds?

Preferiría que **hiciera** menos calor. I'd rather it weren't so hot.

Hazlo como te he dicho. Do it the way I told you.

Remember that subject pronouns are not used very often in Spanish.

hay (there is; there are)

PRESENT
hay

PRESENT PERFECT
ha habido

PRETERITE
hubo

IMPERFECT
había

GERUND
habiendo

PAST PARTICIPLE
habido

EXAMPLE PHRASES

Esta tarde va a **haber** una manifestación. There's going to be a demonstration this evening.

Hay una iglesia en la esquina. There's a church on the corner.

Ha habido una tormenta. There's been a storm.

Hubo una guerra. There was a war.

Había mucha gente. There were a lot of people.

Remember that subject pronouns are not used very often in Spanish.

hay

FUTURE
habrá

CONDITIONAL
habría

PRESENT SUBJUNCTIVE
haya

IMPERFECT SUBJUNCTIVE
hubiera *or* hubiese

IMPERATIVE
not used

EXAMPLE PHRASES

¿**Habrá** suficiente? Will there be enough?

De este modo **habría** menos accidentes. That way there would be fewer accidents.

No creo que **haya** mucha gente en el recital. I don't think there'll be many people at the concert.

Si **hubiera** más espacio, pondría un sofá. I'd have a sofa if there were more room.

Remember that subject pronouns are not used very often in Spanish.

herir (to injure)

	PRESENT		PRESENT PERFECT
(yo)	hiero		he herido
(tú)	hieres		has herido
(él/ella/usted)	hiere		ha herido
(nosotros/as)	herimos		hemos herido
(vosotros/as)	herís		habéis herido
(ellos/ellas/ ustedes)	hieren		han herido

	PRETERITE		IMPERFECT
(yo)	herí		hería
(tú)	heriste		herías
(él/ella/usted)	hirió		hería
(nosotros/as)	herimos		heríamos
(vosotros/as)	heristeis		heríais
(ellos/ellas/ ustedes)	hirieron		herían

GERUND

hiriendo

PAST PARTICIPLE

herido

EXAMPLE PHRASES

Vas a **herir** sus sentimientos. You're going to hurt her feelings.

Me **hiere** que me digas eso. I'm hurt that you should say such a thing.

La **han herido** en el brazo. Her arm's been injured.

Lo **hirieron** en el pecho. He was wounded in the chest.

La **hería** en lo más hondo. She was deeply hurt.

Remember that subject pronouns are not used very often in Spanish.

herir

	FUTURE	CONDITIONAL
(yo)	heriré	heriría
(tú)	herirás	herirías
(él/ella/usted)	herirá	heriría
(nosotros/as)	heriremos	heriríamos
(vosotros/as)	heriréis	heriríais
(ellos/ellas/ ustedes)	herirán	herirían

	PRESENT SUBJUNCTIVE	IMPERFECT SUBJUNCTIVE
(yo)	hiera	hiriera or hiriese
(tú)	hieras	hirieras or hirieses
(él/ella/usted)	hiera	hiriera or hiriese
(nosotros/as)	hiramos	hiriéramos or hiriésemos
(vosotros/as)	hiráis	hirierais or hirieseis
(ellos/ellas/ ustedes)	hieran	hirieran or hiriesen

IMPERATIVE
hiere / herid

Use the present subjunctive in all cases other than these tú and vosotros affirmative forms.

EXAMPLE PHRASES

Mi madre siempre tenía miedo que nos **hiriéramos**. My mum was always scared we'd hurt ourselves.

huir (to escape)

	PRESENT	PRESENT PERFECT
(yo)	huyo	he huido
(tú)	huyes	has huido
(él/ella/usted)	huye	ha huido
(nosotros/as)	huimos	hemos huido
(vosotros/as)	huis	habéis huido
(ellos/ellas/ustedes)	huyen	han huido

	PRETERITE	IMPERFECT
(yo)	hui	huía
(tú)	huiste	huías
(él/ella/usted)	huyó	huía
(nosotros/as)	huimos	huíamos
(vosotros/as)	huisteis	huíais
(ellos/ellas/ustedes)	huyeron	huían

GERUND
huyendo

PAST PARTICIPLE
huido

EXAMPLE PHRASES

No sé por qué me **huye**. I don't know why he's avoiding me.

Salió **huyendo.** He ran away.

Ha huido de la cárcel. He has escaped from prison.

Huyeron del país. They fled the country.

Remember that subject pronouns are not used very often in Spanish.

huir

	FUTURE	CONDITIONAL
(yo)	huiré	huiría
(tú)	huirás	huirías
(él/ella/usted)	huirá	huiría
(nosotros/as)	huiremos	huiríamos
(vosotros/as)	huiréis	huiríais
(ellos/ellas/ustedes)	huirán	huirían

	PRESENT SUBJUNCTIVE	IMPERFECT SUBJUNCTIVE
(yo)	huya	huyera or huyese
(tú)	huyas	huyeras or huyeses
(él/ella/usted)	huya	huyera or huyese
(nosotros/as)	huyamos	huyéramos or huyésemos
(vosotros/as)	huyáis	huyerais or huyeseis
(ellos/ellas/ustedes)	huyan	huyeran or huyesen

IMPERATIVE

huye / huid

Use the present subjunctive in all cases other than these tú and vosotros affirmative forms.

EXAMPLE PHRASES

No quiero que **huyas** como un cobarde. I dont want you to run away like a coward.

¡**Huye**! Si te atrapan, te matarán. Run! If they catch you, they'll kill you.

Remember that subject pronouns are not used very often in Spanish.

imponer (to impose)

	PRESENT		PRESENT PERFECT
(yo)	impongo		he impuesto
(tú)	impones		has impuesto
(él/ella/usted)	impone		ha impuesto
(nosotros/as)	imponemos		hemos impuesto
(vosotros/as)	imponéis		habéis impuesto
(ellos/ellas/ ustedes)	imponen		han impuesto

	PRETERITE		IMPERFECT
(yo)	impuse		imponía
(tú)	impusiste		imponías
(él/ella/usted)	impuso		imponía
(nosotros/as)	impusimos		imponíamos
(vosotros/as)	impusisteis		imponíais
(ellos/ellas/ ustedes)	impusieron		imponían

GERUND

imponiendo

PAST PARTICIPLE

impuesto

EXAMPLE PHRASES

La vista desde el acantilado **impone** un poco. The view from the cliff top is quite impressive.

La minifalda **se está imponiendo** de nuevo. The miniskirt is back in fashion.

Han impuesto la enseñanza religiosa. They have made religious education compulsory.

El corredor nigeriano **se impuso** en la segunda carrera. The Nigerian runner triumphed in the second race.

Mi abuelo **imponía** mucho respeto. My grandfather commanded a lot of respect.

Remember that subject pronouns are not used very often in Spanish.

imponer

	FUTURE	CONDITIONAL
(yo)	impondré	impondría
(tú)	impondrás	impondrías
(él/ella/usted)	impondrá	impondría
(nosotros/as)	impondremos	impondríamos
(vosotros/as)	impondréis	impondríais
(ellos/ellas/ ustedes)	impondrán	impondrían

	PRESENT SUBJUNCTIVE	IMPERFECT SUBJUNCTIVE
(yo)	imponga	impusiera *or* impusiese
(tú)	impongas	impusieras *or* impusieses
(él/ella/usted)	imponga	impusiera *or* impusiese
(nosotros/as)	impongamos	impusiéramos *or* impusiésemos
(vosotros/as)	impongáis	impusierais *or* impusieseis
(ellos/ellas/ ustedes)	impongan	impusieran *or* impusiesen

IMPERATIVE

impón / imponed

Use the present subjunctive in all cases other than these tú and vosotros affirmative forms.

EXAMPLE PHRASES

Impondrán multas de hasta 50 euros. They'll impose fines of up to 50 euros.

imprimir (to print)

	PRESENT	PRESENT PERFECT
(yo)	imprimo	he imprimido
(tú)	imprimes	has imprimido
(él/ella/usted)	imprime	ha imprimido
(nosotros/as)	imprimimos	hemos imprimido
(vosotros/as)	imprimís	habéis imprimido
(ellos/ellas/ustedes)	imprimen	han imprimido

	PRETERITE	IMPERFECT
(yo)	imprimí	imprimía
(tú)	imprimiste	imprimías
(él/ella/usted)	imprimió	imprimía
(nosotros/as)	imprimimos	imprimíamos
(vosotros/as)	imprimisteis	imprimíais
(ellos/ellas/ustedes)	imprimieron	imprimían

GERUND
imprimiendo

PAST PARTICIPLE
imprimido, impreso

EXAMPLE PHRASES

Una experiencia así **imprime** carácter. An experience like that is character-building.

¿**Has imprimido** el documento? Have you printed out the file?

Se imprimieron sólo doce copias del libro. Only twelve copies of the book were printed.

El sillón **imprimía** un cierto aire de distinción al salón. The chair gave the living room a certain air of distinction.

Remember that subject pronouns are not used very often in Spanish.

imprimir

	FUTURE	CONDITIONAL
(yo)	imprimiré	imprimiría
(tú)	imprimirás	imprimirías
(él/ella/usted)	imprimirá	imprimiría
(nosotros/as)	imprimiremos	imprimiríamos
(vosotros/as)	imprimiréis	imprimiríais
(ellos/ellas/ ustedes)	imprimirán	imprimirían

	PRESENT SUBJUNCTIVE	IMPERFECT SUBJUNCTIVE
(yo)	imprima	imprimiera or imprimiese
(tú)	imprimas	imprimieras or imprimieses
(él/ella/usted)	imprima	imprimiera or imprimiese
(nosotros/as)	imprimamos	imprimiéramos or imprimiésemos
(vosotros/as)	imprimáis	imprimierais or imprimieseis
(ellos/ellas/ ustedes)	impriman	imprimieran or imprimiesen

IMPERATIVE

imprime / imprimid

Use the present subjunctive in all cases other than these tú and vosotros affirmative forms.

Remember that subject pronouns are not used very often in Spanish.

ir (to go)

	PRESENT		PRESENT PERFECT
(yo)	voy		he ido
(tú)	vas		has ido
(él/ella/usted)	va		ha ido
(nosotros/as)	vamos		hemos ido
(vosotros/as)	vais		habéis ido
(ellos/ellas/ ustedes)	van		han ido

	PRETERITE		IMPERFECT
(yo)	fui		iba
(tú)	fuiste		ibas
(él/ella/usted)	fue		iba
(nosotros/as)	fuimos		íbamos
(vosotros/as)	fuisteis		ibais
(ellos/ellas/ ustedes)	fueron		iban

GERUND
yendo

PAST PARTICIPLE
ido

EXAMPLE PHRASES

¿Puedo **ir** contigo? Can I come with you?

¿**Vamos** a comer al campo? Shall we have a picnic in the country?

Estoy yendo a clases de natación. I'm taking swimming lessons.

Ha ido a comprar el pan. She's gone to buy some bread.

Anoche **fuimos** al cine. We went to the cinema last night.

Remember that subject pronouns are not used very often in Spanish.

ir

	FUTURE	CONDITIONAL
(yo)	iré	iría
(tú)	irás	irías
(él/ella/usted)	irá	iría
(nosotros/as)	iremos	iríamos
(vosotros/as)	iréis	iríais
(ellos/ellas/ustedes)	irán	irían

	PRESENT SUBJUNCTIVE	IMPERFECT SUBJUNCTIVE
(yo)	vaya	fuera or fuese
(tú)	vayas	fueras or fueses
(él/ella/usted)	vaya	fuera or fuese
(nosotros/as)	vayamos	fuéramos or fuésemos
(vosotros/as)	vayáis	fuerais or fueseis
(ellos/ellas/ustedes)	vayan	fueran or fuesen

IMPERATIVE

ve / id

*Use the present subjunctive in most cases other than these tú and **vosotros** affirmative forms.*
*However, in the 'let's' affirmative form, **vamos** is more common than **vayamos**.*

EXAMPLE PHRASES

El domingo **iré** a Edimburgo. I'll go to Edinburgh on Sunday.

Dijeron que **irían** andando. They said they'd walk.

¡Que te **vaya** bien! Take care of yourself!

Quería pedirte que **fueras** en mi lugar. I wanted to ask you if you'd go instead of me.

No **te vayas** sin despedirte. Don't go without saying goodbye.

Vete a hacer los deberes. Go and do your homework.

Remember that subject pronouns are not used very often in Spanish.

jugar (to play)

	PRESENT		PRESENT PERFECT
(yo)	juego		he jugado
(tú)	juegas		has jugado
(él/ella/usted)	juega		ha jugado
(nosotros/as)	jugamos		hemos jugado
(vosotros/as)	jugáis		habéis jugado
(ellos/ellas/ ustedes)	juegan		han jugado

	PRETERITE		IMPERFECT
(yo)	jugué		jugaba
(tú)	jugaste		jugabas
(él/ella/usted)	jugó		jugaba
(nosotros/as)	jugamos		jugábamos
(vosotros/as)	jugasteis		jugabais
(ellos/ellas/ ustedes)	jugaron		jugaban

GERUND

jugando

PAST PARTICIPLE

jugado

EXAMPLE PHRASES

Juego al fútbol todos los domingos. I play football every Sunday.

Están jugando en el jardín. They're playing in the garden.

Le **han jugado** una mala pasada. They played a dirty trick on him.

Después de cenar **jugamos** a las cartas. After dinner we played cards.

Se jugaba la vida continuamente. She was constantly risking her life.

Remember that subject pronouns are not used very often in Spanish.

jugar

	FUTURE	CONDITIONAL
(yo)	jugaré	jugaría
(tú)	jugarás	jugarías
(él/ella/usted)	jugará	jugaría
(nosotros/as)	jugaremos	jugaríamos
(vosotros/as)	jugaréis	jugaríais
(ellos/ellas/ustedes)	jugarán	jugarían

	PRESENT SUBJUNCTIVE	IMPERFECT SUBJUNCTIVE
(yo)	juegue	jugara or jugase
(tú)	juegues	jugaras or jugases
(él/ella/usted)	juegue	jugara or jugase
(nosotros/as)	juguemos	jugáramos or jugásemos
(vosotros/as)	juguéis	jugarais or jugaseis
(ellos/ellas/ustedes)	jueguen	jugaran or jugasen

IMPERATIVE

juega / jugad

Use the present subjunctive in all cases other than these tú and **vosotros** *affirmative forms.*

EXAMPLE PHRASES

Jugarán contra el Real Madrid. They'll play Real Madrid.

Jugarías mejor si estuvieras más relajado. You'd play better if you were more relaxed.

No **juegues** con tu salud. Don't take risks with your health.

El médico le aconsejó que **jugara** más y leyera menos. The doctor advised him to play more and read less.

Remember that subject pronouns are not used very often in Spanish.

leer (to read)

	PRESENT		PRESENT PERFECT
(yo)	leo		he leído
(tú)	lees		has leído
(él/ella/usted)	lee		ha leído
(nosotros/as)	leemos		hemos leído
(vosotros/as)	leéis		habéis leído
(ellos/ellas/ ustedes)	leen		han leído

	PRETERITE		IMPERFECT
(yo)	leí		leía
(tú)	leíste		leías
(él/ella/usted)	leyó		leía
(nosotros/as)	leímos		leíamos
(vosotros/as)	leísteis		leíais
(ellos/ellas/ ustedes)	leyeron		leían

GERUND

leyendo

PAST PARTICIPLE

leído

EXAMPLE PHRASES

Hace mucho tiempo que no **leo** nada. I haven't read anything for ages.

Estoy leyendo un libro muy interesante. I'm reading a very interesting book.

¿**Has leído** esta novela? Have you read this novel?

Lo **leí** hace tiempo. I read it a while ago.

Antes **leía** mucho más. I used to read a lot more before.

Remember that subject pronouns are not used very often in Spanish.

leer

	FUTURE	CONDITIONAL
(yo)	leeré	leería
(tú)	leerás	leerías
(él/ella/usted)	leerá	leería
(nosotros/as)	leeremos	leeríamos
(vosotros/as)	leeréis	leeríais
(ellos/ellas/ ustedes)	leerán	leerían

	PRESENT SUBJUNCTIVE	IMPERFECT SUBJUNCTIVE
(yo)	lea	leyera or leyese
(tú)	leas	leyeras or leyeses
(él/ella/usted)	lea	leyera or leyese
(nosotros/as)	leamos	leyéramos or leyésemos
(vosotros/as)	leáis	leyerais or leyeseis
(ellos/ellas/ ustedes)	lean	leyeran or leyesen

IMPERATIVE

lee / leed

Use the present subjunctive in all cases other than these tú and vosotros affirmative forms.

EXAMPLE PHRASES

Si os portáis bien, os **leeré** un cuento. If you behave yourselves, I'll read you a story.

Yo **leería** también la letra pequeña. I'd read the small print as well.

Quiero que lo **leas** y me digas qué piensas. I want you to read it and tell me what you think.

No **leas** tan deprisa. Don't read so fast.

Remember that subject pronouns are not used very often in Spanish.

levantar (to lift)

	PRESENT	PRESENT PERFECT
(yo)	levanto	he levantado
(tú)	levantas	has levantado
(él/ella/usted)	levanta	ha levantado
(nosotros/as)	levantamos	hemos levantado
(vosotros/as)	levantáis	habéis levantado
(ellos/ellas/ ustedes)	levantan	han levantado

	PRETERITE	IMPERFECT
(yo)	levanté	levantaba
(tú)	levantaste	levantabas
(él/ella/usted)	levantó	levantaba
(nosotros/as)	levantamos	levantábamos
(vosotros/as)	levantasteis	levantabais
(ellos/ellas/ ustedes)	levantaron	levantaban

GERUND
levantando

PAST PARTICIPLE
levantado

EXAMPLE PHRASES

No me importa **levantarme** temprano. I don't mind getting up early.

Siempre **se levanta** de mal humor. He's always in a bad mood when he gets up.

Hoy **me he levantado** temprano. I got up early this morning.

Levantó la maleta como si no pesara nada. He lifted up the suitcase as if
    it weighed nothing.

Me levanté y seguí caminando. I got up and carried on walking.

Remember that subject pronouns are not used very often in Spanish.

levantar

	FUTURE	CONDITIONAL
(yo)	levantaré	levantaría
(tú)	levantarás	levantarías
(él/ella/usted)	levantará	levantaría
(nosotros/as)	levantaremos	levantaríamos
(vosotros/as)	levantaréis	levantaríais
(ellos/ellas/ ustedes)	levantarán	levantarían

	PRESENT SUBJUNCTIVE	IMPERFECT SUBJUNCTIVE
(yo)	levante	levantara or levantase
(tú)	levantes	levantaras or levantases
(él/ella/usted)	levante	levantara or levantase
(nosotros/as)	levantemos	levantáramos or levantásemos
(vosotros/as)	levantéis	levantarais or levantaseis
(ellos/ellas/ ustedes)	levanten	levantaran or levantasen

IMPERATIVE

levanta / levantad

Use the present subjunctive in all cases other than these tú and vosotros affirmative forms.

EXAMPLE PHRASES

La noticia le **levantará** el ánimo. This news will raise her spirits

Si pudiera **me levantaría** siempre tarde. I'd sleep in every day, if I could.

No me **levantes** la voz. Don't raise your voice to me.

Levanta la tapa. Lift the lid.

Levantad la mano si tenéis alguna duda. Put up your hands if you are unclear about anything.

Remember that subject pronouns are not used very often in Spanish.

llover (to rain)

PRESENT
llueve

PRESENT PERFECT
ha llovido

PRETERITE
llovió

IMPERFECT
llovía

GERUND
lloviendo

PAST PARTICIPLE
llovido

EXAMPLE PHRASES

Hace semanas que no **llueve**. It hasn't rained for weeks.

Está lloviendo. It's raining.

Le **han llovido** las ofertas. He's received lots of offers.

Llovió sin parar. It rained non-stop.

Llovía a cántaros. It was pouring down.

Remember that subject pronouns are not used very often in Spanish.

llover

FUTURE
lloverá

CONDITIONAL
llovería

PRESENT SUBJUNCTIVE
llueva

IMPERFECT SUBJUNCTIVE
lloviera *or* lloviese

IMPERATIVE
not used

EXAMPLE PHRASES

Sabía que le **lloverían** las críticas. She knew she would be much criticized.

Espero que no **llueva** este fin de semana. I hope it won't rain this weekend.

Si no **lloviera** podríamos salir a dar una vuelta. We could go for a walk if it wasn't raining.

Remember that subject pronouns are not used very often in Spanish.

lucir (to shine)

	PRESENT		PRESENT PERFECT
(yo)	luzco		he lucido
(tú)	luces		has lucido
(él/ella/usted)	luce		ha lucido
(nosotros/as)	lucimos		hemos lucido
(vosotros/as)	lucís		habéis lucido
(ellos/ellas/ ustedes)	lucen		han lucido

	PRETERITE		IMPERFECT
(yo)	lucí		lucía
(tú)	luciste		lucías
(él/ella/usted)	lució		lucía
(nosotros/as)	lucimos		lucíamos
(vosotros/as)	lucisteis		lucíais
(ellos/ellas/ ustedes)	lucieron		lucían

GERUND

luciendo

PAST PARTICIPLE

lucido

EXAMPLE PHRASES

Ahí no **luce** nada. It doesn't look very good there.

¡Anda, que **te has lucido**! Well, you've excelled yourself!

Lucían las estrellas. The stars were shining.

lucir

	FUTURE	CONDITIONAL
(yo)	luciré	luciría
(tú)	lucirás	lucirías
(él/ella/usted)	lucirá	luciría
(nosotros/as)	luciremos	luciríamos
(vosotros/as)	luciréis	luciríais
(ellos/ellas/ustedes)	lucirán	lucirían

	PRESENT SUBJUNCTIVE	IMPERFECT SUBJUNCTIVE
(yo)	luzca	luciera or luciese
(tú)	luzcas	lucieras or lucieses
(él/ella/usted)	luzca	luciera or luciese
(nosotros/as)	luzcamos	luciéramos or luciésemos
(vosotros/as)	luzcáis	lucierais or lucieseis
(ellos/ellas/ustedes)	luzcan	lucieran or luciesen

IMPERATIVE

luce / lucid

Use the present subjunctive in all cases other than these tú and vosotros affirmative forms.

EXAMPLE PHRASES

Lucirá un traje muy elegante. She will be wearing a very smart outfit.

Luciría más con otros zapatos. It would look much better with a different pair of shoes.

Quiero que esta noche **luzcas** tú el collar. I want you to wear the necklace tonight.

Remember that subject pronouns are not used very often in Spanish.

morir (to die)

	PRESENT		PRESENT PERFECT
(yo)	muero		he muerto
(tú)	mueres		has muerto
(él/ella/usted)	muere		ha muerto
(nosotros/as)	morimos		hemos muerto
(vosotros/as)	morís		habéis muerto
(ellos/ellas/ ustedes)	mueren		han muerto

	PRETERITE		IMPERFECT
(yo)	morí		moría
(tú)	moriste		morías
(él/ella/usted)	murió		moría
(nosotros/as)	morimos		moríamos
(vosotros/as)	moristeis		moríais
(ellos/ellas/ ustedes)	murieron		morían

GERUND
muriendo

PAST PARTICIPLE
muerto

EXAMPLE PHRASES

¡**Me muero** de hambre! I'm starving!

Se está muriendo. She's dying.

Se le **ha muerto** el gato. His cat has died.

Se murió el mes pasado. He died last month.

Me moría de ganas de contárselo. I was dying to tell her.

Remember that subject pronouns are not used very often in Spanish.

morir

	FUTURE	CONDITIONAL
(yo)	moriré	moriría
(tú)	morirás	morirías
(él/ella/usted)	morirá	moriría
(nosotros/as)	moriremos	moriríamos
(vosotros/as)	moriréis	moriríais
(ellos/ellas/ustedes)	morirán	morirían

	PRESENT SUBJUNCTIVE	IMPERFECT SUBJUNCTIVE
(yo)	muera	muriera *or* muriese
(tú)	mueras	murieras *or* murieses
(él/ella/usted)	muera	muriera *or* muriese
(nosotros/as)	muramos	muriéramos *or* muriésemos
(vosotros/as)	muráis	murierais *or* murieseis
(ellos/ellas/ustedes)	mueran	murieran *or* muriesen

IMPERATIVE
muere / morid

Use the present subjunctive in all cases other than these tú and vosotros affirmative forms.

EXAMPLE PHRASES

Cuando te lo cuente **te morirás** de risa. You'll kill yourself laughing when I tell you.

Yo **me moriría** de vergüenza. I'd die of shame.

Cuando **me muera**... When I die...

¡Por favor, no **te mueras**! Please don't die!

Estoy muerto de miedo. I'm scared stiff.

Remember that subject pronouns are not used very often in Spanish.

mover (to move)

	PRESENT		PRESENT PERFECT
(yo)	muevo		he movido
(tú)	mueves		has movido
(él/ella/usted)	mueve		ha movido
(nosotros/as)	movemos		hemos movido
(vosotros/as)	movéis		habéis movido
(ellos/ellas/ ustedes)	mueven		han movido

	PRETERITE		IMPERFECT
(yo)	moví		movía
(tú)	moviste		movías
(él/ella/usted)	movió		movía
(nosotros/as)	movimos		movíamos
(vosotros/as)	movisteis		movíais
(ellos/ellas/ ustedes)	movieron		movían

GERUND

moviendo

PAST PARTICIPLE

movido

EXAMPLE PHRASES

El perro no dejaba de **mover** la cola. The dog kept wagging its tail.

Se está moviendo. It's moving.

¿**Has movido** ese mueble de sitio? Have you moved that piece of furniture?

No **se movieron** de casa. They didn't leave the house.

Antes **se movía** en esos ambientes. He used to move in those circles.

Remember that subject pronouns are not used very often in Spanish.

mover

	FUTURE	CONDITIONAL
(yo)	moveré	movería
(tú)	moverás	moverías
(él/ella/usted)	moverá	movería
(nosotros/as)	moveremos	moveríamos
(vosotros/as)	moveréis	moveríais
(ellos/ellas/ustedes)	moverán	moverían

	PRESENT SUBJUNCTIVE	IMPERFECT SUBJUNCTIVE
(yo)	mueva	moviera or moviese
(tú)	muevas	movieras or movieses
(él/ella/usted)	mueva	moviera or moviese
(nosotros/as)	movamos	moviéramos or moviésemos
(vosotros/as)	mováis	movierais or movieseis
(ellos/ellas/ustedes)	muevan	movieran or moviesen

IMPERATIVE

mueve / moved

Use the present subjunctive in all cases other than these tú and vosotros affirmative forms.

EXAMPLE PHRASES

Prométeme que no **te moverás** de aquí. Promise me you won't move from here.

No **te muevas**. Don't move.

Mueve un poco las cajas para que podamos pasar. Move the boxes a bit so that we can get past.

Remember that subject pronouns are not used very often in Spanish.

nacer (to be born)

	PRESENT		PRESENT PERFECT
(yo)	nazco		he nacido
(tú)	naces		has nacido
(él/ella/usted)	nace		ha nacido
(nosotros/as)	nacemos		hemos nacido
(vosotros/as)	nacéis		habéis nacido
(ellos/ellas/ ustedes)	nacen		han nacido

	PRETERITE		IMPERFECT
(yo)	nací		nacía
(tú)	naciste		nacías
(él/ella/usted)	nació		nacía
(nosotros/as)	nacimos		nacíamos
(vosotros/as)	nacisteis		nacíais
(ellos/ellas/ ustedes)	nacieron		nacían

GERUND
naciendo

PAST PARTICIPLE
nacido

EXAMPLE PHRASES

Nacen cuatro niños por minuto. Four children are born every minute.

Ha nacido antes de tiempo. It was premature.

Nació en 1980. He was born in 1980.

¿Cuándo **naciste**? When were you born?

En aquella época había muchos más niños que **nacían** en casa. Many more babies were born at home in those days.

Remember that subject pronouns are not used very often in Spanish.

nacer

	FUTURE	CONDITIONAL
(yo)	naceré	nacería
(tú)	nacerás	nacerías
(él/ella/usted)	nacerá	nacería
(nosotros/as)	naceremos	naceríamos
(vosotros/as)	naceréis	naceríais
(ellos/ellas/ ustedes)	nacerán	nacerían

	PRESENT SUBJUNCTIVE	IMPERFECT SUBJUNCTIVE
(yo)	nazca	naciera *or* naciese
(tú)	nazcas	nacieras *or* nacieses
(él/ella/usted)	nazca	naciera *or* naciese
(nosotros/as)	nazcamos	naciéramos *or* naciésemos
(vosotros/as)	nazcáis	nacierais *or* nacieseis
(ellos/ellas/ ustedes)	nazcan	nacieran *or* naciesen

IMPERATIVE

nace / naced

Use the present subjunctive in all cases other than these tú and vosotros affirmative forms.

EXAMPLE PHRASES

Nacerá el año que viene. It will be born next year.

Queremos que **nazca** en España. We want it to be born in Spain.

Si **naciera** hoy, sería tauro. He'd be a Taurus if he were born today.

negar (to deny; to refuse)

	PRESENT		PRESENT PERFECT
(yo)	niego		he negado
(tú)	niegas		has negado
(él/ella/usted)	niega		ha negado
(nosotros/as)	negamos		hemos negado
(vosotros/as)	negáis		habéis negado
(ellos/ellas/ustedes)	niegan		han negado

	PRETERITE		IMPERFECT
(yo)	negué		negaba
(tú)	negaste		negabas
(él/ella/usted)	negó		negaba
(nosotros/as)	negamos		negábamos
(vosotros/as)	negasteis		negabais
(ellos/ellas/ustedes)	negaron		negaban

GERUND
negando

PAST PARTICIPLE
negado

EXAMPLE PHRASES

No lo puedes **negar**. You can't deny it.

Me niego a creerlo. I refuse to believe it.

Me **ha negado** el favor. He wouldn't do me this favour.

Se negó a venir con nosotros. She refused to come with us.

Decían que era el ladrón, pero él lo **negaba**. They said that he was the thief, but he denied it.

Remember that subject pronouns are not used very often in Spanish.

negar

	FUTURE	CONDITIONAL
(yo)	negaré	negaría
(tú)	negarás	negarías
(él/ella/usted)	negará	negaría
(nosotros/as)	negaremos	negaríamos
(vosotros/as)	negaréis	negaríais
(ellos/ellas/ ustedes)	negarán	negarían

	PRESENT SUBJUNCTIVE	IMPERFECT SUBJUNCTIVE
(yo)	niegue	negara or negase
(tú)	niegues	negaras or negases
(él/ella/usted)	niegue	negara or negase
(nosotros/as)	neguemos	negáramos or negásemos
(vosotros/as)	neguéis	negarais or negaseis
(ellos/ellas/ ustedes)	nieguen	negaran or negasen

IMPERATIVE

niega / negad

Use the present subjunctive in all cases other than these tú and vosotros affirmative forms.

EXAMPLE PHRASES

No me **negarás** que es barato. You can't say it's not cheap.

Si lo **negaras**, nadie te creería. If you denied it, nobody would believe you.

No lo **niegues**. Don't deny it.

Remember that subject pronouns are not used very often in Spanish.

oír (to hear)

	PRESENT		PRESENT PERFECT
(yo)	oigo		he oído
(tú)	oyes		has oído
(él/ella/usted)	oye		ha oído
(nosotros/as)	oímos		hemos oído
(vosotros/as)	oís		habéis oído
(ellos/ellas/ustedes)	oyen		han oído

	PRETERITE		IMPERFECT
(yo)	oí		oía
(tú)	oíste		oías
(él/ella/usted)	oyó		oía
(nosotros/as)	oímos		oíamos
(vosotros/as)	oísteis		oíais
(ellos/ellas/ustedes)	oyeron		oían

GERUND
oyendo

PAST PARTICIPLE
oído

EXAMPLE PHRASES

No **oigo** nada. I can't hear anything.

Hemos estado oyendo las noticias. We've been listening to the news.

¿**Has oído** eso? Did you hear that?

Lo **oí** por casualidad. I heard it by chance.

No **oía** muy bien. He couldn't hear very well.

Remember that subject pronouns are not used very often in Spanish.

oír

	FUTURE	**CONDITIONAL**
(yo)	oiré	oiría
(tú)	oirás	oirías
(él/ella/usted)	oirá	oiría
(nosotros/as)	oiremos	oiríamos
(vosotros/as)	oiréis	oiríais
(ellos/ellas/ ustedes)	oirán	oirían

	PRESENT SUBJUNCTIVE	**IMPERFECT SUBJUNCTIVE**
(yo)	oiga	oyera or oyese
(tú)	oigas	oyeras or oyeses
(él/ella/usted)	oiga	oyera or oyese
(nosotros/as)	oigamos	oyéramos or oyésemos
(vosotros/as)	oigáis	oyerais or oyeseis
(ellos/ellas/ ustedes)	oigan	oyeran or oyesen

IMPERATIVE

oye / oíd

*Use the present subjunctive in all cases other than these tú and **vosotros** affirmative forms.*

EXAMPLE PHRASES

Oirías mal. You must have misunderstood.

¡**Oiga**! ¡A ver si mira por dónde va! Excuse me! Why don't you look where you're going?

Óyeme bien, no vuelvas a hacer eso. Now listen carefully; don't do that again.

Remember that subject pronouns are not used very often in Spanish.

oler (to smell)

	PRESENT	PRESENT PERFECT
(yo)	huelo	he olido
(tú)	hueles	has olido
(él/ella/usted)	huele	ha olido
(nosotros/as)	olemos	hemos olido
(vosotros/as)	oléis	habéis olido
(ellos/ellas/ ustedes)	huelen	han olido

	PRETERITE	IMPERFECT
(yo)	olí	olía
(tú)	oliste	olías
(él/ella/usted)	olió	olía
(nosotros/as)	olimos	olíamos
(vosotros/as)	olisteis	olíais
(ellos/ellas/ ustedes)	olieron	olían

GERUND

oliendo

PAST PARTICIPLE

olido

EXAMPLE PHRASES

Huele a pescado. It smells of fish.

El perro **estaba oliendo** la basura. The dog was sniffing the rubbish.

Se ha olido algo. He's started to suspect.

A mí el asunto me **olió** mal. I thought there was something fishy about it.

Olía muy bien. It smelled really nice.

Remember that subject pronouns are not used very often in Spanish.

oler

	FUTURE	**CONDITIONAL**
(yo)	oleré	olería
(tú)	olerás	olerías
(él/ella/usted)	olerá	olería
(nosotros/as)	oleremos	oleríamos
(vosotros/as)	oleréis	oleríais
(ellos/ellas/ustedes)	olerán	olerían

	PRESENT SUBJUNCTIVE	**IMPERFECT SUBJUNCTIVE**
(yo)	huela	oliera *or* oliese
(tú)	huelas	olieras *or* olieses
(él/ella/usted)	huela	oliera *or* oliese
(nosotros/as)	olamos	oliéramos *or* oliésemos
(vosotros/as)	oláis	olierais *or* olieseis
(ellos/ellas/ustedes)	huelan	olieran *or* oliesen

IMPERATIVE
huele / oled
Use the present subjunctive in all cases other than these **tú** *and* **vosotros** *affirmative forms.*

EXAMPLE PHRASES
Con esto ya no **olerá**. This will take the smell away.
Si te **oliera** a quemado, apágalo. If you smell it burning, turn it off.

pagar (to pay; to pay for)

	PRESENT		PRESENT PERFECT
(yo)	pago		he pagado
(tú)	pagas		has pagado
(él/ella/usted)	paga		ha pagado
(nosotros/as)	pagamos		hemos pagado
(vosotros/as)	pagáis		habéis pagado
(ellos/ellas/ ustedes)	pagan		han pagado

	PRETERITE		IMPERFECT
(yo)	pagué		pagaba
(tú)	pagaste		pagabas
(él/ella/usted)	pagó		pagaba
(nosotros/as)	pagamos		pagábamos
(vosotros/as)	pagasteis		pagabais
(ellos/ellas/ ustedes)	pagaron		pagaban

GERUND

pagando

PAST PARTICIPLE

pagado

EXAMPLE PHRASES

Se puede **pagar** con tarjeta de crédito. You can pay by credit card.

¿Cuánto te **pagan** al mes? How much do they pay you a month?

No **han pagado** el alquiler. They haven't paid the rent.

Lo **pagué** en efectivo. I paid for it in cash.

Me **pagaban** muy poco. I got paid very little.

Remember that subject pronouns are not used very often in Spanish.

pagar

	FUTURE	CONDITIONAL
(yo)	pagaré	pagaría
(tú)	pagarás	pagarías
(él/ella/usted)	pagará	pagaría
(nosotros/as)	pagaremos	pagaríamos
(vosotros/as)	pagaréis	pagaríais
(ellos/ellas/ ustedes)	pagarán	pagarían

	PRESENT SUBJUNCTIVE	IMPERFECT SUBJUNCTIVE
(yo)	pague	pagara or pagase
(tú)	pagues	pagaras or pagases
(él/ella/usted)	pague	pagara or pagase
(nosotros/as)	paguemos	pagáramos or pagásemos
(vosotros/as)	paguéis	pagarais or pagaseis
(ellos/ellas/ ustedes)	paguen	pagaran or pagasen

IMPERATIVE

paga / pagad

*Use the present subjunctive in all cases other than these **tú** and **vosotros** affirmative forms.*

EXAMPLE PHRASES

Yo te **pagaré** la entrada. I'll pay for your ticket.

¡Quiero que **pague** por lo que me ha hecho! I want him to pay for what he's done to me!

Si **pagase** sus deudas, se quedaría sin nada. He'd be left with nothing if he paid his debts.

No les **pagues** hasta que lo hayan hecho. Don't pay them until they've done it.

Págame lo que me debes. Pay me what you owe me.

Remember that subject pronouns are not used very often in Spanish.

partir (to cut; to leave)

	PRESENT	PRESENT PERFECT
(yo)	parto	he partido
(tú)	partes	has partido
(él/ella/usted)	parte	ha partido
(nosotros/as)	partimos	hemos partido
(vosotros/as)	partís	habéis partido
(ellos/ellas/ustedes)	parten	han partido

	PRETERITE	IMPERFECT
(yo)	partí	partía
(tú)	partiste	partías
(él/ella/usted)	partió	partía
(nosotros/as)	partimos	partíamos
(vosotros/as)	partisteis	partíais
(ellos/ellas/ustedes)	partieron	partían

GERUND
partiendo

PAST PARTICIPLE
partido

EXAMPLE PHRASES

¿Te **parto** un trozo de queso? Shall I cut you a piece of cheese?
Partiendo de la base de que... Assuming that...
El remo **se partió** en dos. The oar broke in two.
Se partían de risa. They were splitting their sides laughing.

Remember that subject pronouns are not used very often in Spanish.

partir

	FUTURE	CONDITIONAL
(yo)	partiré	partiría
(tú)	partirás	partirías
(él/ella/usted)	partirá	partiría
(nosotros/as)	partiremos	partiríamos
(vosotros/as)	partiréis	partiríais
(ellos/ellas/ustedes)	partirán	partirían

	PRESENT SUBJUNCTIVE	IMPERFECT SUBJUNCTIVE
(yo)	parta	partiera or partiese
(tú)	partas	partieras or partieses
(él/ella/usted)	parta	partiera or partiese
(nosotros/as)	partamos	partiéramos or partiésemos
(vosotros/as)	partáis	partierais or partieseis
(ellos/ellas/ustedes)	partan	partieran or partiesen

IMPERATIVE
parte / partid

Use the present subjunctive in all cases other than these tú and vosotros affirmative forms.

EXAMPLE PHRASES

La expedición **partirá** mañana de París. The expedition will set off from Paris tomorrow.

Eso le **partiría** el corazón. That would break his heart.

No **partas** todavía el pan. Don't slice the bread yet.

Pártelo por la mitad. Cut it in half.

Remember that subject pronouns are not used very often in Spanish.

pedir (to ask for; to ask)

	PRESENT		PRESENT PERFECT
(yo)	pido		he pedido
(tú)	pides		has pedido
(él/ella/usted)	pide		ha pedido
(nosotros/as)	pedimos		hemos pedido
(vosotros/as)	pedís		habéis pedido
(ellos/ellas/ ustedes)	piden		han pedido

	PRETERITE		IMPERFECT
(yo)	pedí		pedía
(tú)	pediste		pedías
(él/ella/usted)	pidió		pedía
(nosotros/as)	pedimos		pedíamos
(vosotros/as)	pedisteis		pedíais
(ellos/ellas/ ustedes)	pidieron		pedían

GERUND
pidiendo

PAST PARTICIPLE
pedido

EXAMPLE PHRASES

¿Cuánto **pide** por el coche? How much is he asking for the car?

La casa **está pidiendo** a gritos una mano de pintura. The house is crying out to be painted.

Hemos pedido dos cervezas. We've ordered two beers.

No nos **pidieron** el pasaporte. They didn't ask us for our passports.

Pedían dos millones de rescate. They were demanding a two-million ransom.

Remember that subject pronouns are not used very often in Spanish.

pedir

	FUTURE	CONDITIONAL
(yo)	pediré	pediría
(tú)	pedirás	pedirías
(él/ella/usted)	pedirá	pediría
(nosotros/as)	pediremos	pediríamos
(vosotros/as)	pediréis	pediríais
(ellos/ellas/ ustedes)	pedirán	pedirían

	PRESENT SUBJUNCTIVE	IMPERFECT SUBJUNCTIVE
(yo)	pida	pidiera or pidiese
(tú)	pidas	pidieras or pidieses
(él/ella/usted)	pida	pidiera or pidiese
(nosotros/as)	pidamos	pidiéramos or pidiésemos
(vosotros/as)	pidáis	pidierais or pidieseis
(ellos/ellas/ ustedes)	pidan	pidieran or pidiesen

IMPERATIVE
pide / pedid

Use the present subjunctive in all cases other than these tú and vosotros affirmative forms.

EXAMPLE PHRASES

Si se entera, te **pedirá** explicaciones. If he finds out, he'll ask you for an explanation.

Nunca te **pediría** que hicieras una cosa así. I'd never ask you to do anything like that.

Y que sea lo último que me **pidas**. And don't ask me for anything else.

Pídele el teléfono. Ask her for her telephone number.

Remember that subject pronouns are not used very often in Spanish.

pensar (to think)

	PRESENT		PRESENT PERFECT
(yo)	pienso		he pensado
(tú)	piensas		has pensado
(él/ella/usted)	piensa		ha pensado
(nosotros/as)	pensamos		hemos pensado
(vosotros/as)	pensáis		habéis pensado
(ellos/ellas/ ustedes)	piensan		han pensado

	PRETERITE		IMPERFECT
(yo)	pensé		pensaba
(tú)	pensaste		pensabas
(él/ella/usted)	pensó		pensaba
(nosotros/as)	pensamos		pensábamos
(vosotros/as)	pensasteis		pensabais
(ellos/ellas/ ustedes)	pensaron		pensaban

GERUND

pensando

PAST PARTICIPLE

pensado

EXAMPLE PHRASES

¿**Piensas** que vale la pena? Do you think it's worth it?

¿Qué **piensas** del aborto? What do you think about abortion?

Está **pensando** en comprarse un piso. He's thinking about buying a flat.

¿Lo **has pensado** bien? Have you thought about it carefully?

Pensaba que vendrías. I thought you'd come.

Remember that subject pronouns are not used very often in Spanish.

pensar

	FUTURE	**CONDITIONAL**
(yo)	pensaré	pensaría
(tú)	pensarás	pensarías
(él/ella/usted)	pensará	pensaría
(nosotros/as)	pensaremos	pensaríamos
(vosotros/as)	pensaréis	pensaríais
(ellos/ellas/ustedes)	pensarán	pensarían

	PRESENT SUBJUNCTIVE	**IMPERFECT SUBJUNCTIVE**
(yo)	piense	pensara or pensase
(tú)	pienses	pensaras or pensases
(él/ella/usted)	piense	pensara or pensase
(nosotros/as)	pensemos	pensáramos or pensásemos
(vosotros/as)	penséis	pensarais or pensaseis
(ellos/ellas/ustedes)	piensen	pensaran or pensasen

IMPERATIVE
piensa / pensad

*Use the present subjunctive in all cases other than these **tú** and **vosotros** affirmative forms.*

EXAMPLE PHRASES
Yo no me lo **pensaría** dos veces. I wouldn't think about it twice.

Me da igual lo que **piensen**. I don't care what they think.

Si **pensara** eso, te lo diría. If I thought that, I'd tell you.

No **pienses** que no quiero ir. Don't think that I don't want to go.

No lo **pienses** más. Don't give it another thought.

Remember that subject pronouns are not used very often in Spanish.

perder (to lose)

	PRESENT		PRESENT PERFECT
(yo)	pierdo		he perdido
(tú)	pierdes		has perdido
(él/ella/usted)	pierde		ha perdido
(nosotros/as)	perdemos		hemos perdido
(vosotros/as)	perdéis		habéis perdido
(ellos/ellas/ ustedes)	pierden		han perdido

	PRETERITE		IMPERFECT
(yo)	perdí		perdía
(tú)	perdiste		perdías
(él/ella/usted)	perdió		perdía
(nosotros/as)	perdimos		perdíamos
(vosotros/as)	perdisteis		perdíais
(ellos/ellas/ ustedes)	perdieron		perdían

GERUND
perdiendo

PAST PARTICIPLE
perdido

EXAMPLE PHRASES

Siempre **pierde** las llaves. He's always losing his keys.

Ana es la que saldrá **perdiendo**. Ana is the one who will lose out.

He perdido dos kilos. I've lost two kilos.

Perdimos dos a cero. We lost two nil.

Perdían siempre. They always used to lose.

Remember that subject pronouns are not used very often in Spanish.

perder

	FUTURE	CONDITIONAL
(yo)	perderé	perdería
(tú)	perderás	perderías
(él/ella/usted)	perderá	perdería
(nosotros/as)	perderemos	perderíamos
(vosotros/as)	perderéis	perderíais
(ellos/ellas/ ustedes)	perderán	perderían

	PRESENT SUBJUNCTIVE	IMPERFECT SUBJUNCTIVE
(yo)	pierda	perdiera *or* perdiese
(tú)	pierdas	perdieras *or* perdieses
(él/ella/usted)	pierda	perdiera *or* perdiese
(nosotros/as)	perdamos	perdiéramos *or* perdiésemos
(vosotros/as)	perdáis	perdierais *or* perdieseis
(ellos/ellas/ ustedes)	pierdan	perdieran *or* perdiesen

IMPERATIVE
pierde / perded

Use the present subjunctive in all cases other than these **tú** *and* **vosotros** *affirmative forms.*

EXAMPLE PHRASES
Date prisa o **perderás** el tren. Hurry up or you'll miss the train.

¡No **te** lo **pierdas**! Don't miss it!

No **pierdas** esta oportunidad. Don't miss this opportunity.

Remember that subject pronouns are not used very often in Spanish.

poder (to be able to)

	PRESENT	PRESENT PERFECT
(yo)	puedo	he podido
(tú)	puedes	has podido
(él/ella/usted)	puede	ha podido
(nosotros/as)	podemos	hemos podido
(vosotros/as)	podéis	habéis podido
(ellos/ellas/ustedes)	pueden	han podido

	PRETERITE	IMPERFECT
(yo)	pude	podía
(tú)	pudiste	podías
(él/ella/usted)	pudo	podía
(nosotros/as)	pudimos	podíamos
(vosotros/as)	pudisteis	podíais
(ellos/ellas/ustedes)	pudieron	podían

GERUND

pudiendo

PAST PARTICIPLE

podido

EXAMPLE PHRASES

¿**Puedo** entrar? Can I come in?

Puede que llegue mañana. He may arrive tomorrow.

No **he podido** venir antes. I couldn't come before.

Pudiste haberte hecho daño. You could have hurt yourself.

¡Me lo **podías** haber dicho! You could have told me!

Remember that subject pronouns are not used very often in Spanish.

poder

	FUTURE	**CONDITIONAL**
(yo)	podré	podría
(tú)	podrás	podrías
(él/ella/usted)	podrá	podría
(nosotros/as)	podremos	podríamos
(vosotros/as)	podréis	podríais
(ellos/ellas/ustedes)	podrán	podrían

	PRESENT SUBJUNCTIVE	**IMPERFECT SUBJUNCTIVE**
(yo)	pueda	pudiera or pudiese
(tú)	puedas	pudieras or pudieses
(él/ella/usted)	pueda	pudiera or pudiese
(nosotros/as)	podamos	pudiéramos or pudiésemos
(vosotros/as)	podáis	pudierais or pudieseis
(ellos/ellas/ustedes)	puedan	pudieran or pudiesen

IMPERATIVE
puede / poded

Use the present subjunctive in all cases other than these tú and vosotros affirmative forms.

EXAMPLE PHRASES
Estoy segura de que **podrá** conseguirlo. I'm sure he'll succeed.

¿**Podrías** ayudarme? Could you help me?

Ven en cuanto **puedas**. Come as soon as you can.

Si no **pudiera** encontrar la casa, te llamaría al móvil. If I weren't able to find the house, I'd call you on your mobile.

Remember that subject pronouns are not used very often in Spanish.

poner (to put)

	PRESENT		PRESENT PERFECT
(yo)	pongo		he puesto
(tú)	pones		has puesto
(él/ella/usted)	pone		ha puesto
(nosotros/as)	ponemos		hemos puesto
(vosotros/as)	ponéis		habéis puesto
(ellos/ellas/ ustedes)	ponen		han puesto

	PRETERITE		IMPERFECT
(yo)	puse		ponía
(tú)	pusiste		ponías
(él/ella/usted)	puso		ponía
(nosotros/as)	pusimos		poníamos
(vosotros/as)	pusisteis		poníais
(ellos/ellas/ ustedes)	pusieron		ponían

GERUND

poniendo

PAST PARTICIPLE

puesto

EXAMPLE PHRASES

¿Dónde **pongo** mis cosas? Where shall I put my things?

¿Qué **pone** en la carta? What does the letter say?

¿Le **has puesto** azúcar a mi café? Have you put any sugar in my coffee?

Todos **nos pusimos** de acuerdo. We all agreed.

Remember that subject pronouns are not used very often in Spanish.

poner

	FUTURE	**CONDITIONAL**
(yo)	pondré	pondría
(tú)	pondrás	pondrías
(él/ella/usted)	pondrá	pondría
(nosotros/as)	pondremos	pondríamos
(vosotros/as)	pondréis	pondríais
(ellos/ellas/ustedes)	pondrán	pondrían

	PRESENT SUBJUNCTIVE	**IMPERFECT SUBJUNCTIVE**
(yo)	ponga	pusiera or pusiese
(tú)	pongas	pusieras or pusieses
(él/ella/usted)	ponga	pusiera or pusiese
(nosotros/as)	pongamos	pusiéramos or pusiésemos
(vosotros/as)	pongáis	pusierais or pusieseis
(ellos/ellas/ustedes)	pongan	pusieran or pusiesen

IMPERATIVE

pon / poned

*Use the present subjunctive in all cases other than these **tú** and **vosotros** affirmative forms.*

EXAMPLE PHRASES

Lo **pondré** aquí. I'll put it here.

¿Le **pondrías** más sal? Would you add more salt?

Ponlo ahí encima. Put it on there.

Remember that subject pronouns are not used very often in Spanish.

prohibir (to ban; to prohibit)

	PRESENT		PRESENT PERFECT
(yo)	prohíbo		he prohibido
(tú)	prohíbes		has prohibido
(él/ella/usted)	prohíbe		ha prohibido
(nosotros/as)	prohibimos		hemos prohibido
(vosotros/as)	prohibís		habéis prohibido
(ellos/ellas/ ustedes)	prohíben		han prohibido

	PRETERITE		IMPERFECT
(yo)	prohibí		prohibía
(tú)	prohibiste		prohibías
(él/ella/usted)	prohibió		prohibía
(nosotros/as)	prohibimos		prohibíamos
(vosotros/as)	prohibisteis		prohibíais
(ellos/ellas/ ustedes)	prohibieron		prohibían

GERUND
prohibiendo

PAST PARTICIPLE
prohibido

EXAMPLE PHRASES

Deberían **prohibirlo**. It should be banned.

Te **prohíbo** que me hables así. I won't have you talking to me like that!

Han prohibido el acceso a la prensa. The press have been banned.

Le **prohibieron** la entrada en el bingo. She was not allowed into the bingo hall.

El tratado **prohibía** el uso de armas químicas. The treaty prohibited the use of chemical weapons.

Remember that subject pronouns are not used very often in Spanish.

prohibir

	FUTURE	CONDITIONAL
(yo)	prohibiré	prohibiría
(tú)	prohibirás	prohibirías
(él/ella/usted)	prohibirá	prohibiría
(nosotros/as)	prohibiremos	prohibiríamos
(vosotros/as)	prohibiréis	prohibiríais
(ellos/ellas/ustedes)	prohibirán	prohibirían

	PRESENT SUBJUNCTIVE	IMPERFECT SUBJUNCTIVE
(yo)	prohíba	prohibiera *or* prohibiese
(tú)	prohíbas	prohibieras *or* prohibieses
(él/ella/usted)	prohíba	prohibiera *or* prohibiese
(nosotros/as)	prohibamos	prohibiéramos *or* prohibiésemos
(vosotros/as)	prohibáis	prohibierais *or* prohibieseis
(ellos/ellas/ustedes)	prohíban	prohibieran *or* prohibiesen

IMPERATIVE
prohíbe / prohibid

*Use the present subjunctive in all cases other than these **tú** and **vosotros** affirmative forms.*

EXAMPLE PHRASES

Lo **prohibirán** más tarde o más temprano. Sooner or later they'll ban it.

Yo esa música la **prohibiría**. If it were up to me, that music would be banned.

"**prohibido** fumar" "no smoking"

querer (to want; to love)

	PRESENT		PRESENT PERFECT
(yo)	quiero		he querido
(tú)	quieres		has querido
(él/ella/usted)	quiere		ha querido
(nosotros/as)	queremos		hemos querido
(vosotros/as)	queréis		habéis querido
(ellos/ellas/ ustedes)	quieren		han querido

	PRETERITE		IMPERFECT
(yo)	quise		quería
(tú)	quisiste		querías
(él/ella/usted)	quiso		quería
(nosotros/as)	quisimos		queríamos
(vosotros/as)	quisisteis		queríais
(ellos/ellas/ ustedes)	quisieron		querían

GERUND
queriendo

PAST PARTICIPLE
querido

EXAMPLE PHRASES

Lo hice sin **querer**. I didn't mean to do it.

Te **quiero**. I love you.

Quiero que vayas. I want you to go.

Tú lo **has querido**. You were asking for it.

No **quería** decírmelo. She didn't want to tell me.

Remember that subject pronouns are not used very often in Spanish.

querer

	FUTURE	CONDITIONAL
(yo)	querré	querría
(tú)	querrás	querrías
(él/ella/usted)	querrá	querría
(nosotros/as)	querremos	querríamos
(vosotros/as)	querréis	querríais
(ellos/ellas/ ustedes)	querrán	querrían

	PRESENT SUBJUNCTIVE	IMPERFECT SUBJUNCTIVE
(yo)	quiera	quisiera or quisiese
(tú)	quieras	quisieras or quisieses
(él/ella/usted)	quiera	quisiera or quisiese
(nosotros/as)	queramos	quisiéramos or quisiésemos
(vosotros/as)	queráis	quisierais or quisieseis
(ellos/ellas/ ustedes)	quieran	quisieran or quisiesen

IMPERATIVE
quiere / quered
*Use the present subjunctive in all cases other than these **tú** and **vosotros** affirmative forms.*

EXAMPLE PHRASES
¿**Querrá** firmarme un autógrafo? Will you give me your autograph?
Querría que no hubiera pasado nunca. I wish it had never happened.
¡Por lo que más **quieras**! ¡Cállate! For goodness' sake, shut up!
Quisiera preguntar una cosa. I'd like to ask something.

Remember that subject pronouns are not used very often in Spanish.

reducir (to reduce)

	PRESENT		PRESENT PERFECT
(yo)	reduzco		he reducido
(tú)	reduces		has reducido
(él/ella/usted)	reduce		ha reducido
(nosotros/as)	reducimos		hemos reducido
(vosotros/as)	reducís		habéis reducido
(ellos/ellas/ustedes)	reducen		han reducido

	PRETERITE		IMPERFECT
(yo)	reduje		reducía
(tú)	redujiste		reducías
(él/ella/usted)	redujo		reducía
(nosotros/as)	redujimos		reducíamos
(vosotros/as)	redujisteis		reducíais
(ellos/ellas/ustedes)	redujeron		reducían

GERUND

reduciendo

PAST PARTICIPLE

reducido

EXAMPLE PHRASES

Al final todo **se reduce** a eso. In the end it all comes down to that.

Le **han reducido** la pena a dos meses. His sentence has been reduced to two months.

Se ha reducido la tasa de natalidad. The birth rate has fallen.

Sus gastos **se redujeron** a la mitad. Their expenses were cut by half.

Remember that subject pronouns are not used very often in Spanish.

reducir

	FUTURE	CONDITIONAL
(yo)	reduciré	reduciría
(tú)	reducirás	reducirías
(él/ella/usted)	reducirá	reduciría
(nosotros/as)	reduciremos	reduciríamos
(vosotros/as)	reduciréis	reduciríais
(ellos/ellas/ ustedes)	reducirán	reducirían

	PRESENT SUBJUNCTIVE	IMPERFECT SUBJUNCTIVE
(yo)	reduzca	redujera or redujese
(tú)	reduzcas	redujeras or redujeses
(él/ella/usted)	reduzca	redujera or redujese
(nosotros/as)	reduzcamos	redujéramos or redujésemos
(vosotros/as)	reduzcáis	redujerais or redujeseis
(ellos/ellas/ ustedes)	reduzcan	redujeran or redujesen

IMPERATIVE

reduce / reducid

Use the present subjunctive in all cases other than these **tú** *and* **vosotros** *affirmative forms.*

EXAMPLE PHRASES

Reducirán la producción en un 20%. They'll cut production by 20%.

Reduzca la velocidad. Reduce speed.

rehusar (to refuse)

	PRESENT		PRESENT PERFECT
(yo)	rehúso		he rehusado
(tú)	rehúsas		has rehusado
(él/ella/usted)	rehúsa		ha rehusado
(nosotros/as)	rehusamos		hemos rehusado
(vosotros/as)	rehusáis		habéis rehusado
(ellos/ellas/ ustedes)	rehúsan		han rehusado

	PRETERITE		IMPERFECT
(yo)	rehusé		rehusaba
(tú)	rehusaste		rehusabas
(él/ella/usted)	rehusó		rehusaba
(nosotros/as)	rehusamos		rehusábamos
(vosotros/as)	rehusasteis		rehusabais
(ellos/ellas/ ustedes)	rehusaron		rehusaban

GERUND

rehusando

PAST PARTICIPLE

rehusado

EXAMPLE PHRASES

Rehúso tomar parte en esto. I refuse to take part in this.

Ha rehusado la oferta de trabajo. He declined the job offer.

Su familia **rehusó** hacer declaraciones. His family refused to comment.

rehusar

	FUTURE	CONDITIONAL
(yo)	rehusaré	rehusaría
(tú)	rehusarás	rehusarías
(él/ella/usted)	rehusará	rehusaría
(nosotros/as)	rehusaremos	rehusaríamos
(vosotros/as)	rehusaréis	rehusaríais
(ellos/ellas/ ustedes)	rehusarán	rehusarían

	PRESENT SUBJUNCTIVE	IMPERFECT SUBJUNCTIVE
(yo)	rehúse	rehusara or rehusase
(tú)	rehúses	rehusaras or rehusases
(él/ella/usted)	rehúse	rehusara or rehusase
(nosotros/as)	rehusemos	rehusáramos or rehusásemos
(vosotros/as)	rehuséis	rehusarais or rehusaseis
(ellos/ellas/ ustedes)	rehúsen	rehusaran or rehusasen

IMPERATIVE

rehúsa / rehusad

Use the present subjunctive in all cases other than these **tú** *and* **vosotros** *affirmative forms.*

reír (to laugh)

	PRESENT	PRESENT PERFECT
(yo)	río	he reído
(tú)	ríes	has reído
(él/ella/usted)	ríe	ha reído
(nosotros/as)	reímos	hemos reído
(vosotros/as)	reís	habéis reído
(ellos/ellas/ustedes)	ríen	han reído

	PRETERITE	IMPERFECT
(yo)	reí	reía
(tú)	reíste	reías
(él/ella/usted)	rio	reía
(nosotros/as)	reímos	reíamos
(vosotros/as)	reísteis	reíais
(ellos/ellas/ustedes)	rieron	reían

GERUND
riendo

PAST PARTICIPLE
reído

EXAMPLE PHRASES

Se echó a **reír**. She burst out laughing.

Se ríe de todo. She doesn't take anything seriously.

¿De qué **te ríes**? What are you laughing at?

Siempre **están riéndose** en clase. They're always laughing in class.

Me reía mucho con él. I always had a good laugh with him.

Remember that subject pronouns are not used very often in Spanish.

reír

	FUTURE	CONDITIONAL
(yo)	reiré	reiría
(tú)	reirás	reirías
(él/ella/usted)	reirá	reiría
(nosotros/as)	reiremos	reiríamos
(vosotros/as)	reiréis	reiríais
(ellos/ellas/ustedes)	reirán	reirían

	PRESENT SUBJUNCTIVE	IMPERFECT SUBJUNCTIVE
(yo)	ría	riera or riese
(tú)	rías	rieras or rieses
(él/ella/usted)	ría	riera or riese
(nosotros/as)	riamos	riéramos or riésemos
(vosotros/as)	riais	rierais or rieseis
(ellos/ellas/ustedes)	rían	rieran or riesen

IMPERATIVE

ríe / reíd

Use the present subjunctive in all cases other than these tú and **vosotros** affirmative forms.

EXAMPLE PHRASES

Te reirás cuando te lo cuente. You'll have a laugh when I tell you about it.

Que **se rían** lo que quieran. Let them laugh as much as they want.

No **te rías** de mí. Don't laugh at me.

¡Tú **ríete**, pero he pasado muchísimo miedo! You may laugh, but I was really frightened.

Remember that subject pronouns are not used very often in Spanish.

reñir (to scold; to quarrel)

	PRESENT		PRESENT PERFECT
(yo)	riño		he reñido
(tú)	riñes		has reñido
(él/ella/usted)	riñe		ha reñido
(nosotros/as)	reñimos		hemos reñido
(vosotros/as)	reñís		habéis reñido
(ellos/ellas/ ustedes)	riñen		han reñido

	PRETERITE		IMPERFECT
(yo)	reñí		reñía
(tú)	reñiste		reñías
(él/ella/usted)	riñó		reñía
(nosotros/as)	reñimos		reñíamos
(vosotros/as)	reñisteis		reñíais
(ellos/ellas/ ustedes)	riñeron		reñían

GERUND
riñendo

PAST PARTICIPLE
reñido

EXAMPLE PHRASES

Se pasan el día entero **riñendo**. They spend the whole day quarrelling.

Ha reñido con su novio. She has fallen out with her boyfriend.

Les **riñó** por llegar tarde a casa. She told them off for getting home late.

Nos **reñía** sin motivo. She used to tell us off for no reason.

Remember that subject pronouns are not used very often in Spanish.

reñir

	FUTURE	CONDITIONAL
(yo)	**reñiré**	reñiría
(tú)	**reñirás**	reñirías
(él/ella/usted)	**reñirá**	reñiría
(nosotros/as)	**reñiremos**	reñiríamos
(vosotros/as)	**reñiréis**	reñiríais
(ellos/ellas/ ustedes)	**reñirán**	reñirían

	PRESENT SUBJUNCTIVE	IMPERFECT SUBJUNCTIVE
(yo)	**riña**	riñera or riñese
(tú)	**riñas**	riñeras or riñeses
(él/ella/usted)	**riña**	riñera or riñese
(nosotros/as)	**riñamos**	riñéramos or riñésemos
(vosotros/as)	**riñáis**	riñerais or riñeseis
(ellos/ellas/ ustedes)	**riñan**	riñeran or riñesen

IMPERATIVE
riñe / reñid

*Use the present subjunctive in all cases other than these **tú** and **vosotros** affirmative forms.*

EXAMPLE PHRASES

Si se entera, te **reñirá**. He'll tell you off if he finds out.

No la **riñas**, no es culpa suya. Don't tell her off, it's not her fault.

¡Niños, no **riñáis**! Children, don't quarrel!

Remember that subject pronouns are not used very often in Spanish.

repetir (to repeat)

	PRESENT	PRESENT PERFECT
(yo)	repito	he repetido
(tú)	repites	has repetido
(él/ella/usted)	repite	ha repetido
(nosotros/as)	repetimos	hemos repetido
(vosotros/as)	repetís	habéis repetido
(ellos/ellas/ustedes)	repiten	han repetido

	PRETERITE	IMPERFECT
(yo)	repetí	repetía
(tú)	repetiste	repetías
(él/ella/usted)	repitió	repetía
(nosotros/as)	repetimos	repetíamos
(vosotros/as)	repetisteis	repetíais
(ellos/ellas/ustedes)	repitieron	repetían

GERUND
repitiendo

PAST PARTICIPLE
repetido

EXAMPLE PHRASES

¿Podría **repetirlo**, por favor? Could you repeat that, please?

Le **repito** que es imposible. I'm telling you again that it is impossible.

Se lo **he repetido** mil veces, pero no escucha. I've told him hundreds of times but he won't listen.

Repetía una y otra vez que era inocente. He kept repeating that he was innocent.

Remember that subject pronouns are not used very often in Spanish.

repetir

	FUTURE	CONDITIONAL
(yo)	repetiré	repetiría
(tú)	repetirás	repetirías
(él/ella/usted)	repetirá	repetiría
(nosotros/as)	repetiremos	repetiríamos
(vosotros/as)	repetiréis	repetiríais
(ellos/ellas/ ustedes)	repetirán	repetirían

	PRESENT SUBJUNCTIVE	IMPERFECT SUBJUNCTIVE
(yo)	repita	repitiera *or* repitiese
(tú)	repitas	repitieras *or* repitieses
(él/ella/usted)	repita	repitiera *or* repitiese
(nosotros/as)	repitamos	repitiéramos *or* repitiésemos
(vosotros/as)	repitáis	repitierais *or* repitieseis
(ellos/ellas/ ustedes)	repitan	repitieran *or* repitiesen

IMPERATIVE

repite / repetid

*Use the present subjunctive in all cases other than these **tú** and **vosotros** affirmative forms.*

EXAMPLE PHRASES

Si sigue así, **repetirá** curso. If she goes on like this, she'll end up having to repeat the year.

Espero que no **se repita**. I hope this won't happen again.

Repetid detrás de mí... Repeat after me...

Remember that subject pronouns are not used very often in Spanish.

resolver (to solve)

	PRESENT		PRESENT PERFECT
(yo)	resuelvo		he resuelto
(tú)	resuelves		has resuelto
(él/ella/usted)	resuelve		ha resuelto
(nosotros/as)	resolvemos		hemos resuelto
(vosotros/as)	resolvéis		habéis resuelto
(ellos/ellas/ustedes)	resuelven		han resuelto

	PRETERITE		IMPERFECT
(yo)	resolví		resolvía
(tú)	resolviste		resolvías
(él/ella/usted)	resolvió		resolvía
(nosotros/as)	resolvimos		resolvíamos
(vosotros/as)	resolvisteis		resolvíais
(ellos/ellas/ustedes)	resolvieron		resolvían

GERUND
resolviendo

PAST PARTICIPLE
resuelto

EXAMPLE PHRASES

Trataré de **resolver** tus dudas. I'll try to answer your questions.

Enfadarse no **resuelve** nada. Getting angry doesn't help at all.

No **hemos resuelto** los problemas. We haven't solved the problems.

Resolvimos el problema entre todos. We solved the problem together.

Remember that subject pronouns are not used very often in Spanish.

resolver

	FUTURE	CONDITIONAL
(yo)	resolveré	resolvería
(tú)	resolverás	resolverías
(él/ella/usted)	resolverá	resolvería
(nosotros/as)	resolveremos	resolveríamos
(vosotros/as)	resolveréis	resolveríais
(ellos/ellas/ ustedes)	resolverán	resolverían

	PRESENT SUBJUNCTIVE	IMPERFECT SUBJUNCTIVE
(yo)	resuelva	resolviera or resolviese
(tú)	resuelvas	resolvieras or resolvieses
(él/ella/usted)	resuelva	resolviera or resolviese
(nosotros/as)	resolvamos	resolviéramos or resolviésemos
(vosotros/as)	resolváis	resolvierais or resolvieseis
(ellos/ellas/ ustedes)	resuelvan	resolvieran or resolviesen

IMPERATIVE
resuelve / resolved

Use the present subjunctive in all cases other than these tú and vosotros affirmative forms.

EXAMPLE PHRASES

No te preocupes, ya lo **resolveremos**. Don't worry, we'll get it sorted.

Yo lo **resolvería** de otra forma. I'd sort it out another way.

Hasta que no lo **resuelva** no descansaré. I won't rest until I've sorted it out.

reunir (to put together; to gather)

	PRESENT		PRESENT PERFECT
(yo)	reúno		he reunido
(tú)	reúnes		has reunido
(él/ella/usted)	reúne		ha reunido
(nosotros/as)	reunimos		hemos reunido
(vosotros/as)	reunís		habéis reunido
(ellos/ellas/ustedes)	reúnen		han reunido

	PRETERITE		IMPERFECT
(yo)	reuní		reunía
(tú)	reuniste		reunías
(él/ella/usted)	reunió		reunía
(nosotros/as)	reunimos		reuníamos
(vosotros/as)	reunisteis		reuníais
(ellos/ellas/ustedes)	reunieron		reunían

GERUND

reuniendo

PAST PARTICIPLE

reunido

EXAMPLE PHRASES

Hemos conseguido **reunir** suficiente dinero. We've managed to raise enough money.

Hace tiempo que no **me reúno** con ellos. I haven't seen them for ages.

Reunió a todos para comunicarles la noticia. He called them all together to tell them the news.

No **reunía** los requisitos. She didn't satisfy the requirements.

Remember that subject pronouns are not used very often in Spanish.

reunir

	FUTURE	CONDITIONAL
(yo)	reuniré	reuniría
(tú)	reunirás	reunirías
(él/ella/usted)	reunirá	reuniría
(nosotros/as)	reuniremos	reuniríamos
(vosotros/as)	reuniréis	reuniríais
(ellos/ellas/ustedes)	reunirán	reunirían

	PRESENT SUBJUNCTIVE	IMPERFECT SUBJUNCTIVE
(yo)	reúna	reuniera or reuniese
(tú)	reúnas	reunieras or reunieses
(él/ella/usted)	reúna	reuniera or reuniese
(nosotros/as)	reunamos	reuniéramos or reuniésemos
(vosotros/as)	reunáis	reunierais or reunieseis
(ellos/ellas/ustedes)	reúnan	reunieran or reuniesen

IMPERATIVE
reúne / reunid

Use the present subjunctive in all cases other than these tú and vosotros affirmative forms.

EXAMPLE PHRASES
Se reunirán el viernes. They'll meet on Friday.

Necesito encontrar un local que **reúna** las condiciones. I need to find premises that will meet the requirements.

Consiguió que su familia **se reuniera** tras una larga separación. She managed to get her family back together again after a long separation.

Antes de acusarle, **reúne** las pruebas suficientes. Get enough evidence together before accusing him.

Remember that subject pronouns are not used very often in Spanish.

rogar (to beg; to pray)

	PRESENT		PRESENT PERFECT
(yo)	ruego		he rogado
(tú)	ruegas		has rogado
(él/ella/usted)	ruega		ha rogado
(nosotros/as)	rogamos		hemos rogado
(vosotros/as)	rogáis		habéis rogado
(ellos/ellas/ustedes)	ruegan		han rogado

	PRETERITE		IMPERFECT
(yo)	rogué		rogaba
(tú)	rogaste		rogabas
(él/ella/usted)	rogó		rogaba
(nosotros/as)	rogamos		rogábamos
(vosotros/as)	rogasteis		rogabais
(ellos/ellas/ustedes)	rogaron		rogaban

GERUND	PAST PARTICIPLE
rogando	rogado

EXAMPLE PHRASES

Les **rogamos** acepten nuestras disculpas. Please accept our apologies.

Te **ruego** que me lo devuelvas. Please give it back to me.

"**Se ruega** no fumar" "Please do not smoke"

Me **rogó** que le perdonara. He begged me to forgive him.

Le **rogaba** a Dios que se curara. I prayed to God to make him better.

Remember that subject pronouns are not used very often in Spanish.

rogar

	FUTURE	CONDITIONAL
(yo)	rogaré	rogaría
(tú)	rogarás	rogarías
(él/ella/usted)	rogará	rogaría
(nosotros/as)	rogaremos	rogaríamos
(vosotros/as)	rogaréis	rogaríais
(ellos/ellas/ustedes)	rogarán	rogarían

	PRESENT SUBJUNCTIVE	IMPERFECT SUBJUNCTIVE
(yo)	ruegue	rogara or rogase
(tú)	ruegues	rogaras or rogases
(él/ella/usted)	ruegue	rogara or rogase
(nosotros/as)	roguemos	rogáramos or rogásemos
(vosotros/as)	roguéis	rogarais or rogaseis
(ellos/ellas/ustedes)	rueguen	rogaran or rogasen

IMPERATIVE
ruega / rogad

Use the present subjunctive in all cases other than these tú and vosotros affirmative forms.

EXAMPLE PHRASES
Ruega por mí. Pray for me.

Remember that subject pronouns are not used very often in Spanish.

romper (to break)

	PRESENT	PRESENT PERFECT
(yo)	rompo	he roto
(tú)	rompes	has roto
(él/ella/usted)	rompe	ha roto
(nosotros/as)	rompemos	hemos roto
(vosotros/as)	rompéis	habéis roto
(ellos/ellas/ustedes)	rompen	han roto

	PRETERITE	IMPERFECT
(yo)	rompí	rompía
(tú)	rompiste	rompías
(él/ella/usted)	rompió	rompía
(nosotros/as)	rompimos	rompíamos
(vosotros/as)	rompisteis	rompíais
(ellos/ellas/ustedes)	rompieron	rompían

GERUND
rompiendo

PAST PARTICIPLE
roto

EXAMPLE PHRASES

La cuerda **se** va a **romper**. The rope is going to snap.

Siempre **están rompiendo** cosas. They're always breaking things.

Se ha roto una taza. A cup's broken.

Se rompió el jarrón. The vase broke.

Remember that subject pronouns are not used very often in Spanish.

romper

	FUTURE	CONDITIONAL
(yo)	romperé	rompería
(tú)	romperás	romperías
(él/ella/usted)	romperá	rompería
(nosotros/as)	romperemos	romperíamos
(vosotros/as)	romperéis	romperíais
(ellos/ellas/ustedes)	romperán	romperían

	PRESENT SUBJUNCTIVE	IMPERFECT SUBJUNCTIVE
(yo)	rompa	rompiera or rompiese
(tú)	rompas	rompieras or rompieses
(él/ella/usted)	rompa	rompiera or rompiese
(nosotros/as)	rompamos	rompiéramos or rompiésemos
(vosotros/as)	rompáis	rompierais or rompieseis
(ellos/ellas/ustedes)	rompan	rompieran or rompiesen

IMPERATIVE
rompe / romped

*Use the present subjunctive in all cases other than these **tú** and **vosotros** affirmative forms.*

EXAMPLE PHRASES

Yo nunca **rompería** una promesa. I'd never break a promise.

Si lo **rompiera**, tendría que pagarlo. If you broke it, you'd have to pay for it.

Rompe con él, si ya no le quieres. If you don't love him any more, finish with him.

Cuidado, no lo **rompas**. Careful you don't break it.

saber (to know)

	PRESENT	PRESENT PERFECT
(yo)	sé	he sabido
(tú)	sabes	has sabido
(él/ella/usted)	sabe	ha sabido
(nosotros/as)	sabemos	hemos sabido
(vosotros/as)	sabéis	habéis sabido
(ellos/ellas/ustedes)	saben	han sabido

	PRETERITE	IMPERFECT
(yo)	supe	sabía
(tú)	supiste	sabías
(él/ella/usted)	supo	sabía
(nosotros/as)	supimos	sabíamos
(vosotros/as)	supisteis	sabíais
(ellos/ellas/ustedes)	supieron	sabían

GERUND
sabiendo

PAST PARTICIPLE
sabido

EXAMPLE PHRASES

No lo **sé**. I don't know.

¿**Sabes** una cosa? Do you know what?

¿Cuándo lo **has sabido**? When did you find out?

No **supe** qué responder. I didn't know what to answer.

Pensaba que lo **sabías**. I thought you knew.

Remember that subject pronouns are not used very often in Spanish.

saber

	FUTURE	CONDITIONAL
(yo)	sabré	sabría
(tú)	sabrás	sabrías
(él/ella/usted)	sabrá	sabría
(nosotros/as)	sabremos	sabríamos
(vosotros/as)	sabréis	sabríais
(ellos/ellas/ustedes)	sabrán	sabrían

	PRESENT SUBJUNCTIVE	IMPERFECT SUBJUNCTIVE
(yo)	sepa	supiera or supiese
(tú)	sepas	supieras or supieses
(él/ella/usted)	sepa	supiera or supiese
(nosotros/as)	sepamos	supiéramos or supiésemos
(vosotros/as)	sepáis	supierais or supieseis
(ellos/ellas/ustedes)	sepan	supieran or supiesen

IMPERATIVE
sabe / sabed

Use the present subjunctive in all cases other than these tú and vosotros affirmative forms.

EXAMPLE PHRASES
Nunca se **sabrá** quién la mató. We'll never know who killed her.

Si no le tuvieras tanto miedo al agua, ya **sabrías** nadar. If you weren't so afraid of water, you'd already be able to swim.

Que yo **sepa**, vive en París. As far as I know, she lives in Paris.

¡Si **supiéramos** al menos dónde está! If only we knew where he was!

Remember that subject pronouns are not used very often in Spanish.

sacar (to take out)

	PRESENT		PRESENT PERFECT
(yo)	saco		he sacado
(tú)	sacas		has sacado
(él/ella/usted)	saca		ha sacado
(nosotros/as)	sacamos		hemos sacado
(vosotros/as)	sacáis		habéis sacado
(ellos/ellas/ ustedes)	sacan		han sacado

	PRETERITE		IMPERFECT
(yo)	saqué		sacaba
(tú)	sacaste		sacabas
(él/ella/usted)	sacó		sacaba
(nosotros/as)	sacamos		sacábamos
(vosotros/as)	sacasteis		sacabais
(ellos/ellas/ ustedes)	sacaron		sacaban

GERUND
sacando

PAST PARTICIPLE
sacado

EXAMPLE PHRASES

¿**Me sacas** una foto? Will you take a photo of me?

Estás sacando las cosas de quicio. You're blowing things out of all proportion.

Ya **he sacado** las entradas. I've already bought the tickets.

Saqué un 7 en el examen. I got a 7 in the exam.

¿De dónde **sacaba** tanto dinero? Where did he get so much money from?

Remember that subject pronouns are not used very often in Spanish.

sacar

	FUTURE	CONDITIONAL
(yo)	sacaré	sacaría
(tú)	sacarás	sacarías
(él/ella/usted)	sacará	sacaría
(nosotros/as)	sacaremos	sacaríamos
(vosotros/as)	sacaréis	sacaríais
(ellos/ellas/ ustedes)	sacarán	sacarían

	PRESENT SUBJUNCTIVE	IMPERFECT SUBJUNCTIVE
(yo)	saque	sacara or sacase
(tú)	saques	sacaras or sacases
(él/ella/usted)	saque	sacara or sacase
(nosotros/as)	saquemos	sacáramos or sacásemos
(vosotros/as)	saquéis	sacarais or sacaseis
(ellos/ellas/ ustedes)	saquen	sacaran or sacasen

IMPERATIVE

saca / sacad

Use the present subjunctive in all cases other than these tú and vosotros affirmative forms.

EXAMPLE PHRASES

Yo no **sacaría** todavía ninguna conclusión. I wouldn't draw any conclusions yet.

Quiero que **saques** inmediatamente esa bicicleta de casa. I want you to get that bike out of the house immediately.

Si te **sacaras** el carnet de conducir, serías mucho más independiente. You'd be much more independent if you got your driving licence.

No **saques** la cabeza por la ventanilla. Don't lean out of the window.

Remember that subject pronouns are not used very often in Spanish.

salir (to go out)

	PRESENT		PRESENT PERFECT
(yo)	salgo		he salido
(tú)	sales		has salido
(él/ella/usted)	sale		ha salido
(nosotros/as)	salimos		hemos salido
(vosotros/as)	salís		habéis salido
(ellos/ellas/ ustedes)	salen		han salido

	PRETERITE		IMPERFECT
(yo)	salí		salía
(tú)	saliste		salías
(él/ella/usted)	salió		salía
(nosotros/as)	salimos		salíamos
(vosotros/as)	salisteis		salíais
(ellos/ellas/ ustedes)	salieron		salían

GERUND

saliendo

PAST PARTICIPLE

salido

EXAMPLE PHRASES

Hace tiempo que no **salimos**. We haven't been out for a while.

Está saliendo con un compañero de trabajo. She's going out with a colleague from work.

Ha salido. She's gone out.

Su foto **salió** en todos los periódicos. Her picture appeared in all the newspapers.

Salía muy tarde de trabajar. He used to finish work very late.

Remember that subject pronouns are not used very often in Spanish.

salir

	FUTURE	CONDITIONAL
(yo)	saldré	saldría
(tú)	saldrás	saldrías
(él/ella/usted)	saldrá	saldría
(nosotros/as)	saldremos	saldríamos
(vosotros/as)	saldréis	saldríais
(ellos/ellas/ ustedes)	saldrán	saldrían

	PRESENT SUBJUNCTIVE	IMPERFECT SUBJUNCTIVE
(yo)	salga	saliera or saliese
(tú)	salgas	salieras or salieses
(él/ella/usted)	salga	saliera or saliese
(nosotros/as)	salgamos	saliéramos or saliésemos
(vosotros/as)	salgáis	salierais or salieseis
(ellos/ellas/ ustedes)	salgan	salieran or saliesen

IMPERATIVE
sal / salid

*Use the present subjunctive in all cases other than these **tú** and **vosotros** affirmative forms.*

EXAMPLE PHRASES
Te dije que **saldría** muy caro. I told you it would work out very expensive.
Espero que todo **salga** bien. I hope everything works out all right.
Si **saliera** elegido... If I were elected...
Por favor, **salgan** por la puerta de atrás. Please leave via the back door.

Remember that subject pronouns are not used very often in Spanish.

satisfacer (to satisfy)

	PRESENT	PRESENT PERFECT
(yo)	satisfago	he satisfecho
(tú)	satisfaces	has satisfecho
(él/ella/usted)	satisface	ha satisfecho
(nosotros/as)	satisfacemos	hemos satisfecho
(vosotros/as)	satisfacéis	habéis satisfecho
(ellos/ellas/ustedes)	satisfacen	han satisfecho

	PRETERITE	IMPERFECT
(yo)	satisfice	satisfacía
(tú)	satisficiste	satisfacías
(él/ella/usted)	satisfizo	satisfacía
(nosotros/as)	satisficimos	satisfacíamos
(vosotros/as)	satisficisteis	satisfacíais
(ellos/ellas/ustedes)	satisficieron	satisfacían

GERUND

satisfaciendo

PAST PARTICIPLE

satisfecho

EXAMPLE PHRASES

No me **satisface** nada el resultado. I'm not at all satisfied with the result.

Ha satisfecho mis expectativas. It came up to my expectations.

Eso **satisfizo** mi curiosidad. That satisfied my curiosity.

Aquella vida **satisfacía** todas mis necesidades. That lifestyle satisfied all my needs.

Remember that subject pronouns are not used very often in Spanish.

satisfacer

	FUTURE	CONDITIONAL
(yo)	satisfaré	satisfaría
(tú)	satisfarás	satisfarías
(él/ella/usted)	satisfará	satisfaría
(nosotros/as)	satisfaremos	satisfaríamos
(vosotros/as)	satisfaréis	satisfaríais
(ellos/ellas/ ustedes)	satisfarán	satisfarían

	PRESENT SUBJUNCTIVE	IMPERFECT SUBJUNCTIVE
(yo)	satisfaga	satisficiera or satisficiese
(tú)	satisfagas	satisficieras or satisficieses
(él/ella/usted)	satisfaga	satisficiera or satisficiese
(nosotros/as)	satisfagamos	satisficiéramos or satisficiésemos
(vosotros/as)	satisfagáis	satisficierais or satisficieseis
(ellos/ellas/ ustedes)	satisfagan	satisficieran or satisficiesen

IMPERATIVE

satisfaz or satisface / satisfaced

Use the present subjunctive in all cases other than these **tú** *and* **vosotros** *affirmative forms.*

EXAMPLE PHRASES

Le **satisfará** saber que hemos cumplido nuestros objetivos. You'll be happy to know that we have achieved our objectives.

Me **satisfaría** mucho más que estudiaras una carrera. I'd be far happier if you went to university.

Remember that subject pronouns are not used very often in Spanish.

seguir (to follow)

	PRESENT		PRESENT PERFECT
(yo)	sigo		he seguido
(tú)	sigues		has seguido
(él/ella/usted)	sigue		ha seguido
(nosotros/as)	seguimos		hemos seguido
(vosotros/as)	seguís		habéis seguido
(ellos/ellas/ ustedes)	siguen		han seguido

	PRETERITE		IMPERFECT
(yo)	seguí		seguía
(tú)	seguiste		seguías
(él/ella/usted)	siguió		seguía
(nosotros/as)	seguimos		seguíamos
(vosotros/as)	seguisteis		seguíais
(ellos/ellas/ ustedes)	siguieron		seguían

GERUND

siguiendo

PAST PARTICIPLE

seguido

EXAMPLE PHRASES

Si **sigues** así, acabarás mal. If you go on like this you'll end up badly.

¿Te **han seguido**? Have you been followed?

Siguió cantando como si nada. He went on singing as if nothing was the matter.

El ordenador **seguía** funcionando a pesar del apagón. The computer went on working in spite of the power cut.

Les **estuvimos siguiendo** mucho rato. We followed them for a long time.

Remember that subject pronouns are not used very often in Spanish.

seguir

	FUTURE	CONDITIONAL
(yo)	seguiré	seguiría
(tú)	seguirás	seguirías
(él/ella/usted)	seguirá	seguiría
(nosotros/as)	seguiremos	seguiríamos
(vosotros/as)	seguiréis	seguiríais
(ellos/ellas/ustedes)	seguirán	seguirían

	PRESENT SUBJUNCTIVE	IMPERFECT SUBJUNCTIVE
(yo)	siga	siguiera or siguiese
(tú)	sigas	siguieras or siguieses
(él/ella/usted)	siga	siguiera or siguiese
(nosotros/as)	sigamos	siguiéramos or siguiésemos
(vosotros/as)	sigáis	siguierais or siguieseis
(ellos/ellas/ustedes)	sigan	siguieran or siguiesen

IMPERATIVE

sigue / seguid

Use the present subjunctive in all cases other than these tú and vosotros affirmative forms.

EXAMPLE PHRASES

Nos seguiremos viendo. We will go on seeing each other.

Quiero que **sigas** estudiando. I want you to go on with your studies.

Si **siguieras** mis consejos, te iría muchísimo mejor. You'd be much better off if you followed my advice.

Siga por esta calle hasta el final. Go on till you get to the end of the street.

Remember that subject pronouns are not used very often in Spanish.

sentir (to feel; to be sorry)

	PRESENT		PRESENT PERFECT
(yo)	siento		he sentido
(tú)	sientes		has sentido
(él/ella/usted)	siente		ha sentido
(nosotros/as)	sentimos		hemos sentido
(vosotros/as)	sentís		habéis sentido
(ellos/ellas/ ustedes)	sienten		han sentido

	PRETERITE		IMPERFECT
(yo)	sentí		sentía
(tú)	sentiste		sentías
(él/ella/usted)	sintió		sentía
(nosotros/as)	sentimos		sentíamos
(vosotros/as)	sentisteis		sentíais
(ellos/ellas/ ustedes)	sintieron		sentían

GERUND

sintiendo

PAST PARTICIPLE

sentido

EXAMPLE PHRASES

Te vas a **sentir** sola. You'll feel lonely.

Siento mucho lo que pasó. I'm really sorry about what happened.

Ha sentido mucho la muerte de su padre. He has been greatly affected by his father's death.

Sentí un pinchazo en la pierna. I felt a sharp pain in my leg.

Me sentía muy mal. I didn't feel well at all.

Remember that subject pronouns are not used very often in Spanish.

sentir

	FUTURE	CONDITIONAL
(yo)	sentiré	sentiría
(tú)	sentirás	sentirías
(él/ella/usted)	sentirá	sentiría
(nosotros/as)	sentiremos	sentiríamos
(vosotros/as)	sentiréis	sentiríais
(ellos/ellas/ustedes)	sentirán	sentirían

	PRESENT SUBJUNCTIVE	IMPERFECT SUBJUNCTIVE
(yo)	sienta	sintiera or sintiese
(tú)	sientas	sintieras or sintieses
(él/ella/usted)	sienta	sintiera or sintiese
(nosotros/as)	sintamos	sintiéramos or sintiésemos
(vosotros/as)	sintáis	sintierais or sintieseis
(ellos/ellas/ustedes)	sientan	sintieran or sintiesen

IMPERATIVE

siente / sentid

Use the present subjunctive in all cases other than these tú and vosotros affirmative forms.

EXAMPLE PHRASES

Al principio **te sentirás** un poco raro. You'll feel a bit strange at first.

Yo **sentiría** mucho que se fuera de la empresa. I'd be really sorry if you left the firm.

No creo que lo **sienta**. I don't think she's sorry.

Sería mucho más preocupante si no **sintiera** la pierna. It would be much more worrying if he couldn't feel his leg.

Remember that subject pronouns are not used very often in Spanish.

ser (to be)

	PRESENT		PRESENT PERFECT
(yo)	soy		he sido
(tú)	eres		has sido
(él/ella/usted)	es		ha sido
(nosotros/as)	somos		hemos sido
(vosotros/as)	sois		habéis sido
(ellos/ellas/ ustedes)	son		han sido

	PRETERITE		IMPERFECT
(yo)	fui		era
(tú)	fuiste		eras
(él/ella/usted)	fue		era
(nosotros/as)	fuimos		éramos
(vosotros/as)	fuisteis		erais
(ellos/ellas/ ustedes)	fueron		eran

GERUND
siendo

PAST PARTICIPLE
sido

EXAMPLE PHRASES

Soy español. I'm Spanish.

Estás siendo muy paciente con él. You're being very patient with him.

Ha sido un duro golpe. It was a major blow.

¿**Fuiste** tú el que llamó? Was it you who phoned?

Era de noche. It was dark.

Remember that subject pronouns are not used very often in Spanish.

ser

	FUTURE	**CONDITIONAL**
(yo)	seré	sería
(tú)	serás	serías
(él/ella/usted)	será	sería
(nosotros/as)	seremos	seríamos
(vosotros/as)	seréis	seríais
(ellos/ellas/ustedes)	serán	serían

	PRESENT SUBJUNCTIVE	**IMPERFECT SUBJUNCTIVE**
(yo)	sea	fuera or fuese
(tú)	seas	fueras or fueses
(él/ella/usted)	sea	fuera or fuese
(nosotros/as)	seamos	fuéramos or fuésemos
(vosotros/as)	seáis	fuerais or fueseis
(ellos/ellas/ustedes)	sean	fueran or fuesen

IMPERATIVE

sé / sed

*Use the present subjunctive in all cases other than these **tú** and **vosotros** affirmative forms.*

EXAMPLE PHRASES

Será de Joaquín. It must be Joaquin's.

Eso **sería** estupendo. That would be great.

O **sea**, que no vienes. So you're not coming.

No **seas** tan perfeccionista. Don't be such a perfectionist.

¡**Sed** buenos! Behave yourselves!

Remember that subject pronouns are not used very often in Spanish.

soler (to be in the habit of; to be accustomed to)

	PRESENT	PRESENT PERFECT
(yo)	suelo	*not used*
(tú)	sueles	
(él/ella/usted)	suele	
(nosotros/as)	solemos	
(vosotros/as)	soléis	
(ellos/ellas/ustedes)	suelen	

	PRETERITE	IMPERFECT
(yo)	*not used*	solía
(tú)		solías
(él/ella/usted)		solía
(nosotros/as)		solíamos
(vosotros/as)		solíais
(ellos/ellas/ustedes)		solían

GERUND	PAST PARTICIPLE
soliendo	*not used*

EXAMPLE PHRASES

Suele salir a las ocho. He usually goes out at eight.

Solíamos ir todos los años a la playa. We used to go to the beach every year.

Remember that subject pronouns are not used very often in Spanish.

soler

	FUTURE	CONDITIONAL
(yo)	*not used*	*not used*
(tú)		
(él/ella/usted)		
(nosotros/as)		
(vosotros/as)		
(ellos/ellas/ ustedes)		

	PRESENT SUBJUNCTIVE	IMPERFECT SUBJUNCTIVE
(yo)	suela	soliera *or* soliese
(tú)	suelas	solieras *or* solieses
(él/ella/usted)	suela	soliera *or* soliese
(nosotros/as)	solamos	soliéramos *or* soliésemos
(vosotros/as)	soláis	solierais *or* solieseis
(ellos/ellas/ ustedes)	suelan	solieran *or* soliesen

IMPERATIVE

not used

soltar (to let go of; to release)

	PRESENT		PRESENT PERFECT
(yo)	suelto		he soltado
(tú)	sueltas		has soltado
(él/ella/usted)	suelta		ha soltado
(nosotros/as)	soltamos		hemos soltado
(vosotros/as)	soltáis		habéis soltado
(ellos/ellas/ ustedes)	sueltan		han soltado

	PRETERITE		IMPERFECT
(yo)	solté		soltaba
(tú)	soltaste		soltabas
(él/ella/usted)	soltó		soltaba
(nosotros/as)	soltamos		soltábamos
(vosotros/as)	soltasteis		soltabais
(ellos/ellas/ ustedes)	soltaron		soltaban

GERUND

soltando

PAST PARTICIPLE

soltado

EXAMPLE PHRASES

Al final logró **soltarse**. Eventually she managed to break free.

No para de **soltar** tacos. He swears all the time.

¿Por qué no **te sueltas** el pelo? Why don't you have your hair loose?

Han soltado a los rehenes. They've released the hostages.

Soltó una carcajada. He burst out laughing.

Remember that subject pronouns are not used very often in Spanish.

soltar

	FUTURE	CONDITIONAL
(yo)	soltaré	soltaría
(tú)	soltarás	soltarías
(él/ella/usted)	soltará	soltaría
(nosotros/as)	soltaremos	soltaríamos
(vosotros/as)	soltaréis	soltaríais
(ellos/ellas/ustedes)	soltarán	soltarían

	PRESENT SUBJUNCTIVE	IMPERFECT SUBJUNCTIVE
(yo)	suelte	soltara or soltase
(tú)	sueltes	soltaras or soltases
(él/ella/usted)	suelte	soltara or soltase
(nosotros/as)	soltemos	soltáramos or soltásemos
(vosotros/as)	soltéis	soltarais or soltaseis
(ellos/ellas/ustedes)	suelten	soltaran or soltasen

IMPERATIVE
suelta / soltad

Use the present subjunctive in all cases other than these **tú** *and* **vosotros** *affirmative forms.*

EXAMPLE PHRASES
Te **soltaré** el brazo si me dices dónde está. I'll let go of your arm if you tell me where he is.

Te dije que lo **soltaras**. I told you to let it go.

No **sueltes** la cuerda. Don't let go of the rope.

¡**Suéltame**! Let me go!

Remember that subject pronouns are not used very often in Spanish.

sonar (to sound; to ring)

	PRESENT	PRESENT PERFECT
(yo)	sueno	he sonado
(tú)	suenas	has sonado
(él/ella/usted)	suena	ha sonado
(nosotros/as)	sonamos	hemos sonado
(vosotros/as)	sonáis	habéis sonado
(ellos/ellas/ustedes)	suenan	han sonado

	PRETERITE	IMPERFECT
(yo)	soné	sonaba
(tú)	sonaste	sonabas
(él/ella/usted)	sonó	sonaba
(nosotros/as)	sonamos	sonábamos
(vosotros/as)	sonasteis	sonabais
(ellos/ellas/ustedes)	sonaron	sonaban

GERUND

sonando

PAST PARTICIPLE

sonado

EXAMPLE PHRASES

¿**Te suena** su nombre? Does her name sound familiar?

Ha sonado tu móvil. Your mobile rang.

Justo en ese momento **sonó** el timbre. Just then the bell rang.

Sonabas un poco triste por teléfono. You sounded a bit sad on the phone.

Estaba sonando el teléfono. The phone was ringing.

Remember that subject pronouns are not used very often in Spanish.

sonar

	FUTURE	CONDITIONAL
(yo)	sonaré	sonaría
(tú)	sonarás	sonarías
(él/ella/usted)	sonará	sonaría
(nosotros/as)	sonaremos	sonaríamos
(vosotros/as)	sonaréis	sonaríais
(ellos/ellas/ustedes)	sonarán	sonarían

	PRESENT SUBJUNCTIVE	IMPERFECT SUBJUNCTIVE
(yo)	suene	sonara or sonase
(tú)	suenes	sonaras or sonases
(él/ella/usted)	suene	sonara or sonase
(nosotros/as)	sonemos	sonáramos or sonásemos
(vosotros/as)	sonéis	sonarais or sonaseis
(ellos/ellas/ustedes)	suenen	sonaran or sonasen

IMPERATIVE
suena / sonad

Use the present subjunctive in all cases other than these **tú** *and* **vosotros** *affirmative forms.*

EXAMPLE PHRASES
Hay que esperar a que **suene** un pitido. We have to wait until we hear a beep.

¡**Suénate** la nariz! Blow your nose!

Remember that subject pronouns are not used very often in Spanish.

temer (to be afraid)

	PRESENT	PRESENT PERFECT
(yo)	temo	he temido
(tú)	temes	has temido
(él/ella/usted)	teme	ha temido
(nosotros/as)	tememos	hemos temido
(vosotros/as)	teméis	habéis temido
(ellos/ellas/ustedes)	temen	han temido

	PRETERITE	IMPERFECT
(yo)	temí	temía
(tú)	temiste	temías
(él/ella/usted)	temío	temía
(nosotros/as)	temimos	temíamos
(vosotros/as)	temisteis	temíais
(ellos/ellas/ustedes)	temieron	temían

GERUND

temiendo

PAST PARTICIPLE

temido

EXAMPLE PHRASES

Me temo que no. I'm afraid not.

Se temen lo peor. They fear the worst.

–Ha empezado a llover. –**Me** lo **temía**. "It's started raining." – "I was afraid it would."

Temí ofenderles. I was afraid of offending them.

Temían por su seguridad. They feared for their security.

Remember that subject pronouns are not used very often in Spanish.

temer

	FUTURE	CONDITIONAL
(yo)	temeré	temería
(tú)	temerás	temerías
(él/ella/usted)	temerá	temería
(nosotros/as)	temeremos	temeríamos
(vosotros/as)	temeréis	temeríais
(ellos/ellas/ustedes)	temerán	temerían

	PRESENT SUBJUNCTIVE	IMPERFECT SUBJUNCTIVE
(yo)	tema	temiera or temiese
(tú)	temas	temieras or temieses
(él/ella/usted)	tema	temiera or temiese
(nosotros/as)	temamos	temiéramos or temiésemos
(vosotros/as)	temáis	temierais or temieseis
(ellos/ellas/ustedes)	teman	temieran or temiesen

IMPERATIVE

teme / temed

Use the present subjunctive in all cases other than these tú and vosotros affirmative forms.

EXAMPLE PHRASES

No **temas**. Don't be afraid.

tener (to have)

	PRESENT		PRESENT PERFECT
(yo)	tengo		he tenido
(tú)	tienes		has tenido
(él/ella/usted)	tiene		ha tenido
(nosotros/as)	tenemos		hemos tenido
(vosotros/as)	tenéis		habéis tenido
(ellos/ellas/ ustedes)	tienen		ha tenido

	PRETERITE		IMPERFECT
(yo)	tuve		tenía
(tú)	tuviste		tenías
(él/ella/usted)	tuvo		tenía
(nosotros/as)	tuvimos		teníamos
(vosotros/as)	tuvisteis		teníais
(ellos/ellas/ ustedes)	tuvieron		tenían

GERUND	PAST PARTICIPLE
teniendo	tenido

EXAMPLE PHRASES

Tengo sed. I'm thirsty.

Están teniendo muchos problemas con el coche. They're having a lot of trouble with the car.

Ha tenido una gripe muy fuerte. She's had very bad flu.

Tuvimos que irnos. We had to leave.

No **tenía** suficiente dinero. She didn't have enough money.

Remember that subject pronouns are not used very often in Spanish.

tener

	FUTURE	CONDITIONAL
(yo)	tendré	tendría
(tú)	tendrás	tendrías
(él/ella/usted)	tendrá	tendría
(nosotros/as)	tendremos	tendríamos
(vosotros/as)	tendréis	tendríais
(ellos/ellas/ustedes)	tendrán	tendrían

	PRESENT SUBJUNCTIVE	IMPERFECT SUBJUNCTIVE
(yo)	tenga	tuviera or tuviese
(tú)	tengas	tuvieras or tuvieses
(él/ella/usted)	tenga	tuviera or tuviese
(nosotros/as)	tengamos	tuviéramos or tuviésemos
(vosotros/as)	tengáis	tuvierais or tuvieseis
(ellos/ellas/ustedes)	tengan	tuvieran or tuviesen

IMPERATIVE

ten / tened

Use the present subjunctive in all cases other than these tú and vosotros affirmative forms.

EXAMPLE PHRASES

Tendrás que pagarlo tú. You'll have to pay for it yourself.

Tendrías que comer más. You should eat more.

No creo que **tenga** suficiente dinero. I don't think I've got enough money.

Si **tuviera** tiempo, haría un curso de catalán. If I had time, I'd do a Catalan course.

Ten cuidado. Be careful.

No **tengas** miedo. Don't be afraid.

Remember that subject pronouns are not used very often in Spanish.

tocar (to touch; to play)

	PRESENT	PRESENT PERFECT
(yo)	toco	he tocado
(tú)	tocas	has tocado
(él/ella/usted)	toca	ha tocado
(nosotros/as)	tocamos	hemos tocado
(vosotros/as)	tocáis	habéis tocado
(ellos/ellas/ustedes)	tocan	han tocado

	PRETERITE	IMPERFECT
(yo)	toqué	tocaba
(tú)	tocaste	tocabas
(él/ella/usted)	tocó	tocaba
(nosotros/as)	tocamos	tocábamos
(vosotros/as)	tocasteis	tocabais
(ellos/ellas/ustedes)	tocaron	tocaban

GERUND
tocando

PAST PARTICIPLE
tocado

EXAMPLE PHRASES

Toca el violín. He plays the violin.

Te **toca** fregar los platos. It's your turn to do the dishes.

Me **ha tocado** el peor asiento. I've ended up with the worst seat.

Le **tocó** la lotería. He won the lottery.

Me **tocaba** tirar a mí. It was my turn.

Remember that subject pronouns are not used very often in Spanish.

tocar

	FUTURE	CONDITIONAL
(yo)	tocaré	tocaría
(tú)	tocarás	tocarías
(él/ella/usted)	tocará	tocaría
(nosotros/as)	tocaremos	tocaríamos
(vosotros/as)	tocaréis	tocaríais
(ellos/ellas/ ustedes)	tocarán	tocarían

	PRESENT SUBJUNCTIVE	IMPERFECT SUBJUNCTIVE
(yo)	toque	tocara or tocase
(tú)	toques	tocaras or tocases
(él/ella/usted)	toque	tocara or tocase
(nosotros/as)	toquemos	tocáramos or tocásemos
(vosotros/as)	toquéis	tocarais or tocaseis
(ellos/ellas/ ustedes)	toquen	tocaran or tocasen

IMPERATIVE

toca / tocad

Use the present subjunctive in all cases other than these **tú** *and* **vosotros** *affirmative forms.*

EXAMPLE PHRASES

Sabía que me **tocaría** ir a mí. I knew I'd be the one to have to go.

No lo **toques**. Don't touch it.

Tócalo, verás que suave. Touch it and see how soft it is.

Remember that subject pronouns are not used very often in Spanish.

torcer (to twist)

	PRESENT		PRESENT PERFECT
(yo)	tuerzo		he torcido
(tú)	tuerces		has torcido
(él/ella/usted)	tuerce		ha torcido
(nosotros/as)	torcemos		hemos torcido
(vosotros/as)	torcéis		habéis torcido
(ellos/ellas/ ustedes)	tuercen		han torcido

	PRETERITE		IMPERFECT
(yo)	torcí		torcía
(tú)	torciste		torcías
(él/ella/usted)	torció		torcía
(nosotros/as)	torcimos		torcíamos
(vosotros/as)	torcisteis		torcíais
(ellos/ellas/ ustedes)	torcieron		torcían

GERUND
torciendo

PAST PARTICIPLE
torcido

EXAMPLE PHRASES

Acaba de **torcer** la esquina. She has just turned the corner.

El sendero **tuerce** luego a la derecha. Later on the path bends round to the right.

Se le **ha torcido** la muñeca. She's sprained her wrist.

Se me **torció** el tobillo. I twisted my ankle.

torcer

	FUTURE	CONDITIONAL
(yo)	torceré	torcería
(tú)	torcerás	torcerías
(él/ella/usted)	torcerá	torcería
(nosotros/as)	torceremos	torceríamos
(vosotros/as)	torceréis	torceríais
(ellos/ellas/ ustedes)	torcerán	torcerían

	PRESENT SUBJUNCTIVE	IMPERFECT SUBJUNCTIVE
(yo)	tuerza	torciera or torciese
(tú)	tuerzas	torcieras or torcieses
(él/ella/usted)	tuerza	torciera or torciese
(nosotros/as)	torzamos	torciéramos or torciésemos
(vosotros/as)	torzáis	torcierais or torcieseis
(ellos/ellas/ ustedes)	tuerzan	torcieran or torciesen

IMPERATIVE
tuerce / torced

Use the present subjunctive in all cases other than these **tú** *and* **vosotros** *affirmative forms.*

EXAMPLE PHRASES
Tuerza a la izquierda. Turn left.
Tuércelo un poco más. Twist it a little more.

traer (to bring)

	PRESENT	PRESENT PERFECT
(yo)	traigo	he traído
(tú)	traes	has traído
(él/ella/usted)	trae	ha traído
(nosotros/as)	traemos	hemos traído
(vosotros/as)	traéis	habéis traído
(ellos/ellas/ustedes)	traen	han traído

	PRETERITE	IMPERFECT
(yo)	traje	traía
(tú)	trajiste	traías
(él/ella/usted)	trajo	traía
(nosotros/as)	trajimos	traíamos
(vosotros/as)	trajisteis	traíais
(ellos/ellas/ustedes)	trajeron	traían

GERUND
trayendo

PAST PARTICIPLE
traído

EXAMPLE PHRASES

¿Me puedes **traer** una toalla? Can you bring me a towel?

Nos **está trayendo** muchos problemas. It's causing us a lot of trouble.

¿**Has traído** lo que te pedí? Have you brought what I asked for?

Traía un vestido nuevo. She was wearing a new dress.

No **trajo** el dinero. He didn't bring the money.

Remember that subject pronouns are not used very often in Spanish.

traer

	FUTURE	CONDITIONAL
(yo)	traeré	traería
(tú)	traerás	traerías
(él/ella/usted)	traerá	traería
(nosotros/as)	traeremos	traeríamos
(vosotros/as)	traeréis	traeríais
(ellos/ellas/ustedes)	traerán	traerían

	PRESENT SUBJUNCTIVE	IMPERFECT SUBJUNCTIVE
(yo)	traiga	trajera or trajese
(tú)	traigas	trajeras or trajeses
(él/ella/usted)	traiga	trajera or trajese
(nosotros/as)	traigamos	trajéramos or trajésemos
(vosotros/as)	traigáis	trajerais or trajeseis
(ellos/ellas/ustedes)	traigan	trajeran or trajesen

IMPERATIVE
trae / traed

*Use the present subjunctive in all cases other than these **tú** and **vosotros** affirmative forms.*

EXAMPLE PHRASES

Me pregunto qué **se traerán** entre manos. I wonder what they're up to.

Se lo **traería** de África. He must have brought it over from Africa.

Dile que **traiga** a algún amigo. Tell him to bring a friend with him.

Trae eso. Give that here.

valer (to be worth)

	PRESENT	PRESENT PERFECT
(yo)	valgo	he valido
(tú)	vales	has valido
(él/ella/usted)	vale	ha valido
(nosotros/as)	valemos	hemos valido
(vosotros/as)	valéis	habéis valido
(ellos/ellas/ustedes)	valen	han valido

	PRETERITE	IMPERFECT
(yo)	valí	valía
(tú)	valiste	valías
(él/ella/usted)	valió	valía
(nosotros/as)	valimos	valíamos
(vosotros/as)	valisteis	valíais
(ellos/ellas/ustedes)	valieron	valían

GERUND	PAST PARTICIPLE
valiendo	valido

EXAMPLE PHRASES

No puede **valerse** por sí mismo. He can't look after himself.

¿Cuánto **vale** eso? How much is that?

¿**Vale**? OK?

No le **valió** de nada suplicar. Begging got her nowhere.

No **valía** la pena. It wasn't worth it.

Remember that subject pronouns are not used very often in Spanish.

valer

	FUTURE	CONDITIONAL
(yo)	valdré	valdría
(tú)	valdrás	valdrías
(él/ella/usted)	valdrá	valdría
(nosotros/as)	valdremos	valdríamos
(vosotros/as)	valdréis	valdríais
(ellos/ellas/ustedes)	valdrán	valdrían

	PRESENT SUBJUNCTIVE	IMPERFECT SUBJUNCTIVE
(yo)	valga	valiera or valiese
(tú)	valgas	valieras or valieses
(él/ella/usted)	valga	valiera or valiese
(nosotros/as)	valgamos	valiéramos or valiésemos
(vosotros/as)	valgáis	valierais or valieseis
(ellos/ellas/ustedes)	valgan	valieran or valiesen

IMPERATIVE
vale / valed

Use the present subjunctive in all cases other than these **tú** *and* **vosotros** *affirmative forms.*

EXAMPLE PHRASES

Valdrá unos 500 euros. It must cost around 500 euros.

Yo no **valdría** para enfermera. I'd make a hopeless nurse.

Valga lo que **valga**, lo compro. I'll buy it, no matter how much it costs.

vencer (to win; to beat)

	PRESENT		PRESENT PERFECT
(yo)	venzo		he vencido
(tú)	vences		has vencido
(él/ella/usted)	vence		ha vencido
(nosotros/as)	vencemos		hemos vencido
(vosotros/as)	vencéis		habéis vencido
(ellos/ellas/ ustedes)	vencen		han vencido

	PRETERITE		IMPERFECT
(yo)	vencí		vencía
(tú)	venciste		vencías
(él/ella/usted)	venció		vencía
(nosotros/as)	vencimos		vencíamos
(vosotros/as)	vencisteis		vencíais
(ellos/ellas/ ustedes)	vencieron		vencían

GERUND

venciendo

PAST PARTICIPLE

vencido

EXAMPLE PHRASES

Tienes que **vencer** el miedo. You must overcome your fear.

El plazo de matrícula **vence** mañana. Tomorrow is the last day for registration.

Finalmente le **ha vencido** el sueño. At last, he was overcome by sleep.

Vencimos por dos a uno. We won two-one.

Le **vencía** la curiosidad. His curiosity got the better of him.

Remember that subject pronouns are not used very often in Spanish.

vencer

	FUTURE	CONDITIONAL
(yo)	venceré	vencería
(tú)	vencerás	vencerías
(él/ella/usted)	vencerá	vencería
(nosotros/as)	venceremos	venceríamos
(vosotros/as)	venceréis	venceríais
(ellos/ellas/ustedes)	vencerán	vencerían

	PRESENT SUBJUNCTIVE	IMPERFECT SUBJUNCTIVE
(yo)	venza	venciera or venciese
(tú)	venzas	vencieras or vencieses
(él/ella/usted)	venza	venciera or venciese
(nosotros/as)	venzamos	venciéramos or venciésemos
(vosotros/as)	venzáis	vencierais or vencieseis
(ellos/ellas/ustedes)	venzan	vencieran or venciesen

IMPERATIVE

vence / venced

Use the present subjunctive in all cases other than these tú and vosotros affirmative forms.

EXAMPLE PHRASES

Nuestro ejército **vencerá**. Our army will be victorious.

No dejes que te **venza** la impaciencia. Don't let your impatience get the better of you.

Remember that subject pronouns are not used very often in Spanish.

venir (to come)

	PRESENT		PRESENT PERFECT
(yo)	vengo		he venido
(tú)	vienes		has venido
(él/ella/usted)	viene		ha venido
(nosotros/as)	venimos		hemos venido
(vosotros/as)	venís		habéis venido
(ellos/ellas/ ustedes)	vienen		han venido

	PRETERITE		IMPERFECT
(yo)	vine		venía
(tú)	viniste		venías
(él/ella/usted)	vino		venía
(nosotros/as)	vinimos		veníamos
(vosotros/as)	vinisteis		veníais
(ellos/ellas/ ustedes)	vinieron		venían

GERUND

viniendo

PAST PARTICIPLE

venido

EXAMPLE PHRASES

Vengo andando desde la playa. I've walked all the way from the beach.

La casa **se está viniendo** abajo. The house is falling apart.

Ha venido en taxi. He came by taxi.

Vinieron a verme al hospital. They came to see me in hospital.

La noticia **venía** en el periódico. The news was in the paper.

Remember that subject pronouns are not used very often in Spanish.

venir

	FUTURE	CONDITIONAL
(yo)	vendré	vendría
(tú)	vendrás	vendrías
(él/ella/usted)	vendrá	vendría
(nosotros/as)	vendremos	vendríamos
(vosotros/as)	vendréis	vendríais
(ellos/ellas/ustedes)	vendrán	vendrían

	PRESENT SUBJUNCTIVE	IMPERFECT SUBJUNCTIVE
(yo)	venga	viniera or viniese
(tú)	vengas	vinieras or vinieses
(él/ella/usted)	venga	viniera or viniese
(nosotros/as)	vengamos	viniéramos or viniésemos
(vosotros/as)	vengáis	vinierais or vinieseis
(ellos/ellas/ustedes)	vengan	vinieran or viniesen

IMPERATIVE
ven / venid

*Use the present subjunctive in all cases other than these **tú** and **vosotros** affirmative forms.*

EXAMPLE PHRASES
¿**Vendrás** conmigo al cine? Will you come to the cinema with me?
A mí me **vendría** mejor el sábado. Saturday would be better for me.
¡**Venga**, vámonos! Come on, let's go!
No **vengas** si no quieres. Don't come if you don't want to.
¡**Ven** aquí! Come here!

Remember that subject pronouns are not used very often in Spanish.

ver (to see)

	PRESENT		PRESENT PERFECT
(yo)	veo		he visto
(tú)	ves		has visto
(él/ella/usted)	ve		ha visto
(nosotros/as)	vemos		hemos visto
(vosotros/as)	veis		habéis visto
(ellos/ellas/ ustedes)	ven		han visto

	PRETERITE		IMPERFECT
(yo)	vi		veía
(tú)	viste		veías
(él/ella/usted)	vio		veía
(nosotros/as)	vimos		veíamos
(vosotros/as)	visteis		veíais
(ellos/ellas/ ustedes)	vieron		veían

GERUND

viendo

PAST PARTICIPLE

visto

EXAMPLE PHRASES

No **veo** muy bien. I can't see very well.

Están viendo la televisión. They're watching television.

No **he visto** esa película. I haven't seen that film.

¿**Viste** lo que pasó? Did you see what happened?

Los **veía** a todos desde la ventana. I could see them all from the window.

Remember that subject pronouns are not used very often in Spanish.

ver

	FUTURE	CONDITIONAL
(yo)	**veré**	**vería**
(tú)	**verás**	**verías**
(él/ella/usted)	**verá**	**vería**
(nosotros/as)	**veremos**	**veríamos**
(vosotros/as)	**veréis**	**veríais**
(ellos/ellas/ ustedes)	**verán**	**verían**

	PRESENT SUBJUNCTIVE	IMPERFECT SUBJUNCTIVE
(yo)	**vea**	**viera** or **viese**
(tú)	**veas**	**vieras** or **vieses**
(él/ella/usted)	**vea**	**viera** or **viese**
(nosotros/as)	**veamos**	**viéramos** or **viésemos**
(vosotros/as)	**veáis**	**vierais** or **vieseis**
(ellos/ellas/ ustedes)	**vean**	**vieran** or **viesen**

IMPERATIVE

ve / ved

*Use the present subjunctive in all cases other than these **tú** and **vosotros** affirmative forms.*

EXAMPLE PHRASES

Eso ya se **verá**. We'll see.

No **veas** cómo se puso. He got incredibly worked up.

¡Si **vieras** cómo ha cambiado todo aquello! If you could see how everything has changed.

Veamos, ¿qué le pasa? Let's see now, what's the matter?

Remember that subject pronouns are not used very often in Spanish.

verter (to pour)

	PRESENT		PRESENT PERFECT
(yo)	vierto		he vertido
(tú)	viertes		has vertido
(él/ella/usted)	vierte		ha vertido
(nosotros/as)	vertemos		hemos vertido
(vosotros/as)	vertéis		habéis vertido
(ellos/ellas/ ustedes)	vierten		han vertido

	PRETERITE		IMPERFECT
(yo)	vertí		vertía
(tú)	vertiste		vertías
(él/ella/usted)	vertió		vertía
(nosotros/as)	vertimos		vertíamos
(vosotros/as)	vertisteis		vertíais
(ellos/ellas/ ustedes)	vertieron		vertían

GERUND
vertiendo

PAST PARTICIPLE
vertido

EXAMPLE PHRASES

Primero **viertes** el contenido del sobre en un recipiente. First you empty out the contents of the packet into a container.

Me **has vertido** agua encima. You've spilt water on me.

Vertió un poco de leche en el cazo. He poured some milk into the saucepan.

Se **vertían** muchos residuos radioactivos en el mar. A lot of nuclear waste was dumped in the sea.

Remember that subject pronouns are not used very often in Spanish.

verter

	FUTURE	CONDITIONAL
(yo)	verteré	vertería
(tú)	verterás	verterías
(él/ella/usted)	verterá	vertería
(nosotros/as)	verteremos	verteríamos
(vosotros/as)	verteréis	verteríais
(ellos/ellas/ustedes)	verterán	verterían

	PRESENT SUBJUNCTIVE	IMPERFECT SUBJUNCTIVE
(yo)	vierta	vertiera or vertiese
(tú)	viertas	vertieras or vertieses
(él/ella/usted)	vierta	vertiera or vertiese
(nosotros/as)	vertamos	vertiéramos or vertiésemos
(vosotros/as)	vertáis	vertierais or vertieseis
(ellos/ellas/ustedes)	viertan	vertieran or vertiesen

IMPERATIVE

vierte / verted

*Use the present subjunctive in all cases other than these **tú** and **vosotros** affirmative forms.*

EXAMPLE PHRASES

Se vertirán muchas lágrimas por esto. A lot of tears will be shed over this.

Ten cuidado no **viertas** el café. Be careful you don't knock over the coffee.

Por favor, **vierta** el contenido del bolso sobre la mesa. Please empty out your bag on the table.

Remember that subject pronouns are not used very often in Spanish.

vestir (to dress)

	PRESENT		PRESENT PERFECT
(yo)	visto		he vestido
(tú)	vistes		has vestido
(él/ella/usted)	viste		ha vestido
(nosotros/as)	vestimos		hemos vestido
(vosotros/as)	vestís		habéis vestido
(ellos/ellas/ustedes)	visten		han vestido

	PRETERITE		IMPERFECT
(yo)	vestí		vestía
(tú)	vestiste		vestías
(él/ella/usted)	vistió		vestía
(nosotros/as)	vestimos		vestíamos
(vosotros/as)	vestisteis		vestíais
(ellos/ellas/ustedes)	vistieron		vestían

GERUND
vistiendo

PAST PARTICIPLE
vestido

EXAMPLE PHRASES

Tengo una familia que **vestir** y que alimentar. I have a family to feed and clothe.

Viste bien. She's a smart dresser.

Estaba **vistiendo** a los niños. I was dressing the children.

Me he vestido en cinco minutos. It took me five minutes to get dressed.

Remember that subject pronouns are not used very often in Spanish.

vestir

	FUTURE	CONDITIONAL
(yo)	vestiré	vestiría
(tú)	vestirás	vestirías
(él/ella/usted)	vestirá	vestiría
(nosotros/as)	vestiremos	vestiríamos
(vosotros/as)	vestiréis	vestiríais
(ellos/ellas/ustedes)	vestirán	vestirían

	PRESENT SUBJUNCTIVE	IMPERFECT SUBJUNCTIVE
(yo)	vista	vistiera or vistiese
(tú)	vistas	vistieras or vistieses
(él/ella/usted)	vista	vistiera or vistiese
(nosotros/as)	vistamos	vistiéramos or vistiésemos
(vosotros/as)	vistáis	vistierais or vistieseis
(ellos/ellas/ustedes)	vistan	vistieran or vistiesen

IMPERATIVE

viste / vestid

Use the present subjunctive in all cases other than these tú and vosotros affirmative forms.

EXAMPLE PHRASES

Se vistió de princesa. She dressed up as a princess.

Vestía pantalones vaqueros y una camiseta. He was wearing jeans and a T-shirt.

Su padre **vestirá** de uniforme. Her father will wear a uniform.

¡**Vístete** de una vez! For the last time, go and get dressed!

Remember that subject pronouns are not used very often in Spanish.

vivir (to live)

	PRESENT		PRESENT PERFECT
(yo)	vivo		he vivido
(tú)	vives		has vivido
(él/ella/usted)	vive		ha vivido
(nosotros/as)	vivimos		hemos vivido
(vosotros/as)	vivís		habéis vivido
(ellos/ellas/ ustedes)	viven		han vivido

	PRETERITE		IMPERFECT
(yo)	viví		vivía
(tú)	viviste		vivías
(él/ella/usted)	vivió		vivía
(nosotros/as)	vivimos		vivíamos
(vosotros/as)	vivisteis		vivíais
(ellos/ellas/ ustedes)	vivieron		vivían

GERUND

viviendo

PAST PARTICIPLE

vivido

EXAMPLE PHRASES

Me gusta **vivir** sola. I like living on my own.

¿Dónde **vives**? Where do you live?

Siempre **han vivido** muy bien. They've always had a very comfortable life.

Vivían de su pensión. They lived on his pension.

Remember that subject pronouns are not used very often in Spanish.

vivir

	FUTURE	CONDITIONAL
(yo)	viviré	viviría
(tú)	vivirás	vivirías
(él/ella/usted)	vivirá	viviría
(nosotros/as)	viviremos	viviríamos
(vosotros/as)	viviréis	viviríais
(ellos/ellas/ ustedes)	vivirán	vivirían

	PRESENT SUBJUNCTIVE	IMPERFECT SUBJUNCTIVE
(yo)	viva	viviera or viviese
(tú)	vivas	vivieras or vivieses
(él/ella/usted)	viva	viviera or viviese
(nosotros/as)	vivamos	viviéramos or viviésemos
(vosotros/as)	viváis	vivierais or vivieseis
(ellos/ellas/ ustedes)	vivan	vivieran or viviesen

IMPERATIVE
vive / vivid

Use the present subjunctive in all cases other than these **tú** *and* **vosotros** *affirmative forms.* .

EXAMPLE PHRASES
Viviremos en el centro de la ciudad. We'll live in the city centre.
Si pudiéramos, **viviríamos** en el campo. We'd live in the country if we could.
Si **vivierais** más cerca, nos veríamos más a menudo. We'd see each other
   more often if you lived nearer.
¡**Viva**! Hurray!

Remember that subject pronouns are not used very often in Spanish.

volcar (to overturn)

	PRESENT		PRESENT PERFECT
(yo)	vuelco		he volcado
(tú)	vuelcas		has volcado
(él/ella/usted)	vuelca		ha volcado
(nosotros/as)	volcamos		hemos volcado
(vosotros/as)	volcáis		habéis volcado
(ellos/ellas/ ustedes)	vuelcan		han volcado

	PRETERITE		IMPERFECT
(yo)	volqué		volcaba
(tú)	volcaste		volcabas
(él/ella/usted)	volcó		volcaba
(nosotros/as)	volcamos		volcábamos
(vosotros/as)	volcasteis		volcabais
(ellos/ellas/ ustedes)	volcaron		volcaban

GERUND
volcando

PAST PARTICIPLE
volcado

EXAMPLE PHRASES

Se vuelca en su trabajo. She throws herself into her work.
Se han volcado con nosotros. They've been very kind to us.
El camión **volcó**. The lorry overturned.

volcar

	FUTURE	CONDITIONAL
(yo)	volcaré	volcaría
(tú)	volcarás	volcarías
(él/ella/usted)	volcará	volcaría
(nosotros/as)	volcaremos	volcaríamos
(vosotros/as)	volcaréis	volcaríais
(ellos/ellas/ustedes)	volcarán	volcarían

	PRESENT SUBJUNCTIVE	IMPERFECT SUBJUNCTIVE
(yo)	vuelque	volcara or volcase
(tú)	vuelques	volcaras or volcases
(él/ella/usted)	vuelque	volcara or volcase
(nosotros/as)	volquemos	volcáramos or volcásemos
(vosotros/as)	volquéis	volcarais or volcaseis
(ellos/ellas/ustedes)	vuelquen	volcaran or volcasen

IMPERATIVE

vuelca / volcad

*Use the present subjunctive in all cases other than these **tú** and **vosotros** affirmative forms.*

EXAMPLE PHRASES

Si sigues moviéndote, harás que **vuelque** el bote. If you keep on moving like that, you'll make the boat capsize.

Ten cuidado, no **vuelques** el vaso. Be careful not to knock over the glass.

Vuelca el contenido sobre la cama. Empty the contents onto the bed.

volver (to return)

	PRESENT		PRESENT PERFECT
(yo)	vuelvo		he vuelto
(tú)	vuelves		has vuelto
(él/ella/usted)	vuelve		ha vuelto
(nosotros/as)	volvemos		hemos vuelto
(vosotros/as)	volvéis		habéis vuelto
(ellos/ellas/ustedes)	vuelven		han vuelto

	PRETERITE		IMPERFECT
(yo)	volví		volvía
(tú)	volviste		volvías
(él/ella/usted)	volvió		volvía
(nosotros/as)	volvimos		volvíamos
(vosotros/as)	volvisteis		volvíais
(ellos/ellas/ustedes)	volvieron		volvían

GERUND
volviendo

PAST PARTICIPLE
vuelto

EXAMPLE PHRASES

Mi padre **vuelve** mañana. My father's coming back tomorrow.

Se **está volviendo** muy pesado. He's becoming a real pain in the neck.

Ha vuelto a casa. He's gone back home.

Me volví para ver quién era. I turned round to see who it was.

Volvía agotado de trabajar. I used to come back exhausted from work.

Remember that subject pronouns are not used very often in Spanish.

volver

	FUTURE	CONDITIONAL
(yo)	volveré	volvería
(tú)	volverás	volverías
(él/ella/usted)	volverá	volvería
(nosotros/as)	volveremos	volveríamos
(vosotros/as)	volveréis	volveríais
(ellos/ellas/ ustedes)	volverán	volverían

	PRESENT SUBJUNCTIVE	IMPERFECT SUBJUNCTIVE
(yo)	vuelva	volviera or volviese
(tú)	vuelvas	volvieras or volvieses
(él/ella/usted)	vuelva	volviera or volviese
(nosotros/as)	volvamos	volviéramos or volviésemos
(vosotros/as)	volváis	volvierais or volvieseis
(ellos/ellas/ ustedes)	vuelvan	volvieran or volviesen

IMPERATIVE

vuelve / volved

*Use the present subjunctive in all cases other than these **tú** and **vosotros** affirmative forms.*

EXAMPLE PHRASES

Todo **volverá** a la normalidad. Everything will go back to normal.

Yo **volvería** a intentarlo. I'd try again.

No quiero que **vuelvas** a las andadas. I don't want you to go back to your old ways.

No **vuelvas** por aquí. Don't come back here.

¡**Vuelve** a la cama! Go back to bed!

Remember that subject pronouns are not used very often in Spanish.

zurcir (to darn)

	PRESENT		PRESENT PERFECT
(yo)	zurzo		he zurcido
(tú)	zurces		has zurcido
(él/ella/usted)	zurce		ha zurcido
(nosotros/as)	zurcimos		hemos zurcido
(vosotros/as)	zurcís		habéis zurcido
(ellos/ellas/ustedes)	zurcen		han zurcido

	PRETERITE		IMPERFECT
(yo)	zurcí		zurcía
(tú)	zurciste		zurcías
(él/ella/usted)	zurció		zurcía
(nosotros/as)	zurcimos		zurcíamos
(vosotros/as)	zurcisteis		zurcíais
(ellos/ellas/ustedes)	zurcieron		zurcían

GERUND
zurciendo

PAST PARTICIPLE
zurcido

EXAMPLE PHRASES

¿Quién le **zurce** las camisas? Who darns his shirts?

Se pasa el día **zurciéndole** la ropa. She spends the whole day darning his clothes.

Remember that subject pronouns are not used very often in Spanish.

zurcir

	FUTURE	CONDITIONAL
(yo)	zurciré	zurciría
(tú)	zurcirás	zurcirías
(él/ella/usted)	zurcirá	zurciría
(nosotros/as)	zurciremos	zurciríamos
(vosotros/as)	zurciréis	zurciríais
(ellos/ellas/ ustedes)	zurcirán	zurcirían

	PRESENT SUBJUNCTIVE	IMPERFECT SUBJUNCTIVE
(yo)	zurza	zurciera or zurciese
(tú)	zurzas	zurcieras or zurcieses
(él/ella/usted)	zurza	zurciera or zurciese
(nosotros/as)	zurzamos	zurciéramos or zurciésemos
(vosotros/as)	zurzáis	zurcierais or zurcieseis
(ellos/ellas/ ustedes)	zurzan	zurcieran or zurciesen

IMPERATIVE
zurce / zurcid

Use the present subjunctive in all cases other than these **tú** *and* **vosotros** *affirmative forms.*

EXAMPLE PHRASES
¡Que te **zurzan**! Get lost!

How to use the Verb Index

The verbs in bold are the model verbs which you will find in the Verb Tables. All the other verbs follow one of these patterns, so the number next to each verb indicates which pattern fits this particular verb. For example, **acampar** (*to camp*) follows the same pattern as **hablar** (number 118 in the Verb Tables).

All the verbs are in alphabetical order. Superior numbers ([1] etc) refer you to notes on page 247. These notes explain any differences between verbs and their model.

tener	214	traicionar	118	trotar	118	verificar	194
tensar	118	tramitar	118	tumbar	118	**verter**	230
tentar	162	tranquilizar	64	turnarse	118	**vestir**	232
tenir	180	transcurrir	158	tutear	118	viajar	118
tergiversar	118	transformar	118	unir	234	vibrar	118
terminar	118	transmitir	234	untar	118	viciar(se)	118
timar	118	transportar	118	usar	118	vigilar	118
tirar	118	trasladar	118	utilizar	64	vindicar	194
tiritar	118	trasnochar	118	vaciar	92	violar	118
titubear	118	traspapelar(se)	118	vacilar	118	visitar	118
titular(se)	118	traspasar	118	vacunar	118	vitorear	118
tocar	216	trasplantar	118	vagar	156	**vivir**	234
tolerar	118	tratar	118	**valer**	222	volar	60
tomar	118	trazar	64	valorar	118	**volcar**	236
topar(se)	118	trepar	118	variar	92	**volver**	238
torcer	218	trillar	118	velar	118	vomitar	118
torear	118	trinchar	118	**vencer**	224	votar	118
torturar	118	triplicar	194	vendar	118	zambullirse	112
toser	52	triturar	118	vender	52	zampar(se)	118
tostar	60	triunfar	118	vengar(se)	156	zanjar	118
trabajar	118	trocear	118	**venir**	226	zarpar	118
traducir	54	tronar[1]	60	ventilar	118	zumbar	118
traer	220	tronchar(se)	118	**ver**	228	**zurcir**	240
tragar	156	tropezar	86	veranear	118	zurrar	118

Notes

[1] The verbs **anochecer, atardecer, granizar, helar, llover, nevar, nublarse** and **tronar** are used almost exclusively in the infinitive and third person singular forms.

[2] The **past participle** of the verb **pudrir** is **podrido**.